# Cinema and Technology

# Cinema and Technology
## Cultures, Theories, Practices

Edited by
Bruce Bennett, Marc Furstenau and Adrian Mackenzie

Introduction, selection and editorial matter © Bruce Bennett, Marc Furstenau and Adrian Mackenzie 2008
Individual chapters © contributors

All rights reserved. No reproduction, copy or transmission of this publication may be made without written permission.

No portion of this publication may be reproduced, copied or transmitted save with written permission or in accordance with the provisions of the Copyright, Designs and Patents Act 1988, or under the terms of any licence permitting limited copying issued by the Copyright Licensing Agency, Saffron House, 6-10 Kirby Street, London EC1N 8TS.

Any person who does any unauthorized act in relation to this publication may be liable to criminal prosecution and civil claims for damages.

The editor's and publishers have made every effort to contact the copyright holders, but if any have been inadvertently overlooked the publishers will be pleased to make the necessary arrangement at the first opportunity.

The authors have asserted their rights to be identified as the authors of this work in accordance with the Copyright, Designs and Patents Act 1988.

First published 2008 by
PALGRAVE MACMILLAN

Palgrave Macmillan in the UK is an imprint of Macmillan Publishers Limited, registered in England, company number 785998, of Houndmills, Basingstoke, Hampshire RG21 6XS.

Palgrave Macmillan in the US is a division of St Martin's Press LLC, 175 Fifth Avenue, New York, NY 10010.

Palgrave Macmillan is the global academic imprint of the above companies and has companies and representatives throughout the world.

Palgrave® and Macmillan® are registered trademarks in the United States, the United Kingdom, Europe and other countries.

ISBN-13: 978-0-230-52477-4      hardback
ISBN-10: 0-230-52477-X           hardback

This book is printed on paper suitable for recycling and made from fully managed and sustained forest sources. Logging, pulping and manufacturing processes are expected to conform to the environmental regulations of the country of origin.

A catalogue record for this book is available from the British Library.

Library of Congress Cataloging-in-Publication Data

  Cinema and technology : cultures, theories, practices/edited by
    Bruce Bennett, Marc Furstenau and Adrian Mackenzie.
    p. cm.
  Includes index.
  ISBN 978-0-230-52477-4
  1. Technology in motion pictures.  2. Cinematography—Technological
    innovations.   I. Bennett, Bruce, 1970–   II. Furstenau, Marc, 1963–
    III. Mackenzie, Adrian, 1962–

PN1995.9.T43C56   2008
791.43'656—dc22                                              2008020596

Printed and bound in Great Britain by
CPI Antony Rowe, Chippenham and Eastbourne

# Contents

*Notes on Contributors* vii

*Acknowledgements* xi

Introduction 1

I Format 19

1 The Perilous Gauge: Canadian Independent Film Exhibition and the 16mm Mobile Menace 23
*Peter Lester*

2 BMW Films and the Star Wars Kid: 'Early Web Cinema' and Technology 37
*Andrew Clay*

3 On Some Limits to Film Theory (Mainly from Science) 53
*James Elkins*

II Norms 71

4 Socially Combustible: Panicky People, Flammable Films and the Dangerous New Technology of the Nickelodeon 75
*Paul S. Moore*

5 Cinema and Its Doubles: Kittler v. Deleuze 88
*Jan Harris*

6 Genomic Science in Contemporary Film: Institutions, Individuals and Genre 105
*Kate O'Riordan*

III Scanning 125

7 Cinema as Technology: Encounters with an Interface 129
*Aylish Wood*

8 *Demonlover*: Interval, Affect and the Aesthetics of Digital Dislocation 142
*Maja Manojlovic*

9 'Into the décor': Attention and Distraction, Foreground and
   Background                                                      157
   *Christopher Rodrigues*

10 Children, Robots, Cinephilia and Technophobia                   168
   *Bruce Bennett*

## IV  Movement                                                    183

11 Lola and the Vampire: Technologies of Time and Movement
   in German Cinema                                                187
   *Michelle Langford*

12 Inbetweening: Animation, Deleuze, Film Theory                   201
   *Bill Schaffer*

13 Affective Troubles and Cinema                                   214
   *Marie-Luise Angerer*

14 Afterword—Digital Cinema and the Apparatus:
   Archaeologies, Epistemologies, Ontologies                       226
   *Thomas Elsaesser*

Bibliography                                                       241

Index                                                              254

# Notes on Contributors

**Marie-Luise Angerer** was born in Bregenz/Austria in 1958. She studied communication sciences, history of art, philosophy, Romance languages and literature in Vienna and completed her post-doctoral thesis at the University of Salzburg. In 2000 she was appointed Professor of Media and Cultural Studies at the Academy of Media Arts Cologne. From 2000 to 2004 she was the academy's vice-principal (Teaching and Research), and in February 2007, she was elected principal of the academy. She is a jury member of the Bundeskulturstiftung (federal cultural foundation) and a member of the Board of Trustees of Deutsches Hygiene-Museum Dresden. Selected publications are *The Body of Gender* (ed.) 1995, *Body Options, Körper.Spuren.Medien.Bilder*, 1999 (2nd edition, 2000), *Future Bodies* (co-edited with Kathrin Peters, Zoe Sofoulis, 2002) and *Das Begehren nach dem Affekt* (2007) (http://www.khm.de/personen/staff/angerer/).

**Bruce Bennett** is Lecturer in Film Studies at Lancaster University. His areas of research include film theory, Georges Bataille and general economy, James Cameron, border films and politics. His publications include 'Towards a General Economics of Cinema', in S. Bruce, V. Wagner (eds), *Fiction and Economy* (Palgrave Macmillan, 2007), and 'Screening Unlivable Lives: The Cinema of Borders' (co-written with Imogen Tyler), in A. Imre, K. Marciniak, A. O'Healy (eds.), *Transnational Feminism in Film and Media: Visibility, Representation and Sexual Differences* (Palgrave Macmillan, 2007). He is currently working on a book on the director Michael Winterbottom, entitled *The Cinema of Michael Winterbottom: Politics, Aesthetics, Media* (Wallflower Press).

**Andrew Clay** is Senior Lecturer in Critical Technical Practices at De Montfort University, Leicester. He has published articles on crime and masculinity in British cinema and is preparing a book on Lewis Gilbert. He is currently researching the theory and practice of online film.

**James Elkins** is E. C. Chadbourne Professor in the Department of Art History, Theory, and Criticism, School of the Art Institute of Chicago. He writes on art and non–art images; his recent books include *On the Strange Place of Religion in Contemporary Art, Visual Studies: A Skeptical*

*Introduction, What Happened to Art Criticism?*, and *Master Narratives and Their Discontents*. He is editing two book series for Routledge: *The Art Seminar* (conversations on different subjects in art theory) and *Theories of Modernism and Postmodernism in the Visual Arts* (short monographs on the shape of the twentieth century); currently he is organizing a seven-year series called the 'Stone Summer Theory Institute' (imagehistory.org) (jameselkins@fastmail.jp).

**Thomas Elsaesser** is Professor in the Department of Media and Culture and Director of Research Film and Television at the University of Amsterdam. His most recent books as (co-) editor include *Cinema Futures: Cain, Abel or Cable?* (1998), *The BFI Companion to German Cinema* (1999), *The Last Great American Picture Show* (2004) and *Harun Farocki – Working on the Sightlines* (2004). His books as author include *Fassbinder's Germany: History, Identity, Subject* (1996), *Weimar Cinema and After* (2000), *Metropolis* (2000), *Studying Contemporary American Film* (2002, with Warren Buckland), *Filmgeschichte und Frühes Kino* (2002), *European Cinema: Face to Face with Hollywood* (2005), *Terror und Trauma* (2007) and *Filmtheorie zur Einführung* (2007, with Malte Hagener).

**Marc Furstenau** is Assistant Professor in the School for Studies in Art and Culture, Carleton University, Ottawa. His areas of research include cinema, new media, communication theory and visual culture studies. He has published on new video technologies, photographic theory and film and philosophy, and is preparing a book on cinema and communication.

**Jan Harris** is the author (with P. Taylor) of *Digital Matters: Theory and Culture of the Matrix* (Routledge, 2005) and *Critical Theories of Mass Media: Then & Now* (Open University, 2007). His research is concerned with the impact of new media on cultural forms, and the philosophy of technology.

**Michelle Langford** is Lecturer in Film Studies in the School of English, Media and Performing Arts at the University of New South Wales, where her research interests include German and Iranian cinemas as well as theories of cinematic temporality and gesture. Her current research looks at the allegorical dimensions of Iranian cinema. She is author of *Allegorical Images: Tableau, Time and Gesture in the Cinema of Werner Schroeter* (Bristol: Intellect, 2006) and has also published on Iranian cinema in the journal *Camera Obscura*.

**Peter Lester** is a doctoral candidate in the Department of Communication Studies at Concordia University, Montreal. He is currently finishing his dissertation on small gauge, travelling film exhibition in Canada during the interwar years.

**Adrian Mackenzie** (Institute for Cultural Research, Lancaster University) does social research in areas of new media and wirelessness, writing *Transductions: Bodies and Machines at Speed* (London: Continuum, 2002); He has studied the cultural life of software, and how software acquires cultural value, publishing *Cutting Code: Software and Sociality* (New York: Peter Lang, 2006). He has published widely on the cultural life of wireless networks, looking at how artists, activists, development projects and community groups develop alternative communication infrastructures (*Wirelessness: Radical Network Empiricism* (MIT, 2008)). He also works on digital video, focusing on video codecs and the increasing mobility of video materials.

**Maja Manojlovic** is a Ph.D. candidate in Cinema and Media Studies at the UCLA Department of Film, Television and Digital Media.

**Paul S. Moore** is Assistant Professor of Sociology at Ryerson University in Toronto. His work on the regulation and promotion of early film exhibition in North America argues that mass culture was first established as urban, regional practices. He has published articles in *City & Community*, *Urban History Review* and the *Canadian Journal of Film Studies*, as well as a forthcoming book from SUNY Press Horizons of Cinema Series, *Now Playing: Early Movie Showmanship and the Regulation of Fun*.

**Kate O'Riordan** is Lecturer in Media and Film at the University of Sussex, where she is the co-director of the Centre for Material Digital Culture. Her research is a cultural study of science and technology that deploys sexuality and gender as its key analytical categories. Kate has made numerous interventions, and published widely, in the areas of embodiment and digital media (ICTs) and embodiment and human biotechnology (genomics and cloning). Publications include *Queer Online: Media Technology and Sexuality* (Peter Lang, 2007) and *Human Cloning in the Media: From Science Fiction to Science Practice* (Routledge, 2007).

**Christopher Rodrigues** lectures in media arts at the University of Plymouth and is Programme Leader for the new MA in Contemporary

Film Practice. He is currently researching the iconography of background and attention in cinema and co-writing a book with Rod Stoneman (Galway Film School) on film stills.

**Bill Schaffer** teaches film and animation studies at the University of Newcastle, Australia. He has given numerous papers and addresses in animation studies in Europe and Australia. His most recent publication in the area is 'Animation 1: The Control Image' in *The Illusion of Life II* (Cholodenko, 2007). He is currently working towards an integrated model of the moving image that accounts for both the referential indexicality of cinematography and the generative indexicality of animation in terms responsive to the advent of digital images.

**Aylish Wood** is Senior Lecturer in Film Studies at the University of Kent. She has published a number of articles (Screen, New Review of Film and Video, Film Criticism and Animation: An Interdisciplinary Journal) and book chapters on the impact of digital technologies on contemporary cinema. Her recently published book *Digital Encounters* (2007) is a cross-media study of digital technologies in cinema, games and installation art, with an emphasis on the agency of viewers.

# Acknowledgements

This volume originated from a conference at Lancaster University in 2005 entitled 'Cinema and Technology.' The conference was organized by staff and students at the Institute for Cultural Research, Lancaster University, including Professor Annette Kuhn, Coralie Claeysen, June Rye, Nick Gebhardt, Charlie Gere, Richard Rushton, Jonathan Munby, Lesley Anne Rose, and the editors of this book. Funding was provided by the Faculty of Arts and Social Sciences, Lancaster University, and the British Academy. We would also like to thank all of the contributors for their hard work, the anonymous readers who provided very helpful and constructive comments, and Steve Rifkin for the index. We would like especially to thank Annette Kuhn for the encouragement and assistance that she offered in the initiation of this book project.

# Introduction

## Cinema and technology

The technological character of cinema has long been the source of both anxiety and excitement, but the scope of the analysis of cinema and technology has remained quite limited. Although certain critical models have claimed to account for cinema's technological identity, film theorists and critics have tended to push the issue of technology to the margins of film studies and related disciplines, in favour of putatively more important formal, aesthetic and political questions. In recent years, however, technology has become a central issue in film studies, as cinema has been forced to contend with technological developments in other, related media, and with the emergence of the so-called 'new media'. These have generally been understood to pose a significant challenge to the old medium of film and have led to announcements of the 'death' of cinema, or at least its profound reconfiguration. 'Computer media', as Lev Manovich has declared, 'redefine the very identity of cinema' (Manovich, 2001, p. 293). Manovich describes a new technical logic that is emerging, which governs this process of redefinition. 'As traditional film technology is universally being replaced by digital technology', Manovich argues, 'the logic of the film-making process is being redefined' (Manovich, 2001, p. 300). Manovich presents what he calls the 'new principles of digital filmmaking', which amount to a 'new language of cinema'. According to such an argument, cinema is a primarily technological phenomenon, and changes to the medium are the direct effects of technological forces.[1]

The chapters collected in this book are all concerned with the relationship between cinema and technology. At the same time, they recognize the limitations of any attempt to make technology into a foundation that *explains* cinema. While this collection is concerned with cinema *as* technology, as a particular technological phenomenon or assemblage, it is primarily interested in the relationship between cinema *and* a broader domain of technology, or with cinema as one particular site within extensive technological configurations or within broader networks of technological activity or interaction. In this context, critical reflections on cinema may be concerned with the technical and infrastructural dimensions of film production and distribution – such as the ongoing struggle for dominance of different film gauges or the status of animation (computer-generated or conventional) within theories of film. Equally, they may be concerned with cinema as a privileged platform for thinking about technologized culture that is explored through films that are 'about' technology, or perhaps with thinking about cinema as a migratory array of effects, affects and narrative and aesthetic frameworks that are adopted and deployed in different media (contexts) such as, for example, video games, websites, TV programmes and gallery installations.

Understood within the context of such a dispersed field of activity, we are reluctant simply to say that cinema *is* a 'technology', distinguishing it thereby from other phenomena. The term 'technology' itself, moreover, is notoriously difficult to define. Theoretical, political, social, cultural and economic struggles over the value, meaning and scope of 'technology' are ongoing (and much the same can be said of the term 'cinema'). Technology is, as Ursula Franklin has observed, 'a multifaceted entity. It includes activities as well as a body of knowledge, structures as well as the act of structuring. Our language itself', she admits, 'is poorly suited to describe the complexity of technological interactions' (1999, pp. 5–6). Technology is an extensive and wide-ranging factor in culture. For some philosophers and theorists, such as Bernard Stiegler, every act and artefact is 'technological' in some way (Stiegler, 1994; 2001), which is to say that humans are essentially technological, or 'anthropotechnical'. By contrast, from the standpoint of many cultural historians and sociologists, 'technology' is a figure that only emerges at certain points within political economies of innovation, when the values of a practice, equipment or system are not yet settled. Things are 'technological', that is, while their value and meaning are still being contested. Once that negotiation is settled they are quickly incorporated into existing infrastructures, media or institutions, and are no longer alien, uncanny, extrinsic – no longer visible *as* technology.[2]

Cinema, it is often claimed, has been only intermittently visible *as* technology (rather than as 'art' or as 'entertainment', or even as an 'industry' or a 'business'), becoming so only at times of crisis or contestation. Cinema is understood to have been most visible as technology at its inception, at the point of innovation, when it was highly contested. 'In the first moments of the history of cinema', Stephen Heath has claimed, 'it is the technology which provides the immediate interest' (1980, p. 1). The early cinema was, in Tom Gunning's phrase, a 'cinema of attractions', which 'directly solicits spectator attention', drawing attention to its status as technology (1990, p. 58). In its first years, Gunning argues, 'the cinema itself was an attraction. Early audiences went to exhibitions to see machines demonstrated . . . rather than to view films' (1990, p. 58). The contemporary cinema seems to have returned to its original technological status, described as a new cinema of digital attractions, experienced now as technical spectacle, or as 'technological film' (Cubitt, 2004).[3] Cinema is once again contested, and the designation 'technological' indicates its precarious status. Cinema becomes visible (again) *as* technology just as it is supposedly coming to an end.

But the end of cinema is an event that has been rehearsed, declared and examined repeatedly from the moment of cinema's putative 'birth' (or perhaps even earlier). After attending the first commercial film screening by Auguste and Louis Lumière in Paris in December 1895, theatre owner and magician Georges Méliès made repeated attempts to buy a *cinématographe* from their father, Antoine Lumière. Lumière *père* refused on the grounds that 'interest in the new medium would be short-lived, and that it would be best for the family to exploit it exclusively until its popularity waned' (Ezra, 2000, p. 12). Subsequent forecasts of the death of cinema have typically been associated with technological and commercial shifts (and accompanying changes in audience behaviour) such as the arrival of radio, the spread of television sets, the adoption of home video recorders and video cameras and now the use of file-sharing software such as BitTorrent to distribute films and TV programmes over the Internet or the growth of websites such as *YouTube* and *Google Video*, which promise rapid access to a superabundance of heterogeneous audio-visual material. Cinema dies repeatedly at the moments in which the technological armature of cinema becomes visible through these continual shifts. There are also contingent reasons why certain shifts or foregroundings register as significant or fatal, whereas others that have little to do with specific technological transformations remain invisible or unnoticed – the various international celebrations of cinema's centenary in 1995, for example, prompted a great deal of reflection upon the fragile state of the medium.

This book appears at a moment when cinema is once again perceived to be under the threat of extinction, dissipation or reconfiguration from the incursions of various digital technologies that are having an effect on all stages of film-making, from conceptualisation and pre-production, through sound and image production and registration, post-production, to the distribution, marketing and screening of films. The technological identity of cinema is once again foregrounded and reconceived in relation to questions about the continuing distinctiveness and significance of the medium. The question, though, of what is at stake varies depending on one's perspective, as several recent examples reveal. The experience of shooting *Inland Empire* (2006) on digital video and then editing the film digitally has led director David Lynch to announce that the comparatively slow process of working with celluloid film is 'death, death, death. I can hardly stand even thinking about it' (quoted in Figgis, 2007, p. 18). On the other hand, the near-simultaneous release in the US in January 2006 of Steven Soderbergh's *Bubble* (2006) in cinemas, on DVD and on pay TV was declared 'the biggest threat to the viability of the cinema industry today' by John Fithian, Chair of the US National Association of Theater Owners[4], and led to the boycotting of the film by several North American cinema chains. In the UK, the simultaneous release on 9 March 2006 of *The Road to Guantánamo* (Michael Winterbottom, Mat Whitecross, 2006) in cinemas, on DVD, on free-to-air network TV and over the Internet for streaming or downloading took this development further, exploiting the political possibilities of new distribution technologies in order to reach a wide range of audiences through different media or channels. While eliciting less direct criticism from the film industry, Winterbottom's distribution strategy was widely hailed as making 'cinema history'.[5]

The deaths or moments of crisis (or historical transformation) that these dramatic comments refer to are driven by a range of factors such as consumer expectations and demands, economics and changing business models, aesthetic and political strategies, as well as by technological change (and, of course, each critical moment or death is different, since the technological grounds are different). They are, however, presented as the result primarily of technological novelty and innovation. One of the premises of this book is that such sensationalism misrecognizes technology as a periodically disruptive and autonomous force or mechanism, rather than an object of social and political negotiation, the struggles over the control of which are revealed in the examples above. Academic writing on cinema is just as liable to this sensationalism and to a fetishization of the 'new' (as represented by the discourse of the 'digital', or the digital turn) as journalistic or promotional commentary. This book certainly addresses the impact of digital technologies upon the production, perception and experience of film images, but seeks to place it within a continuous history of transformation and experimentation, contest and struggle. We are concerned with the complex field of engagement and interaction, where the meaning and value of technology emerges as the effect of its use rather than as the result of its inherent properties.

While academic discourse is susceptible to the rhetoric of innovation and invention, there is an equally strong tendency to play down the effects of technological change, or to overlook its significance. This is partly the result of the fact that academic discourse is (or academics are) slow to register changes for a variety of reasons. In the field of film studies this is sometimes articulated as politicized resistance or as self-conscious cinephilia, and in some respects this slow and focused response is valuable. A sceptical refusal of the rhetoric of revolutionary change and shocking novelty can open a space for critical reflection. It is more typically the case, though, that announcements of innovation and radical change, in the press and in promotional material, are taken at face value. By the time the manifestations of technological transformations become 'visible', the shifts seem to have already taken place, generating the desire to account for this apparent change. A failure to recognize that these shifts are constant, however, can mean that academic writing on cinema is relegated to the role of describing their putative after-effects, examining the after-images, either with a celebratory tone, with the romantic sense that one is working at the 'cutting edge', the threshold of the future, or with a sense of resignation at the inefficacy of academic interventions in the face of these apparently irresistible revolutionary movements. Writing about new developments in cinema technology can convey the seductive impression of currency in documenting technological change as it happens, but the fact is that all too often such writing is complicit with or suborned to the neoliberal capitalist spectacle of radical progress, joining the journalistic and promotional chorus, failing to consider whether the claims are legitimate and failing to address or dispute the very logic of the rhetoric of innovation.[6]

Writing and thinking about cinema and technology thus requires a certain mobility of approach in response to this shifting, evasive and dispersed issue, which is constituted and reconstituted within specific regimes of discourse. Each of the chapters collected here is concerned with accounting for cinema as inevitably bound up with processes of technological interaction. While open to technological forces, though, it is never wholly determined by those forces, nor reducible to a basic technological identity. While most historical and critical accounts of cinema accept its technological character – that its origins are in a technological breakthrough or innovation (or, more correctly, that it emerges within and is constituted by continuing parallel processes of technological breakthroughs, accidents, errors and dead ends) – this gives way to quite different assumptions about the significance of this technological character or grounding.

## Cinema as technology?

To claim that cinema is basically technological, to understand it *as* a technology, seems little more than common sense. It is a set of technical contraptions, perhaps the most elementary being the camera and the screen. Yet even these are not essential: structural/materialist film-makers such as Stan Brakhage, Norman McLaren and Len Lye have eschewed a camera to work directly on film with paints, dyes, scalpels and collaged materials, while digital animators work with 'virtual cameras' in producing animations. In simplest terms, though, cinema may be understood as a technical process for the registration and subsequent projection of moving images, the origins of which may be found in earlier technologies. Hence, the emergence of cinema is often presented as a sort of technological culmination. 'The beginning of film history', writes David Cook, 'is the end of something else: the successive stages of technological development throughout the nineteenth century whereby simple optical devices used for entertainment grew into sophisticated machines which could convincingly represent empirical reality in motion' (1996, p. 1).

Cinema, from this perspective, is *first of all* technological. It represents the apparent fulfilment of a desire for the mechanical reproduction of motion in the field of vision, the complex realization of the technical possibilities that were merely suggested by earlier 'simpler' optical devices such as Joseph Plateau's 'Phenakistoscope', George Horner's 'daedalum', Eadweard Muybridge's 'Zoopraxinoscope' or Étienne-Jules Marey's 'Chronophotographe'. On the basis of these technical devices, cinema emerges, first as a technology, and only later as an aesthetic medium. 'The most important reason the motion pictures came into being', argue Jack Ellis and Virginia Wright Wexman, 'had nothing to do with their artistic potential' (2001, p. 1). The possibility of cinema, they argue, became apparent through a process of technological 'demonstration':

> The theory underlying the motion picture was demonstrated in a succession of optical toys. Its tools and materials were invented out

of a desire to make visual records of life and to study the movements of animals, including humans. Its capacity to provide peep-show entertainment attracted impresarios and paying customers to what scientists and inventors had made available.
(Ellis and Wexman, 2001, p. 1)

The subsequent history of cinema is then conceived as a move away from these technological origins towards the aesthetic possibilities that have been created, as it moves from the hands of the 'scientist and inventors' who had created it to the 'impresarios' who began to exploit it for 'paying customers', as it ceases to be a 'technology' and becomes instead an 'art'. After the initial period of wonder, when the technology itself was the attraction, new aesthetic possibilities began to emerge. According to Ellis and Wexman, 'as the novelty of lifelike movement began to pale, the technicians and entrepreneurs who had discovered how to project moving images onto the screen stumbled onto an old interest latent in audiences – the story. They began to offer simple narratives in a new form' (2001, p. 1).

On the basis of such effectively teleological and deterministic accounts, critical discussion of cinema and technology has been oriented around two loosely divergent responses to cinema's technological character. The first line of argument insists that for various reasons technology is largely irrelevant in relation to the aesthetic and semiotic analysis of films and an appreciation of their cultural significance. It is a distraction from or a substitute for critical engagement, or, for David Cook, it is simply the case that no technical developments of any consequence have taken place for over a century, since the basic technological foundation was originally established. 'By 1896', he claims,

> all the basic technological principles of film recording and projection had been discovered and incorporated into existing machines – which, with certain obvious exceptions like the introduction of light-sensitive sound, have remained essentially unchanged from that day to this. Thus, the history of cinema as an art form begins, for if our understanding of the machines was sophisticated, knowledge of how to use them was primitive indeed.
> (Cook, 1996, p. 13)

The pattern of technological *origin* and subsequent aesthetic *development* was established early in the history of film theory. In *The Photoplay*, first published in 1916, Hugo Münsterberg argued that thinking about cinema *as/and* technology was an unhelpful distraction. Posing the problem of film in exclusively aesthetic and psychological terms, he asked whether 'the moving pictures bring us an independent art, controlled by esthetic laws of its own' (Münsterberg, 1970, p. 43). It was a question that he thought had been ignored by those who had so far undertaken to explain the 'moving pictures' in merely technological terms. 'If this so far neglected problem is ours', he wrote,

> we evidently need not ask in our further discussions about all which books on moving pictures have so far put in the foreground, namely the physical technique of producing the pictures on the film or of projecting the pictures on the screen, or anything else which belongs to the technical or physical or economic aspect of the photoplay industry.
>
> (Münsterberg, 1970, p. 43)

To approach cinema from the perspective of its technological constitution, Münsterberg insisted, was to mistake means and ends, distracting the theorist from the primary object of enquiry. The other arts, he maintained, were not considered in terms of their technical or physical basis. 'If we try to understand and to explain the means by which music exerts its powerful effects', he insists, 'we do not reach our goal by describing the structure of the piano and of the violin, or by explaining the physical laws of sound' (Münsterberg, 1970, pp. 44–5). Similarly, if cinema is understood to have achieved the status of art, then it must not be reduced to its technological basis. What Münsterberg sought was 'an insight into the means by which the moving pictures impress us and appeal to us. Not the physical means and technical devices are in question, but the mental means' (1970, p. 39).

Münsterberg and other early film theorists were concerned with directing attention to cinema's aesthetic potential, which could only be realized, they claimed, by overcoming the merely technological capacities of cinema. The idea that film-makers have been preoccupied with pushing at and trying to overcome the technical boundaries of the medium underpins many progressive or teleological accounts of film history. In the era of 'classical' film theory, a central task was to confront those who would dismiss the movies as mere technology, and to celebrate their aesthetic potential. In his 1933 book, *Film as Art*, Rudolf Arnheim explicitly challenged those who would reduce the motion picture camera to the status of a recording instrument, and who rejected the possibility of a cinematic art. 'It is worthwhile', wrote Arnheim,

'to refute thoroughly and systematically the charge that photography and film are only mechanical reproductions and that they therefore have no connection to art' (1971, p. 9).[7]
Later film theorists would find other reasons for distinguishing between the technological and other more significant aspects of the cinematic phenomenon. Christian Metz, for instance, advocated a methodological division of labour, isolating those aspects of cinema that were most amenable to, or that were most in need of, analysis. Elaborating a semiotics of cinema, he insisted that its purview be necessarily limited. 'The cinematic object', he wrote, 'is . . . immense and heteroclite, and sufficiently large so that some of its dimensions – for example the economic and technological – are excluded from the domain of semiotic analysis' (1974, p. 17). The legacy of Metzian semiotics is found in the many formalist projects that followed, but more broadly in the basic textualism that characterized much film theory in subsequent decades. This is part of the more general tendency, though, that has pushed technological questions to the margins of film studies, as it has sought to describe cinema in formal, aesthetic or social and cultural terms, which have been understood as distinct and separate (or separable) from technological issues.

A second line of argument claims that technology is of key importance, a permanent determining factor on cinematic form and meaning. The most influential form of this argument was developed in the pages of various French journals in the 1960s and 1970s, and was stated perhaps most explicitly by Marcellin Pleynet, at the time an editor of the journal *Tel Quel*, in an interview in *Cinéthique* from 1969. Pleynet insisted that cinema was the inheritor of the 'scientific' technique for the reproduction of perspective, and that it could not be understood as a 'neutral' technology. The camera was 'a tool that spreads the bourgeois ideology before anything else' (quoted in Casetti, 1999, p. 186). Such a claim was the basis for what came to be called 'apparatus' theory, and for the various subsequent accounts of cinema as 'mental machinery', which was understood to reproduce the basic structures of human perception and cognition, with the effect that natural and cinematic vision become confused. The central task of film theory, then, was to reveal the technological basis, and ideological effects, of such confusion. An explicitly political project, the task was to subject cinema to a rigorous ideological analysis. In order to do this, in order to reveal and challenge cinema's political function and ideological effects, the source of those effects had to be exposed. It was, as Francesco Casetti has said, in his account of apparatus theory, 'to analyse the functioning of the basic machinery and the modes of representation of the cinema' (1999, p. 196).[8]

The argument was presented most compellingly and influentially in what is perhaps one of the most widely read essays on cinematic technology, Jean-Louis Baudry's 'Ideological Effects of the Basic Cinematic Apparatus'. Baudry provides a critical account of the cinematic process, which he describes as a process of effacement or disavowal, and considers the 'ideological effects' of obscuring the technological character of cinematic production. Any effective critical analysis of cinema, he argues, must begin with an analysis of its technological constitution – it 'must first establish the place of the instrumental base in the set of operations which combine in the production of a film' (Baudry, 1986, p. 287). However, the analysis of films had tended to proceed from the other direction. 'It is strange', he writes,

> (but is it so strange?) that emphasis has been placed almost exclusively on their influence, on the effects that they have as finished products, their content, the field of the signified if you like; the technical bases on which these effects depend and the specific characteristics of these bases have, however, been ignored.
> (Baudry, 1986, p. 287)

Baudry sought to reverse the traditional approach, beginning not with the finished product, but with the apparatus of production. He shifted the traditional perspective of film theory, turning his attention specifically to the question of technology. His primary concern was not the film itself (or films themselves) but rather the efforts to produce the film. To the degree that he was concerned with the 'finished product', it was to demonstrate how films obscure, or 'conceal', the facts of their production. What Baudry aimed to describe is all that occurs between the initial moment of inscription – and so this is a restricted model of cinema in some ways, one that begins with a camera – and the final moment of projection, everything that is concealed at that final moment. 'Between "objective reality" and the camera, site of inscription', he writes, 'and between the inscription and projection are situated certain operations, a work which has as its result a finished product' (Baudry, 1986, p. 287). From this perspective, cinema comes to be seen less as a set of specific, discrete aesthetic objects, the effects and influences of which we may consider from various perspectives, and more as a generalizable process, an operation or set of operations, which generates objects that seem, but *only* seem, to be autonomous objects of enquiry, about whose effects we may speculate without having to consider the facts of their generation.

For Baudry, then, a proper account of cinema begins with the question of production or generation, making visible the labour that produced the object. 'Cinematographic specificity', Baudry insists, 'thus refers to a work, that is, to a process of transformation' (1986, p. 287). The site of specificity has been shifted from the object, from 'the work', understood as a noun, to 'work', understood as a verb. Theoretical enquiry shifts from the object to the production of that object, to the transformation by the cinematic apparatus of 'objective reality' into an 'object', an epistemological process already described by Plato, in what Baudry presents as the proto-cinematic scenario at the centre of *The Republic*. In a follow-up essay, 'The Apparatus', Baudry says:

> One constantly returns to the scene of the cave. As a matter of fact, isn't it curious that Plato, in order to . . . make understood what sort of illusion underlies our direct contact with the real, would imagine or resort to an apparatus that doesn't merely evoke but quite precisely describes in its mode of operation the cinematographic apparatus and the spectator's place in relation to it.
> 
> (1986, p. 302)

Baudry's recourse to Plato, as carefully historicized as he might have imagined it to be, nevertheless subjects his argument to certain philosophical risks, and the process of concealment that he describes suggests too rigid a mode of spectatorial engagement. To argue that technology may be 'concealed' in such a manner is to restrict cinematic technology to technical, material manifestations, to inevitably find the source of ideological effects in the devices themselves (the camera that we never see, the projector hidden behind us in the theatre), whereas, in its understanding of technology as a practice/process, this book is concerned with opening up notions of technology to embrace the plurality of viewing practices and modes of spectatorship and affect and to consider the vast, dense network of screens scattered unevenly but profusely across the globe. The book is concerned with the fact that the technological process has, for the most part, *not* been concealed, but has remained highly visible in many areas of moving image culture (even while it may remain historically and critically obscure) both within mainstream narrative cinema – we might cite, for example, the popular preoccupation with stars from the early 1900s onwards, which suggests, at the very least, a more or less complex recognition of the constructedness of fiction films, or, more recently, the loading of DVD videos with 'demystifying' documentaries about various aspects of a film's production – and in the expanded 'cinematic' field beyond. It is not the 'concealment' of the devices that is the ideological issue, but rather the social and political struggles and negotiations over the arrangement, deployment and usage of cinematic and moving image technology.

Nevertheless, apparatus theory's insistence on the acknowledgement of the processes, techniques and materiality of film production *is* a crucial starting point. Baudry's emphasis on the 'work' of cinematic production, and Jean-Louis Comolli's subsequent efforts to place the cinematic apparatus within a more carefully delineated historical context, were important steps in the elaboration of a technological analysis of cinema. For Comolli, one cannot study technology outside of a context of use. 'As soon as one interprets a technical process "for its own sake"', he insists, 'by cutting it off from the signifying practice where it is not just a factor but an *effect* . . . it becomes an ahistorical empirical object' (Comolli, 1986, p. 430; emphasis in original). Despite such declarations, however, apparatus theorists have been roundly criticized for effectively producing a logic of technological determinism and a too rigid account of the spectatorial experience. Robert Stam has complained that apparatus theory 'at times imbued the cinematic machine with an abstract and malevolent intentionality, falling into a kind of neo-Platonic condemnation of emotional manipulation. But real-life spectators', he insists, 'were never the pathetically deluded, shackled captives of a high-tech version of Plato's cave decreed by apparatus theorists' (Stam, 2000, p. 139).

An account of cinema and technology cannot ignore the importance and the significance of apparatus theory, but it must avoid, as James Lastra has insisted, the pitfalls revealed in its theoretical excesses. While acknowledging that Baudry and Comolli 'each in his way attempts to focus upon the conjuncture between devices and particular cultural contexts, each winds up reinstating a kind of technological determinism' (Lastra, 2000, p. 11). In his careful historical account of the relation between sound technologies and the American cinema, Lastra has offered a corrective to such determinism. In his account of cameras and other recording devices as technologies in use, Lastra insists that 'we need to recognize that in spite of their apparent material intransigence, representational devices, however familiar, are neither static nor self-defining' (2000, p. 61). By contrast, he insists, the arguments of Baudry and Comolli,

> about the aesthetic or social ideologies 'inherent' in photography, or, more commonly, in cameras and lenses, necessarily reduce the heterogeneous field covered by those terms by naturalizing one particular

historical tradition of representation as the exclusively determinant one. Instead, we should understand devices as constitutively situated in networks of assumptions, habits, practices and modes of representation that extend well beyond instrument-centered definitions of technology.

(Lastra, 2000, pp. 61–2)

Accounts of cinematic technologies have been preponderantly 'instrument-centred', and this is reflected in most analyses of the latest technological developments. The so-called 'digital cinema' is typically described in fundamentally technological terms, the overweening force of which radically limits or determines its aesthetic potential and cultural significance, and produces specific ideological effects. 'The ruling ideology of computer-generated imagery', writes Wheeler Winston Dixon, 'is above all that of synthetic creation' (1998, p. 112). The technology is conceived of as an autonomous, malevolent force that we must resist, 'or we become passive viewers at the service of a narcotizing series of images that seek to control and pacify our emotions' (Dixon, 1998, p. 186). Dixon describes, in terms that recall the excesses of apparatus theory, 'the transparency of the cinematic/video construct [which] is at once alluring and dangerously seductive, a spectacle that we must control, before it controls us' (1998, p. 186). In the digital era, according to Sean Cubitt, '[i]t is no longer the case that films in some way respond to, refract, express, or debate reality or society. Mass entertainment has abandoned the task of making sense of the world, severing the cords that bound the two together' (2004, p. 245). Digital cinema, he claims, 'subordinates the phenomenon to the subject-object nexus of the commodity, so that we stand in awe of the object nature of the object, and surrender to that' (Cubitt, 2004, p. 269). In terms that are inevitably deterministic, these effects are presented as the direct result of technological change. Lev Manovich describes the 'distinct logic of a digital moving image. This logic', he insists, 'subordinates the photographic and the cinematic to the painterly and the graphic, destroying cinema's identity as a media art' (Manovich, 2001, p. 295). Focussing on the devices themselves, Manovich elaborates an instrument-centred account, so that 'digital technology redefines what can be done with cinema' (2001, p. 305). Such sweeping claims obscure the far more complex and heterogeneous fields of technological use, the networks of interaction and the arenas of struggle and contest, where the possible meanings and effects of technology are subject to constant renewal and reformulation.

## 'New' understandings of cinema and technology?

Could cinema be understood along different lines from those laid down by apparatus theory or by histories of cinematic technology? In one sense, this book offers an extended and varied experiment into the possibility of understanding specificities without lifting cinema out of the material conditions of its experience. What would this new dispensation look like? What would be at stake? Several chapters in this volume indicate a preliminary requirement of any nuanced account of the complicated conjunction of cinema and technology. It is necessary to pay attention to how technology is invoked in relation to cinema. What counts as technology is not historically stable or invariant. 'Technology' appears in conjunction with cinema under quite specific conditions. Given that any practice or thing in human and non-human affairs potentially has a technical dimension, the problem is always to specify what determines that a specific practice or thing becomes something 'technological'. Hence, whenever someone claims that technology is the basis, the foundation, the driving force or the agent of change in relation to cinema, it is necessary to examine what is at stake in these claims. What does this invocation do? Where does it occur? In the name of what, and at what intersections of force? Conversely, whenever someone claims that cinema has nothing to do with the apparatus, the supports, the substrates, the formats, the surfaces of projection or display and so on, then it might be necessary to ask how technology has been rendered invisible and with what effects.

There are many ways one might go about doing this, and we offer a variety of approaches in this collection. One could investigate, as James Elkins does in his chapter on the limits of film theory, things that look like films yet have very little to do with cameras and perceptible action in the world. Elkins' investigation of visualization in high-energy physics and astronomy discovers cinematic aspects of contemporary scientific knowledge production. The worlds of the ultra-small, the astronomically large, the extremely short-lived or the excruciatingly slow seem a long way from the life-worlds of most cinema. The practices of scientific visualization deploy an apparatus that differs greatly from anything imagined in most accounts of film, and indeed visual culture more generally. Yet they are recognizably cinematic in form. In moving in this direction, Elkins extends the limits of what we are prepared to see as filmic or cinematic.

Another way of understanding invocations of technology and cinema is to analyse how film theory and film studies themselves respond to technology. Marie-Louise Angerer in 'Affective Troubles and Cinema' heads in this direction. She analyses how recent film and media theory re-orients itself to technology by redefining and re-conceptualizing visual experience in terms of affect and corporeality. Angerer contends that the turn to affect in so much cultural and media studies work on audio-visual media responds to an alteration in contemporary or recent-past conditions of experience. The upsurge of affect-related theorization of media claims to re-conceptualize spectators along radically different lines. For Angerer it attests more to the stunning of perception by high rates of image-sound flow, themselves generated by patterns of densely networked image-sound production. Affect-based theory disguises rather than specifies these patternings. Again, like Elkins, Angerer explores a limit case. If Elkins poses the problem of things that look like a film yet come from a radically different apparatus, Angerer poses the problem of people who seem be experiencing a film yet are understood as doing or being something radically different (for example, as a 'sensorimotor nexus of the body open ... to its own indeterminacy' (Hansen, 2004, p. 7)). She highlights the issue of how far we are prepared to go in saying experience is cinematic or cinematographic, yet still recognizably a matter of experience.

In the light of these two limit cases, we might say that what is really needed is a reflexively mediated analysis of the historically specific circumstances in which technology is called on (or rejected) in explaining or representing something about cinema. These circumstances will not always be broadly shared, coherent or general. Many of the chapters in this book discuss local or limited circumstances and specific appeals to technology. This can mean analysing just one dimension or feature of cinema such as the legal constraints on early cinema architecture in Paul Moore's history of early cinema in Toronto; the industrial and economic discourses around competing film gauges described by Peter Lester; or the blending of Web and cinematic systems of distribution in car advertising of the late 1990s analysed by Andrew Clay. One effect of such historically specific accounts is to remind us of the variety of practices and processes that might become 'technological'. Any point in the circuits of production, circulation, consumption, regulation, representation and identity might enter a phase of 'technologization'.

The circumstances under which technology and cinema come into conjunction appear on screen in various ways. Several chapters in this book develop accounts of how cinematic forms and figures are deeply imbued with technological traits. These range from highly general figures and forms of cinema such as the double, which Jan Harris approaches through a reading of Gilles Deleuze and Friedrich Kittler, to temporal restructurings of narrative affected by technological accidents, as described in Michelle Langford's account of Weimar cinema. Screen space itself is being reorganized in the wake of interactive technologies and point-click controls. We are faced with the 'multiplying interface' described by Aylish Wood, and the complex spaces of the digitally animated image analysed by Bill Schaffer.

The fears and hopes generated by technological change are often given compelling cinematic expression, and film-makers have long sought to reproduce the affective experiences of inhabiting a highly technologized world. Maja Manojlovic addresses the question of affect in cinema, through the notion of the 'interval', describing the emergence of a new 'digital' aesthetic. Christopher Rodrigues traces the history of such 'affective' style, looking at the tradition of the European art film, and the play between attention and distraction that has been mobilized by various film-makers, as a strategy for engaging the viewer, drawing our attention to the technological effects of cinematic representation.

The cinematic image is also a significant site of empathetic engagement, where we are able often to gaze into the faces of others, a technologically mediated experience that is at once intimate and puzzling. This experience is described by Bruce Bennett, who traces the recent history of the familiar scenario of human/robot relationships, which can be read as an allegory for cinematic engagement itself. Robot doubles are giving way, though, to the possibilities of genetic reproduction, which Kate O'Riordan considers in her account of the figurations of genomic science, an increasingly compelling subject for film-makers.

There is no singular outlook presented here. We are concerned, instead, with revealing the very many ways in which the question of technology may be raised in relation to cinema, and to offer a few preliminary answers. The concept of technology developed in this book could be described as event-driven, designed to account for the rapid appearances and disappearances of cinema *as* technology and for the manifold relations and intersections of cinema *and* technology. Such an approach aims to maximize specificity yet maintain openness to ongoing revision and alteration. The contributors to this book explore a variety of sites of technological engagement and consider a wide range of objects and activities: science films and the limits of cinematic images, Web cinema, the regulation of early cinema-going, perception of sound and light at film media interfaces, DVD formats, genetic technology in cinema, the aesthetics of digital cinema, digital video cameras in practice, film distribution networks, new narrative structures associated with database logics, animation, new approaches to film history, spectatorship and affectivity, changing film formats and the fictional representations of technology and the body. In his chapter that concludes this book, Thomas Elsaesser makes the case for a 'wider agenda' for film studies, arguing that film scholars need to attend to a 'different range of issues'. Film exists, he says, within an 'expanded field', comprising a diverse set of practices and discourses. This book traverses this expanded field as it explores the complex relationships between cinema and technology.

## Notes

1. There is a large and rapidly expanding literature on the effects of new digital technology on cinema, most of which describes the 'challenges' that such technologies pose, or the radical transformations they have produced. Jay David Bolter and Richard Grusin, for instance, describe cinema as '[a]rguably the most important artform of the twentieth century', but insist that its aesthetic status has been put at risk, that it is 'especially challenged by new media' (1999, p. 147). The response, they argue, has been to try to 'absorb computer graphics into its traditional structure', transforming cinema into a more explicitly technological phenomenon and foregrounding its status *as* a technology. Anne Friedberg has claimed that '[t]he cinema screen has been replaced by its digital other, the computer screen' (2000, p. 439). Cinema, she argues, 'has been dramatically transformed. It has become embedded in – or perhaps lost in – the new technologies that surround it' (p. 439). For a counter argument, see John Belton's essay, 'Digital Cinema: A False Revolution' (2002).
2. The classic work on the complex negotiations and struggles over the value and meaning of the newly emerging electric communication media in the latter half of the nineteenth century is Carolyn Marvin's *When Old Technologies Were New*. Marvin begins by insisting that '[n]ew technologies is a historically relative term', and seeks to temper contemporary accounts by carefully historicizing the reception and deployment of 'new' media. 'We are not the first generation', she insists, 'to wonder at the rapid and extraordinary shifts in the dimension of the world and the human relationships it contains as a result of new forms of communication' (Marvin, 1988, p. 3). Her task is to reveal those aspects of electric media history that have, as she says, 'been rendered invisible', and to introduce 'issues that may have been overlooked when the social history of . . . media is framed exclusively by the instrument-centred perspective that governs its conventional starting point' (Marvin, 1988, p. 4). Marvin focuses less on 'the evolution of technical efficiencies' than on 'a series of arenas for negotiating issues crucial to the conduct of social life', asking questions about who garners the authority to determine the value and meaning of technologies. 'Changes in the speed, capacity and performance of communications devices', she insists, 'tell us little about these questions' (Marvin, 1988, p. 4).
3. See also Wanda Strauven's new collection of essays, *The Cinema of Attractions Reloaded* (2006), and Tom Brown's 'The DVD of Attractions?' (2007).
4. See www.boingboing.net/2006/01/18/big_theater_chains_r.html.

5. See, for example, 'Winterbottom Film Makes Cinema History', *Guardian Unlimited*, February 14, 2006 (Figgis, 2007).
6. The historian of technology, David Edgerton, has long been critical of what he calls the 'innovation-centred' accounts of technology. In his recent book, *The Shock of the Old*, he complains that 'too often the agenda for discussing the past, present and future of technology is set by the promoters of new technology' (2006, p. ix). He argues instead for a 'history of technology-in-use' (2006, p. xi), which would focus on the far more significant fact of duration over the moments of invention and innovation, which are in fact quite rare. Edgerton is primarily concerned with those technologies that are no longer visible *as* technology, obscured by the powerful and self-interested discourse of the new. 'By thinking about the history of technology-in-use', he argues, 'a radically different picture of technology . . . becomes possible. A whole invisible world of technologies appears' (2006, p. xi).
7. Arnheim was quite sensitive, though, to the movement from novelty to familiarity, the passage of an object from the status of 'technical gadget', whose value and significance is in question, to familiar cultural entity, whose character is no longer puzzling or in dispute. In his 1935 essay, 'A Forecast of Television', he notes that the 'new gadget seems magical and mysterious. It arouses curiosity: How does it work? What does it do to us?' (1971, p. 188). Such questions recede, though, once the basic patterns of use have been established, when the strange technology has become an unremarkable commodity. 'To be sure', he notes, 'when the television sets will have appeared on the birthday tables and under the Christmas trees, curiosity will abate. Mystery asks for explanation only as long as it is new' (1971, p. 188).
8. Casetti (1999) offers a detailed account of the complex and competing arguments developed by the various 'apparatus' theorists. See pp. 184–96.

# I
# Format

To discuss cinema in relation to formats might seem to restrict a critical engagement with film to questions of technical standards. A format is the physical vehicle for the transmission or distribution of specific recorded information, but it is always much more than that, since the dominance or disappearance of a particular format, such as 'Technicolor' or 'Eastmancolor', is as much a matter of economics, marketing and aesthetics as it is a question of functionality. A format is thus the provisional crystallization of a complex set of histories, processes and interests. Typically, however, formats are regarded as largely unimportant, functioning merely to make information available/perceptible to our ears or eyes. While each successive format may be understood to be an improvement on the last – offering ever greater verisimilitude, for example, or easier access to the means of production – and while there are those who argue for the superior aesthetic qualities of some formats over others – celluloid film, for example, offers a richer, more precise image than the digital projection systems that are increasingly popular in cinemas – the format itself is often understood as simply the subordinate material support for the primary aesthetic object, the recording itself, an integral object (or text?) capable of distribution in any number of suitable formats.

Much recent work endeavours to account for the aesthetic reconfigurations associated with format-change across a range of media and the chapters included in this section are engaged with the challenge of understanding and theorizing the significance of formats and reformattings at different historical junctures. Many critics and theorists argue that the latest technological developments in communications and entertainment media and the proliferation of new formats of cinematic exhibition, such as DVD players and flat-screen video displays, video iPods and computer game consoles, are transforming the cinema, perhaps even jeopardizing its existence. This claim is something of a commonplace, of course, and such questions as to whether cinema is being vitiated by the sorts of 'format wars' that characterize the histories of other media, or whether, in being reduced to a variety of alterable formats, cinema will lose its particular aesthetic character, are by now familiar points of discussion. If cinema is understood to have derived its identity from the relative historical stability of its format, then any changes in the format might seem to have a radical effect on the character of the medium. Such claims, however, belie the fact that the cinematic format has been subject to many changes and should be understood as the site of considerable and constant transformation. One has only to consider the very many competing film gauges – not only the well-known standards of IMAX, 70mm, 35mm, 16mm and 8mm, but the less well-known alternatives, including 9.5mm and 28mm, the latter introduced by Pathé in 1911 as an alternative for the burgeoning non-theatrical market (Mebold and Tepperman, 2003, pp. 137–8). Cinema is also exported to other formats, as films are shown on broadcast television and as they have been made available in the form of videocassettes (Betamax and VHS), laserdiscs, DVD, Blu-Ray discs and now in the various video compression formats for the distribution of moving images on the Internet and exhibition on various portable devices. Recent digital developments should be understood not as radically new, though, but as part of a long history of cinematic reformatting, or of what Toby Miller has described as 'occasionality', the many and varied, and often highly contested, sites for the consumption or even possession of moving imagery that emerge with each new format (Miller, 2001, p. 306). As Miller argues, the moving image has never been restricted to one particular format. It has, rather, been available in a wide variety of modes, each of which has provided various degrees of accessibility, portability and reproducibility, each providing a different sense of 'occasion'.

In this respect, a format is not merely the specific material substrate or medium such as the celluloid filmstrip, but should be understood as the changing material circumstances according to which we are in a constant state of renegotiating our relationship with and understanding of the cinematic phenomenon. The value of thinking about cinema in relation to formats and technical changes – how the image is 'formatted' – is that it gives on to a range of questions about how films are funded, produced, distributed and watched and actively used by audiences. Formatting thus refers to various stages in the physical manufacture and circulation of films, and it also refers to the processes of the organization of information and interpretation of data – how meaning is made. Formatting, in this more global sense, is the intimate relation between style, technology and experience. The chapters in this section are all on questions of format, understood not as the unchanging substrate of the cinematic apparatus, but rather as a dynamic field of both technological and discursive change.

Peter Lester's chapter offers a survey of the exhibition of 16mm film in Canada, challenging the tendency of histories of cinema to associate the 16mm gauge almost entirely with educational films. This very specific case study highlights the way that normative values are attached to particular formats and offers an instructive example of the commercial, legal and institutional pressures that are factors in the dominance of one particular format, such as 35mm film, over other competing formats. Lester's chapter also reveals how critical accounts of cinema are shaped by these pressures.

Andrew Clay describes the migration of the cinema to the alternate formats of the computer and the Web, resulting in such hybrid forms as the 'advermovie' or 'webvert'. These constitute one of the most recent re-configurations of the relationship between Hollywood cinema and commodity production, but, Clay suggests, there are also significant parallels between the attractions of early cinema and this contemporary 'cinema of distractions'. 'Advermovies' thus offer an example of contemporary cinema undergoing reformatting, but also indicate that this process of reconfiguration is integral to the medium's history.

As James Elkins suggests in his chapter on scientific films, film formats comprise highly divergent ways of seeing and hearing. Terms such as picture, film, still and motion bear within them formatted norms of seeing. Other formats sometimes look cinematic in their handling of motion, frame and picture, but the scale of events they encounter and register may lie well beyond the turns (terms?) of camera-screen-eye experience. The Rapatronic camera, the scanning, tunnelling electron microscope or the interferometer radio telescope array can deliver films that appear simply to show us the normally visible world in greater detail. However, many norms of perception (contrasts between light and shadow as defining objects, the linear flow of time, the difference between movement and stillness) and many assumptions about the world in which things become perceptible simply do not apply at these different scales of events. Could we say then that every cinematic format embodies a different norm of seeing? Or alternately, should we say that every technology of seeing can be subjected to cinematic formatting?

# 1
# The Perilous Gauge: Canadian Independent Film Exhibition and the 16mm Mobile Menace

*Peter Lester*

> Our viewpoint is that the 16mm is not a little exhibitor or a little trouble; the 16mm is as benign and harmless as a cancer and that gradually it will eat out the territory of the little exhibitor and spread to the zones of the big fellows.
>
> Ray Lewis, 'Ray Presents', editorial voice for
> *Canadian Moving Picture Digest*, 29 October 1938

Advocates of 35mm motion picture technology have always been quick to spot looming threats to the format, yet it has proved to be remarkably resilient. Today, over a century since its inception and subsequent adoption by the film industry as its standard format, the fundamental characteristics of the medium remain surprisingly intact. Cameras and projectors have improved and their employment has been mastered – yet the core principles of the technology itself have changed very little. The reign of 35mm as the dominant standard has, however, been marked by frequent 'cultural disturbances', be they real or imagined, which have set off panics heralding the end of the format and the death of the medium. The recent challenge posed by emergent digital technologies, for instance, is but the latest in a series of such disturbances that have, to varying degrees, represented perceived threats to the format's dominant position, a history that includes such developments as the introduction of television and the later widespread availability of home video technologies. Crucial to this tension that has consistently plagued 35mm's dominance is a recognition that the conflicts posed by these competing media forms represent far more than mere issues of technological performance. Beyond the obvious technological tone to these debates, they bear with them considerable social and political implications. The discourses surrounding these media *mêlées* ultimately function as sites of contestation over competing venues of cultural consumption and participation, over the formation of audience groupings and over issues of actual filmic content (as opposed to technological form). The result has been governing industrial and popular discourses that all too frequently find themselves expressed in seemingly paranoid dispositions. However, despite all the talk of a technological *coup d'état*, 35 mm has yet to be usurped and, for now, continues to enjoy its dominant industrial position.

But perhaps there is something different about the recent move towards digital film production and exhibition. That 35 mm will remain the dominant standard in the film industry is far from assured. Digital film production has already established itself as a legitimate alternative to traditional film-making technologies, and there is currently serious discussion of a full transition to digital theatrical exhibition in the coming years – a transition that, according to the rhetoric of the National Association of Theatre Owners, the largest exhibition trade organization in the world, would appear all but inevitable.

A separate (though not entirely unrelated) challenge perceived by dominant forces in the industry that threatens its status quo is the issue of film piracy. Even the most casual moviegoer could not have failed to notice the massive anti-piracy campaign waged in recent years by the Motion Picture Association of America, and a visit to the association's website makes it abundantly clear how much importance it attaches to this issue.[1] While there is nothing particularly novel about the issue of piracy itself, its recently assumed prominence in the discourse of the film industry is noteworthy. What is interesting about piracy is that this issue, more than any other, is where the industry's rhetoric of moral outrage is most clearly evidenced and articulated. Much of the language present in the contemporary discourses surrounding piracy and the 'evils' it represents seems to replicate the tone and content that frequently characterized previous historical discourses surrounding threats posed by competing technologies. 'Rogue' cultural practices, such as piracy, facilitated by 'new media' technologies are frequently framed as unprecedented threats that the industry must confront, when in reality these threats are very much prefigured in a number of historical instances. There appears too often an assumption that digital technologies and their related 'new media' configurations, along with the practices associated with them (be they perceived as 'legit' or not) present somehow entirely new challenges to dominant models of communication. While perhaps an argument could be made that the sheer scale and scope of the 'digital revolution' certainly merits it a certain distinctiveness, this tendency nevertheless obscures the reality that contemporary debates surrounding the nature and function of film technology and its relationship to the practice of film exhibition echo earlier moments of cultural and technological disturbance. The interest here is not so much in the veracity of the claims and assumptions that appear throughout these historical debates as in the acknowledgement that by putting too much stock in the rhetoric of these discourses we run the risk of in fact overlooking the true impact that emergent technologies have had, and will continue to have, upon alternative spheres of moving image culture and practice. Given that at our current historical juncture, 35 mm's reign may actually be in question due to the very real threat represented by digital technologies, a consideration of previous historical threats that it has faced seems appropriate. And it is on this topic that this chapter seeks to make a contribution, through a detailed examination of the impact of the introduction of 16 mm technology on the cultural landscape of film exhibition in Canada in the interwar period, and the concerted efforts by segments of the industry at large to curtail and contain this rival format that threatened the interests of these dominant forces.

The history of 16 mm is particularly relevant to a discussion of competing technological forms, as its introduction as a means of film exhibition was perhaps the first to pose what many in the film industry perceived as a threat to the dominance of the standard 35 mm gauge. It was by no means, however, the first actual alternative to 35 mm. Although 35 mm had quickly established itself as the dominant industrial format, as early as 1899 film companies were experimenting with a wide range of film stock widths. A 1930 paper published in *The Society of Motion Picture Engineer's Journal* lists the variety of alternative film formats available at the turn of the century, from as small as 12.7 mm to as large as 95.25 mm (cited in Graham, 1989, p. 49). However, due to insufficient demand and products to sustain them, these 'substandard' formats failed to gain much of a foothold and subsequently mostly faded into the footnotes of history. The reliable 35 mm format was the standard in urban theatres, but more and more, entrepreneurial individuals were experimenting with the concept of mobile, or travelling, cinema and began showing films outdoors and in public halls across the country, originally with 35 mm projectors and then later with more portable smaller-width gauges. The 35 mm format, while generally a high-quality film stock, was also cumbersome and expensive – suited for theatrical exhibition, but hardly ideal for life on the road. It was also made of a nitrate stock and was therefore highly flammable. The French company

Pathé invented a slow-burning cellulose acetate film in 1915, which made its way to Canada by 1916. This safety base film was somewhat more conducive to non-theatrical environments, which were often previously restricted for fire and safety precautions. By 1917, Pathé had developed a more lightweight 28 mm format, with non-theatrical audiences in mind. But it was the 16 mm format, introduced to Canada by Kodak in 1923, that really took off as a viable alternative to 35 mm. Like the 28 mm before it, 16 mm had its genesis in a greater desire for flexibility and accessibility. While its smaller size lent it an increased capacity for portability, its projection accordingly suffered from decreased image quality. The intention was never to supplant 35 mm, but rather to complement it. Whereas 35 mm was the standard in theatres, 16 mm offered a flexibility more in tune with the needs of the growing ranks of amateur film-makers and non-theatrical exhibition markets. On this issue there is no real debate: 35 mm was suited for theatres, and 16 mm was suited for less conventional arenas of exhibition.

What becomes interesting, however, is the manner in which the term 'non-theatrical' and its associated film gauge, 16 mm, became increasingly perceived by many as synonymous with a particular form of motion picture – the 'educational' film. It is certainly true that some of the first uses of 16 mm in Canada were in the educational market. According to the Dominion Bureau of Statistics, by 1937 there were 260 projectors in schools across the nation (Gray, 1973, p. 12). This was also a period that saw a growing number of organizations such as university programs, governmental departments, forestry and agriculture associations, church missionaries and many other groups touring rural areas with 16 mm films for educational purposes. The 1930s also witnessed the rapid proliferation of film societies in Canada, the first appearing in Toronto, Ottawa and Vancouver in 1934 and others following in major centres over the next few years. The National Film Society was formed in 1935 with a mandate to 'encourage and promote the study, appreciation and use of motion pictures as educational and cultural factors' (Gray, 1973, p. 27).

While 16 mm was certainly facilitating an important educational function during the 1920s and 1930s, what perhaps is far too regularly forgotten is that the technology was simultaneously being employed by travelling, independent showmen, who served up film programs of a decidedly more entertaining nature, specifically for non-theatrical audiences. While established movie theatres have long been considered the domain for Hollywood fare, the circuits maintained by the itinerant 16 mm exhibitors during this period represented a considerable challenge to this de facto hegemonic position. They represented a separate sphere of leisure activity, specifically for audiences who were isolated from permanent movie theatres. Furthermore, they provided an alternative structure of distribution to the established systems of motion picture circulation, which were established and maintained by the dominant forces in the film industry. Many of these exhibitors screened Hollywood feature film programs to groups of five or six circuit points on a regular weekly basis (Gray, 1973, p. 13). A wide variety of motion pictures were available in 16mm format in the 1930s. Castle Films' series of short colour cartoons such as *Sinbad the Sailor* and *Aladdin's Lamp* were popular selections, for instance. *Felix the Cat* was not an uncommon visitor to non-theatrical screens. Full feature films were also in circulation, such as *Silas Marner*, *The Mill on the Floss* and the Laurel and Hardy film *March of the Toys*. By 1939, some 300 16mm titles, both sound and silent, were in circulation throughout Canada (Gray, 1973, p. 19).

Movies were, of course, 'non-theatrical' before they were 'theatrical'. The invention of the medium obviously predates the introduction of venues specifically built to house them. The earliest screenings of motion pictures were by sheer necessity 'non-theatrical' and many of them were open air, such as the first exhibition of Edison's Vitascope in Ottawa's West End Park or the early screenings at Montreal's Sohmer Park. But as the film industry developed, and theatres were built specifically to screen motion pictures, this by no means meant that the process of non-theatrical exhibition became immediately relegated to the status of archaic cultural activity, even for films considered to be 'entertainment'. In particular 16mm technology played a large role in ensuring this continuity of screen practice, despite the determined efforts of the established theatrical film industry to lay exclusive claim to this sector of moviegoers. The controversies surrounding 16mm film exhibition and the perceived threat it posed to the 35mm theatrical format in Canada were perhaps never more clearly pronounced than in the 1930s, and it is to this period that I would now like to turn.

The history of the Canadian film industry, and the American influence upon it, has been thoroughly documented and analysed by Manjunath Pendakur in his seminal *Canadian Dreams and American Control: The Political Economy of the Canadian Film Industry*. His text carefully traces the roots of dependency in the industry and reveals the web of tensions between American corporate interests and Canadian entrepreneurial capitalists, particularly in the exhibition and distribution sectors. The focus is distinctly theatrical, however, and noticeably absent is any discussion of either non-theatrical screening activity or tensions resulting from the 16 mm format. This is a rather peculiar omission, given the standpoint of the independent theatrical exhibitor, at least as expressed by Ray Lewis, editor of *Canadian Moving Picture Digest*, that in 1938, 16 mm constituted 'a peril much more serious than anything else to contend with' (Lewis, 29 October 1938). *Canadian Moving Picture Digest* was a trade publication primarily designed for exhibitors and producer/distributors in Canada. Lewis' regular column, 'Ray Presents', frequently addressed pressing issues of the day relevant to the interests of 'the little exhibitor', whom she and the publication claimed to represent. For Lewis and other influential figures in the trade press, the greatest peril independent theatre exhibitors faced in the late 1930s was not, as Pendakur would have it, the stranglehold imposed on their industry by American corporate interests – the threat from above – but rather the threat from below – the 16 mm 'fire' that had, as Harold Kay, a Toronto-based independent theatre owner and member of the Independent Theatres Association of Ontario, wrote in the trade journal *Canadian Independent*, 'burst its bounds . . . leapt out and threatens to burn the house down' (Kay, 1 November 1938). Whether the independent 35 mm theatre owners truly felt that the threat posed by 16 mm exhibitors was on par with the rhetoric employed by the trade press is not entirely known, but it is evident that it was a phenomenon they were not taking lightly. An examination of the trade press, embodied in the inflammatory rhetoric of individuals such as Ray Lewis and Harold Kay and in the organizational behaviour of the independent exhibitors, reveals how embedded and deterministic conceptions of the 'hereditary' function of specific media, in this case the place of 16 mm film within the film industry in Canada, continue to manifest and reinforce themselves.

Canadian exhibitors and distributors first united for the pursuit of common interests in 1924 when the Motion Picture Exhibitors and Distributors of Canada was formed. However, as Pendakur (pp. 79–80) is quick to point out, the Cooper Organization, as it was called, after its first president, Col. John Cooper, was essentially a branch plant of the American Motion Picture Producers and Distributors of America, and its actual role was to safeguard the American industry's interests in Canada. In an industry plagued by rivalry between competing local capitalists and American monopoly power, Pendakur (p. 80) reveals that the organization spoke in a language of self-regulation and of unifying common interests. It engaged in such activities as lobbying against censorship, amusement taxes and especially potential quota laws. But the organization was run entirely by American interests, namely the Famous Players chain, and it by no means represented the interests of the independent Canadian-owned theatres. In fact, it often ran counter to their best interests. For example, in 1925 Cooper initiated a standard contract, similar to the American version that was used by film exchanges when selling pictures to exhibitors. Pendakur (p. 85) reveals that this uniform contract in effect gave coercive power to distributors and helped to curtail any power of independent exhibitors.

The increasingly oppressive market conditions experienced by independent exhibitors were eventually acknowledged by the federal government, which launched an inquiry under the Federal Combines Investigation Act in September 1930. The general conclusion was that a combine did in fact exist and that all US distributors in Canada as well as Famous Players were complicit. However, no resulting court cases succeeded in altering the industrial structure in any meaningful way. Independent exhibitors were feeling squeezed out of the market, yet they had no effective means of doing anything. It seems bewildering, then, given this hostile market environment, that the trade press, which spoke for the 'little exhibitor', should single out small-scale 16mm operators as the primary threat to their existence, rather than the obvious foreign-capital behemoth that had them in a headlock.

Unquestionably 16mm had seen a surge in popularity during the 1930s. In Ontario in 1924, the Inspection Branch of the Ontario Treasury Department began to issue licenses for operating 16mm projectors and 16mm film exchanges. In 1938, the activities of the branch merged with the Ontario Board of Censors to form the Motion Picture Censorship and Theatre Inspection Branch. According to available records, during the years 1938–40, the branch had approximately 100 active 16mm licenses in the province, 19 of which were issued for film exchanges. Most of the film exchanges were based in Toronto (15 of 19) and 2 were out of province (Montreal and Winnipeg). Unfortunately, it is difficult to determine exactly how many of the companies that were issued licenses were stable theatrical operations and how many were travelling exhibitors. The majority, however, would appear to be itinerant and rural, rather than stable and urban.[2] Although 100 may not seem like that large a number, the records indicate that approximately only 16 licenses had been issued prior to 1938, under the auspices of the Inspection Branch of the Ontario Treasury Board. There were likely significant numbers of unlicensed operators both before and after 1938, but without question that year certainly appears to be a watershed for the widespread use of 16mm film.

While the National Film Board tends to receive credit for its innovative use of mobile theatre vans during World War II, independent entrepreneurs had been doing the very same thing privately for years. Essentially updating the model created by turn-of-the-century itinerant showmen like John C. Green (aka Belsaz the Magician) and John Schuberg, these outfits simply employed contemporary automotive and 16 mm technology to make the job that much easier. Consider, for example, one such travelling organization: Superior Road Attractions. As detailed in the Canadian edition of *Box Office* in August 1938, this company invested $4000 in a truck, a generator and 16 mm projection equipment (*Box Office*, 1938). It was the project of Superior Films Ltd, a Canadian distribution company (licensed by the Inspection Branch) and under the management of Harry Price. The travelling unit functioned very much like the National Film Board model would a few years later. It was a one-man show: the driver was also the projectionist and outfitted with a 9 × 12 foot screen. This particular unit travelled the Ottawa Valley and other communities not serviced by theatres. Shows were held both in open air and in town halls and lodges. Specializing in one-night shows, patrons apparently frequently asked for return engagements.

These were the typical activities of a 16 mm travelling projectionist. On the surface, there should be nothing immediately alarming about this behaviour for established independent theatre owners. But increasingly the concern was that these 16 mm operators would begin to set up shop in permanent locations, and in more urbanized settings – where established theatres already were struggling to survive amid the hostility of monopolies and vertical integration of the industry. Harold Kay, writing in *Canadian Independent*, revealed an initial suspicion among exhibitors when 16 mm first started making itself noticed. But as he himself admitted, 'I, for one, was slow to believe it could be a serious competitor to the regulation film', citing a limited supply of feature subjects and noting that 'theatre comforts [are] too well developed' (Kay, 1938). He felt that 16 mm would be confined to rural districts and to areas that were at least ten miles from an established theatre. But he went on to describe the chaotic situation that had evolved into '40 itinerant exhibitors in Ontario fighting for territory, overlapping, crowding each other for show dates . . .', and worst of all, 'covering up each other's posters!' His primary concern, and those of other like-minded individuals, was that 16 mm was creeping in 'where it doesn't belong' – essentially, into towns, 'closer and closer to established theatres' (Kay, 1938). What is interesting is that there simply doesn't appear to be evidence that this was happening on any significant scale. Kay was capable of citing only two semi-permanent 16 mm showplaces: one, a 150-seat venue in Welland, Ontario, and the other, a 183-seat theatre in Grand Valley, which was putting on only three shows a week. Of the two, only Welland appears to have had established 35 mm theatres anyway.

Kay's argument was that theatre owners contributed to their communities, and this was an issue that would frame much of the subsequent debate. Theatre owners paid 15-cent seat taxes, business taxes and real estate taxes and provided local jobs. They were also obliged to pay a considerable amount of money on safety renovations for their theatres – a significant burden, he felt, which 16 mm operators managed to unfairly avoid.

> If the Motion Picture Bureau can step in and regulate the 35 mm theatres for the safety and comfort of the patrons, why are 16 mm showplaces permitted to run practically unregulated, in fire traps without proper exits in untaxed town halls by exhibitors who pay negligible license fees per year, take the town's money and move on?
>
> (Kay, 1938)

Theatre owners frequently referred to 16 mm outfits as 'unfair' competition. A 20 June meeting of the directors of the Independent Theatres Association of Ontario addressed the detrimental effects that 16 mm was causing their industry as 'further competition to an already depressed box office' (*Box Office*, 1938). The overriding concern was that its increasing presence would in fact be detrimental because 'its use cannot be confined to outlying situations as originally planned' (*Box Office*, 1938). The 'outlying situations' referred to in these comments imply that 16 mm was originally conceived as a medium designed for employment in remote, non-urban settings. But there is nothing inherent in the technology that should dictate geographic limitations on its usage. While it may have originally been intended for amateur usage, this by no means implied that its employment be limited to rural, or more peripheral, locations away from city centres. Furthermore,

> It is feared that clubs, schools, churches and fraternal organizations with negligible taxes and expenses would set up exhibition units in competition to highly-taxed theatres expensively staffed and equipped and employing union operators. This sort of competition, the Board of Directors felt, would mean the slow bleeding of the regular exhibitor.
>
> (*Box Office*, 1938)

The independent exhibitors consistently lobbied the government to play a greater role in the licensing and regulation of both 16 mm films and their associated screening environments. The Inspection Branch had been issuing operational licenses since 1924, but in terms of actual regulation, it was felt that greater government intervention was required. A meeting of the Motion Picture Branch of the Toronto-based Board of Trade was held on 16 June 1938, and a resolution was passed stating, 'Resolved that if 16 mm theatres are allowed by the governments of the provinces of Canada, they should be subject to the same regulations as 35 mm theatres' (*Box Office*, 1938). Shortly thereafter, the Province of Ontario clarified its admittedly occasionally nebulous stance on 16 mm projection and explicitly stated that

> Any exchange distributing this product shall pay an annual tax of $50. Public halls showing 16 mm shall pay a yearly license fee of $10. Travelling exhibitions shall pay an annual license fee of $10. . . . All 16 mm theatres are subject to the same building law regulations as govern theatres operating 35 mm films.
>
> (*Canadian Independent*, 1938)

The last section is perhaps the most important, given that maintaining standard safety regulations in theatres is what owners frequently cited as the most expensive operating cost, aside from taxes. Strangely, despite the rhetoric of the independent owners and its enshrinement in the government's enactments, the evidence doesn't really indicate that 16 mm theatres were a widespread phenomenon. But the threat alone was enough to constitute an action and a regulatory response.

It should be noted that despite the regulatory actions of Ontario, and also of Manitoba and Nova Scotia, which implemented similar measures, independent 35 mm exhibitors were still generally not satisfied that the threat had been contained. Trade press editorials by Harold Kay, Ray Lewis and others continued to sound the alarm of impending doom. In fact, it became increasingly obvious that increased governmental regulation of 16 mm operations was not really the end that was desired. The root of the hostility towards 16 mm is ultimately revealed as more complex than a mere fear of competition. Something far more significant seemed to be at stake, as suggested by the inflammatory language and vivid images of Ray Lewis, as in the quote that serves as an epigraph to this chapter:

> Our viewpoint is that the 16 mm is not a little exhibitor or a little trouble; the 16 mm is as benign and harmless as a cancer and that

gradually it will eat out the territory of the little exhibitor and spread to the zones of the big fellows.

(Lewis, 29 October 1938)

Lewis was perhaps the most vocal of the opponents of 16mm in the trade press. Her regular rants about the evils of the medium and the immediate peril it represented are rich with hyperbolic metaphors of biblical proportions. At one point she described 16mm as a young, adopted child who will one day grow up and eat his masters (Lewis, 29 October 1938). The next month, 16mm emerged as an octopus with vicious tentacles, and the only way to kill was to 'knife it in its one soft spot – between its eyes, as its head darts toward you' (Lewis, 12 November 1938). And she was perhaps at her most provocative when in 1938 she linked the activities of 16mm showmen with those of Nazi Germany by declaring that she was '. . . full of resentment toward the bullying spirit which seeks to grab Czechoslovakia, or to grab generally. We know that "bull" in our own Industry. Horn in on the grab! Stop it' (Lewis, 24 September 1938). She justified her hyperbole when she stated, 'no language is too strong with which to condemn this unethical, unbusinesslike and unfair competition' (Lewis, 12 November 1938). Unlike many of the vocal opponents of 16mm's perceived encroachments who lobbied for increased governmental regulation and taxation, Lewis rejected further legislative control. In her opinion, this did not actually help the independent exhibitor; in fact it did a great disservice by acknowledging and recognizing 16mm as part of the motion picture industry. Legislative control was not the appropriate venue to 'cure the 16mm sickness'. 'Too much time has been wasted in tolerating its presence and growth, but THERE IS STILL TIME TO ROOT IT OUT' (Lewis, 29 October 1938; her emphasis). She felt the industry needed to regulate itself and that it shouldn't always run to the government for assistance. This language of self-regulation and anti-interventionism echoes that of the misleadingly named Motion Picture Exhibitors and Distributors of Canada, which, as Pendakur has shown, in effect safeguarded American interests in the Canadian industry. This harmony of thought would reappear in the 1940s when a movement was afoot to create a new association of Canadian exhibitors, one more representative of Canadian, independent interests. Lewis denounced the newly minted Independent Motion Picture Exhibitors Association – an organization of militant independents that actually represented small Canadian exhibitors' interests – as 'unpatriotic' for seeking to alter the structure of the industry, when they should be focusing on beating Hitler (cited in Pendakur, 1990, p. 104). Later that year, a new association formed, the Motion Picture Theatres

Association of Ontario, which was for all intents and purposes little different from the original Motion Picture Exhibitors and Distributors of Canada, and Lewis threw her support behind it right away – strange behaviour for an individual who supposedly gave a voice to the 'little exhibitors' of Canada.

However, where Lewis' comments are at their most insightful is in her assertions regarding film gauge, screening environment and cinematic content. Lewis rejected legislative control and further regulation to control 16 mm. The way she saw it, the problem was not how to control 16 mm as a competitor to theatrical motion pictures – the problem was to disallow the practice completely, to refuse to accept that 16 mm could screen anything other than educational films, in environments far removed from towns and theatres. This is the crux of her argument – that 16 mm should be a strictly educational medium and remain in the non-theatrical milieu. 'It has no place in the picture business' (Lewis, 29 October 1938). And conversely, the field of 35 mm theatrical motion pictures is strictly for entertainment. 'We are showmen, not educationalists. . . . Motion pictures (as we produce them) have no place in churches or schools' (Lewis, 29 October 1938). Here she falls back on the classic argument that such buildings are not safe enough and that should accidents occur, the industry as a whole would suffer as a result of the backlash. Her proposed solution to the problem was not to further regulate 16 mm operators, and in the process legitimize them, but instead to delegitimize them. This would be achieved by forging producer-distributor alliances and agreeing not to make or distribute 16 mm film of a non-educational (i.e., 'entertaining') value and in the process further sequester 16 mm operators to 'where they belong' – out in the country, showing films about farming. Lewis was in effect invoking a misconceived and simplistic understanding of media technology that served to prescribe specific exclusive functions for particular media and dictated the environments or milieus in which these technologies could be employed. By reinforcing these notions, her intent was to no doubt effectively curtail the increasing scope of 16 mm's employment into spheres of activity that served to threaten the interests of Canadian theatrical exhibitors.

Small-scale independent exhibitors likely had much more in common with their 16 mm counterparts than with the American-owned Famous Players theatrical chain. Why was such an alliance or association across 'gauge lines' never once considered? Why did something as trivial as the width of film cause such intense hostility? Certainly at some level the hostility shown towards both non-theatrical and theatrical 16 mm film operators in the 1930s is emblematic of a genuine concern for a potential new form of competition in an already tight market, but it is more fundamentally representative of a malaise far from unique to the particular historical circumstance. This historical circumstance is representative of far more than a simple technological battle between a dominant medium and an emergent one. A more comprehensive understanding of this particular historical circumstance would reveal, rather, that the determined efforts of the Canadian trade press and theatrical organizations to effectively limit the activities of 16 mm operators were fundamentally rooted in a desire to manage the operation of their industry and to safeguard their interests. The 16 mm exhibition led to the development of separate spheres of cultural activity and new models of screening practice and effectively offered up alternative circuits of distribution. These activities crossed into territory 'where they didn't belong' and threatened to agitate the dominant, entrenched systems of film exhibition that governed the activities of the industry.

Interestingly, in the eyes of many, it is now 16 mm that faces the threat of extinction with the rapid proliferation of new emergent audiovisual technologies. But, as a special section dedicated to the medium in a recent edition of *Cinema Journal* shows, claims of 16 mm's demise have been grossly overstated. The contributors collectively argue that 16 mm will continue to persist as a relevant residual media format in various spheres of cultural activity, and in some institutional settings, will even continue to enjoy a dominant position (Hendershot, 2006, pp. 109–40). With regard to 35 mm, its dominant industrial position is far from assured. But what this moment in Canadian film history hopefully demonstrates is that deterministic concepts of technological development, coupled with hyperbolic discourses of fear and paranoia towards potentially competing media forms, reveal very little about actual cultural practice and in fact obscure far more than they illuminate. To view such debates and discourses in such simplistic terms runs the risk of ultimately clouding the far more complex manners in which technological change affects audio-visual screening practice, and the spheres and environments in which it takes place.

## Acknowledgements

I would like to thank Charles Acland and the editors of this collection, Marc Furstenau, Bruce Bennett and Adrian Mackenzie, for their various comments and suggestions in the writing of this chapter.

## Notes

1. See www.mpaa.org.
2. Figures are from *Licenses for 16mm Films (1924–1968)*, produced by the Motion Picture Censorship and Theatre Inspection Branch, Ontario. Source: Archives of Ontario.

# 2
# BMW Films and the Star Wars Kid: 'Early Web Cinema' and Technology

*Andrew Clay*

The Web sits on the Internet connecting dispersed users as potential producers as well as consumers of moving image culture. The Web both expands existing cinema and becomes a cinema itself. Films on the Web and 'Web films'[1] invite us to consider a new technological apparatus of cinematic time and space. Web cinema consists of diverse digital video cultural practices including car manufacturers such as Volvo, Mercedes-Benz and BMW, who have become film producers, and young people who 'cut and paste' with desktop video technologies as hybrid 'prosumers' (producers-consumers) of user-generated content for media-sharing websites such as *YouTube*.[2] This online cinema is also part of the expanding market economy of modernity where the old and the new are the dialectical 'novel as the ever-same' that Walter Benjamin invokes to lay bare the myth of progress (Leslie, 2000, p. 60). Politically, these tensions constitute a problem whereby democratic participation is accompanied by deepening consumerism and irresponsible media.

Cinema began as a technology of public projection, but it continues to develop as a screen-based media culture. In particular, there are two distinctive ongoing technological realignments of cinema. The first is the convergence of the feature film with television. Films provide content for television, and the television set has emerged as a display device for 'home cinema', creating a privatized electronic cinema in a domestic setting. At the same time, a second shift has begun with the development of computer and network audio-visual technologies. This is potentially a much more radical development because it has disconnected film culture from the commodity of the feature film.

Web cinema originates with short films on digital video distributed via telecommunication networks for display on the screens of computers and mobile devices. It is just one of many identifiable moving image practices that are facilitated by these technologies. The short videos that circulate as films in this context are reminiscent of the first steps of the infant 'living photographs' of early cinema. With hindsight of cinema's maturity as a theatrical screen, we might expect the short Web film to prove to be only a temporary divagation from the mainstream of feature film culture as Web cinema (film as specific content of the Web medium) develops into an increasingly sophisticated entertainment form.

Historically, we are in a period of 'early Web cinema' characterized by a renaissance of short film-making that we first encounter at the birth of cinema. Once again, as in Gunning and Gaudreault's conception of early cinema as a 'cinema of attractions' (Gunning, 1990), the technology of the moving image itself is a fascination for audiences reconfigured as users. The sense of the 'newness' of Web cinema is an experience of a technological shift. At the beginning of cinema, the Lumière Cinématographe was a combined camera, printer and projector in the control of showmen. At the emergence of Web cinema, the computer is a personal moving image screen and video production workstation under the command of users networked together via the Internet, which has been opened up to market forces and traditional commodity consumption and production, but which also facilitates a democratized access to cultural production. As Marshall (2004, p. 27) observes, the Web is a medium where 'the professional and the corporate intersects with the personal and the idiosyncratic'. In this context, Web cinema is where the audience, whether at home, at work, or increasingly in wireless spaces elsewhere, snatches short bursts of online video material, in effect a 'cinema of distractions', a utopian non-work plenitude of 'digitextuality' or 'click fetishism'.[3]

I use the term 'distraction' here as 'concentration elsewhere' to refer to the switching of attention between tasks facilitated by the personal computer (PC). The viewer's relationship with the short video 'film' is casual 'Entertainment Snacking' between regular 'meals' of feature films and television programmes.[4] The word 'distraction' in this chapter is not used entirely in the same context as Benjamin's 'perception in the state of distraction' that Manovich argues has become 'perfectly realized' in the application of computer media (2001, p. 176).

Rightly, Manovich identifies how users of computer media oscillate between viewing and using as they interface with the obtrusive hypertext machine while accessing linear content, and Harries (2002) adds the hybrid 'viewsing' mode of spectatorship to refer to the integration of viewing and using on the Web. These are valid observations about the condition of viewing films on the Web, where the technology of on-demand Web video can produce an 'unsatisfactory experience' so that the 'user ends up viewing little and doing even less' (Harries, 2002, p. 178). However, Benjamin's concept of a distractive state is misapplied by Manovich and Harries. As discussed by Bogard (2000), Benjamin's concept of distraction describes how people can be trained in good habits that are disruptive of existing power structures. Viewers, according to Benjamin, can be shocked out of the immersive contemplation of art to become habitually self-aware. Bogard identifies 'escape' and 'capture' as keywords in relation to the dialectical nature of distraction. To depart from Benjamin, Web cinema is not distractive in the formalist sense of montage superseding the bad habits of classical narrative, but in the way that we are trained to become habitual viewers in a new technological context, watching short films or other video material as an escape from work and at the same time being captured as consumers exposed to advertising or seduced by the invitation to produce as a participant in user-generated content. In Web cinema, and other forms of online production such as writing blogs and wikis or recording podcasts, leisure becomes work.

In addition, early Web cinema is also a cinema of attractions. The 'visual curiosity' of novice spectators of early cinema was for the 'exhibitionism' and 'exciting spectacle' of life-like photographic movement (Gunning, 1990). Similarly, there is a curiosity about early Web cinema on the basis of an exhibitionism that addresses experienced viewers not in terms of the magic of illusionism but in terms of the seductive possibility of what they might be able to see. The viewing of cinema by an individual on a monitor screen echoes the format of the pre-cinematic kinetoscope, while the mobile Internet locates the spectator once more in a position of private amusement in a public space.

My project to write a history of Web cinema as it unfolds around us is informed by the work of Walter Benjamin and takes *The Arcades Project* in particular as a model or stepping-off point for theoretical and historical enquiry.[5] There are two reasons for this reference to Benjamin. Firstly, in *The Arcades Project*, Benjamin developed a way of working in fragments and used a model of history consisting of non-linear, montage-like juxtapositions and alignments of cultural objects – a technique that is particularly suited to writing about the Internet as a dynamic network and the Web as a hypertextual medium. The volume and diversity of the objects of study discourage a more complete approach – every day on *YouTube*, for example, 70,000 new videos are uploaded by users and 70 million videos are watched. Secondly, Benjamin's object of study was the Paris Passages of the early nineteenth century, the development of the arcades that he regards as the original temples of commodity capitalism and that we can see as the precursors of the department store, the shopping mall and e-commerce. The arcades are *ur*-forms, the original forms of modernity, and the Internet is a new electronic space of modernity where the surfer replaces the *flâneur*.

For Benjamin, technology is potentially progressive in the sense that there is a promising creative potential for change, for the satisfaction of desires as yet unfulfilled and for the accomplishment of a classless society However, technology is retarded by the limits of convention that promotes the new with the old that has just now become obsolete (Buck-Morss, 1989, pp. 115–116). Thus, the ruins, fossils and traces of the old can be discovered in commodity forms as the 'new as the eversame', the fusion of the old and the new, the major 'dialectical image' that Benjamin detects as antithetical elements made physical in the material culture of modern life.

However, Benjamin did not fully apply these ideas to film. In the 1930s he began to address the technologies of mechanical reproduction, photography and film, as progressive democratizations of the reception and production of images. With specific reference to film, he valued the shock effect of cinematic montage whose disorienting effect on the audience makes familiar reality unfamiliar. The awakening of the viewer from the slumber of the phantasmagoria of commodity fetishism is a revelation whereby the 'camera introduces us to unconscious optics as does psychoanalysis to unconscious impulses' (Benjamin, 2005, p. 117).

Benjamin was realistic enough to recognize that the commercial nature of the film industry threatened the creative and progressive potential of film technology. His circumspection was justified and the radical potential ascribed to technologies such as film to facilitate the fulfilment of social utopia and desire for a 'classless society' has not yet been realized. The technology of mechanical reproduction has not accomplished Benjamin's analysis of its historical destiny to shock the people out of their 'unaware dreaming'. Most feature films are still produced within the general system of commodity capitalism, but our engagement with films as commodities goes way beyond their exchange-value (such as the price of a ticket or DVD). Films have use-value to us as spectators because of the aesthetic experiences we gain from them, and the cultural capital we generate as movie audiences.

Benjamin was less interested in Marx's 'commodity-in-the-market', with its emphasis on price, than in 'commodity-on-display', the appropriation of the representational or symbolic value of things by the consumer. In this sense, commodities are 'fetishes-on-display', the transformation of everyday desirables as objects. Commodities for Benjamin were also 'dialectical images', contradictory conflations of old and new. Web films, for instance, have symbolic value for audiences, for example, by referencing the cult[ure] of *Star Wars* as the aesthetic representation of life. They are also dialectically old and new, through the operations of genre, for example, (identified as conventional, but different) or sampling from existing moving image material.

In terms, then, of our symbolic engagement with films as commodities, we have used technology to *materialize* the aesthetic experience of cinema-going. I grew up watching films on television, and I learned to love film. I received a film education, watching a range of films from different cultures and historical periods in my 'home cinema' as well as visiting public cinemas. In both cases the engagement with the *physical* existence of film as celluloid, and the series of commercial exchanges associated with it, were quite remote. They were more experiences than material engagements with physical objects. The introduction of the videocassette recorder (VCR) and films on Video Home System (VHS) tape and subsequently on disc formats began to change this.

Since the introduction of the VCR, it is widely possible to 'possess' film or at least the right to own a viewing copy. Subsequently, the cinematic heritage has developed more physically through the ownership of films in personal video collections as well as a memory-based recall of viewing experience. This physicality, of 'getting our hands on' film, is further developed using the Web and the 'next point' of the technological materialization of the film and video experience – mobile devices that can store downloaded moving image products. Television and the computer have been used to bring cinema into the home, and mobile devices such as phones, laptops, PDAs and multimedia jukeboxes are bringing cinema into new public spaces outside of cinemas. The Web, like television, is not just a viewing space of aesthetic experience, but it is also the source of material objects that can be saved and archived. The Web continues the expansion of cinema from experience to materialism, through the downloading of films to the hard discs of the PC.

Furthermore, in contradiction to the common view that digital media promote dematerialization, digital technologies such as the Web do not dematerialize films as commodities but instead allow them to be re-materialized as part of a historical process, most recently subject to the conditions of 'hypercontextualization'. Peter Lunenfeld (2002) uses this term to identify the real interactive potential of cinema and new technologies whereby the film text is just one element in a wider network of intertextual commodities such as DVDs, videogames and websites – a condition of marketing, promotion and responsive consumer participation.

Benjamin recognized a growing trend for readers to become writers in published media that began in the press with letters to editors. In the same line of argument he pointed to the progressive potential of film to offer 'everyone the opportunity to rise from passer-by to movie extra' so that 'any man might even find himself part of a work of art' (1935, p. 114). However, the development of video and computer technology has facilitated a level of participation in cinema that goes beyond the ability to appear as oneself in a film. Digital video technology enables the production of Web cinema, and Web technology provides distribution channels and exhibition spaces. The real 'jolt' of Web cinema is the invitation to participate so that spectators become film-makers just as readers have become writers.

The 'Star Wars Kid' (SWK) is an illustration of this trajectory at play in Web cinema. SWK culture began in November 2002 when a 15-year-old French-Canadian, Ghyslain Raza, recorded himself in a school video studio, imitating a Jedi warrior from *Star Wars*. In April 2003, about two minutes of this video was transferred to a computer and linked to the *Kazaa* website by fellow pupils, and so it became part of the peer-to-peer (P2P) network file sharing community. A few days later an 'original remix', the first clone, created by Bryan Dube was also added. Using his desktop video skills, Dube added *Star Wars* music, graphics and effects to Raza's video footage. Immediately the video was being linked, downloaded and virally e-mailed on a massive scale. Since then, hundreds of SWK movies involving digital manipulation of the original video, often inserted into found film and television footage, have been made available via dedicated websites such as *Jedimaster.net* and *Spindulik.com*. Titles such as *Bravekid*, *Star Wars Kong* and *Bend It Like Ghyslain* give some indication of the hybridizing nature of this Web video culture and how its participants engage with their moving image heritage, and compete over technological competency and wit.

It is at this point that we can begin to juxtapose and align two disparate examples of moving image experience, materialism and participation on the Web – BMW Films and the SWK – as technological manifestations of the expanding market economy in which the potential of digital technology and social organization for cinematic practice is realized. In both cases, we see hypercontextualized films that contain highly resonant commodity-fetishes – luxury cars and Internet icons.

## Advermovies and BMW films

Manufacturers of prestige cars such as BMW, Mercedes-Benz and Volvo have become producers of Web cinema. Guided by their advertising agencies, these corporations are exploring new branding opportunities, using the Web to harness aspirational products and creative ideas to the cultural capital of film for younger audiences who are embracing the new technologies. This has created 'advermovies' as a fusion of advertising and entertainment (advertainment). Typically, mass media channels such as television, cinema and newspaper advertising are used to create awareness of online films. Volvo's campaigns, for instance, have used television adverts as 'teaser trailers' to drive audiences to websites to view short films, including the fake documentary *Mystery of Dalarö* (Carlos Soto, 2003)[6], the drama *Route V50* (Stephen Frears, 2004) and the 'Life on Board Project' (2004–05) documentaries.

Web advermovies are short films placed at the centre of hypercontextual branding campaigns using corporate and personalized media. The audience is simultaneously empowered and targeted as users and consumers through media products that are novel and continuous, newly responsive but also intrinsically commercialized, and it is the connectivity and two-way communication of networked media that allows this to take place. The mass media is used to inform the public that the hypercontextual product is 'in play', but it is the on-demand nature of the Web that facilitates closer relationships between the corporate and the personal.

The 'Lucky Star' campaign run for Mercedes-Benz provides a useful example. This promotion centred on the cinematic release of *Lucky Star* (Michael Mann, 2002), a trailer for a non-existent film that functioned as a subtle advert for the SL-Class car that appears in the 'film/trailer'. At the end of the film, viewers were directed to an 'Official Site' that supported the illusion of a forthcoming major Hollywood feature film release starring Benicio del Toro and directed by Michael Mann, including an opportunity to watch a 'Director's Cut' of the trailer (the online advermovie). The showing of *Lucky Star* in cinemas energized a campaign that had already started prior to its release. Viral marketing, where 'infected' people online will pass on information to each other using, for example, e-mail attachments, was used to lead Web users to fake fan sites created by the advertisers. This 'alternate reality' strategy is often used in hypercontextual marketing of commodities such as films, especially online, where it is possible to use the Web to create content that looks authentic enough to provide immersive, interactive cross-media play typical of 'alternate reality games' (ARGs).[7]

*Lucky Star* is simultaneously an advert, film and trailer. As a commodity-on-display, however, it is its aesthetic representation as film that is uppermost. The film's primary value is its 'borrowed credibility' (Leigh, 2002) from the cultural heritage of the commodity fetishism of film. There is a long tradition of advertisements that are directed by film directors, but they have evaded categorization as films. On the other hand, as short films and not 'long adverts', Web advermovies, because they have been available to download, have been materialized as cinematic experience. This materialization of advertising as film-making has been crucial to the impact of advermovies as a distinctive practice of Web cinema that creates value from the elevation of mass media advertising to the status of film art. BMW's online branding campaign was convincingly called 'BMW Films', not 'BMW Adverts'. However, the conviction of these adverts as films has been seen as an encroachment on the artistic worth of cinema because of the 'blurring [of] the lines between art and commerce, between novelty and expansionism' (Leigh, 2002). The worry expressed here is about a clandestine, 'shady' use of the product placement opportunities of cinema and the Web that compromises artistic expression. It would be right to question the assumptions behind such categories as 'film art' and 'advertising commerce' deployed in this anxiety, but this categorization is clearly at work in the branding of prestige cars with Hollywood *auteurs*.

The 'largesse' of corporations who provide 'free' digitextual content to be experienced as novel and advanced applications of moving image Web technologies can be seen as one of the freedoms of modernity. Instead of messages about products, consumers are given media products to appropriate, discuss and generally make sense of accordingly. This includes such examples of formal experimentation as Mercedes-Benz's *7 Years Later* (Jan Wentz, 2003), self-promoted as 'more than just a film' and 'cinema in your head' (http://www.mercedes-benz.com/7yearslater).[8] This Web film is broken down into smaller sequences that can be ordered in different combinations according to how the user responds with clicks to prompted decision-making. The user's version of the film can then be shared via e-mail or among the community of registrants. Thus, we witness the fault lines of the dialectical play of oppression and liberation at the collision of the corporate and the personal in the form of the advermovie. Mercedes-Benz's *7 Years Later* is a symbolically new and different 'escape' from the conventionality of film, but the 'viewser' is also 'captured' as a participant distributor of the branded advertainment experience.

The BMW Films campaign 'The Hire', which began in 2001, is similarly dialectical. On a weblog devoted to movies,[9] a fan of the BMW films posted his negotiated response to these advermovies:

> [S]ure, in the end all they are (with the possible exception of Powderkeg) is adverts for expensive cars, but you don't see me running out to buy a BMW because of it. I'm just sitting back grateful that someone, somewhere, is still making cool car chases in movies – for whatever reason.
>
> (Reid, 2002)

Thus, bloggers can claim to be impervious to advertising if the logic of the campaign is to make them purchase a BMW. However, they cannot see that by their positive response to 'cool car chases', they are being transformed and are serving the purpose of the branding strategy.

'The Hire' campaign centres on a series of eight short films (generally six to eight minutes long) that were produced by BMW of North America for the designated website *BMWfilms.com* in two seasons between 2001 and 2002. The project was coordinated by Hollywood creative David Fincher as executive producer of the films and advertising agency Fallon Worldwide whose solution was designed to give 'people a chance to discover BMW on their own terms – at the hands of the world's hottest film directors with a dialled-up entertainment factor, and a "seek-it-out" media seduction via the Internet' (Fallon Worldwide, 2005).

This was a conventional, elaborate, hypertextual campaign using the mass media to drive follow-up interest to the *BMWfilms.com* website, where the films could be marketed virally or with promotional DVDs and an immersive ARG could be played. Ten million films were downloaded from the site, two million people registered online and tens of thousands volunteered survey information to the company (Hespos, 2002). The effectiveness of *BMWfilms.com* and its significance as Web cinema is the way that it achieved the quality threshold that made the technology an attraction for movie fans. This was done by marshalling optimum resources along each stage of the production workflow. Each BMW short film had a budget of over one million dollars (Primedia, 2001) and was directed by a feature film director with an international reputation or action film credentials, such as John Woo, Ang Lee and Tony Scott. Each film showcased a particular model of BMW and starred Clive Owen as an enigmatic driver for hire.

Once the films were completed, the widescreen print was transferred to digibeta masters that were given to a specialist production company to prepare for Internet delivery using Media 100 proprietary software and hardware (Business Wire, 2001). The video compression maintained the high-quality widescreen cinematic qualities of the source films in various formats for streaming and downloads of DVD quality. The online files were carefully hosted on dedicated servers for high traffic use at all times for a worldwide audience. A custom application, 'BMW Film Player', could also be downloaded from the site to play the films in widescreen format and access the special features such as audio commentary and 'making of' documentaries that are typically found on DVD.

What conclusions can be drawn about the BMW advermovies or 'moviemercials' – as short films, Internet branding, old forms in new contexts, the 'novel as the ever-same'? There is certainly novelty in the notion of *'BMWfilms.com* presents' since it is unusual to be part of an audience for films that are financed by car manufacturers.[10] Although BMW are not in the business of making films, Web technology has allowed BMW to make Hollywood cinema by circumventing theatrical distribution. In relation to cinema, they have shifted their marketing and promotion from conventional product placement, such as in the 'James Bond' series of feature films, to producing their own short films where branded properties are brought more centrally into filmic representation. This has created a major new genre of early Web cinema, the hybrid advermovie.

The BMW cars that are aestheticized in 'The Hire' films are fetish commodities-on-display, but not to the extent that their presence is obtrusive or lacks integration. Instead, it is the films themselves that are on show, not as great adverts but as Web cinema that has achieved distinction through the deployment of high-quality technological resources and Hollywood cultural capital. Thus, it is the films themselves that have symbolic value more than the luxury cars that appear in them. For instance, one of the films, *Hostage* (John Woo, 2002), won 'Best Action Short' at the Los Angeles International Short Film Festival, and the series has been adapted in comic book form by Dark Horse Comics, a leading producer of licensed television and film properties. In fact it could be argued that the cars themselves are the least interesting elements of the BMW films. This is in contrast to the SWK, whose presence demands our attention and our complicity in the viral distribution of his humiliation.

The BMW films, then, have emerged as a significant constituent of novel Web cinema, but at the same time their fascination is continuous with the development of Hollywood cinema. It is this continuity that contributes the 'ever-same' to the novelty of the Web advertisement format of BMW films. For example, most of the films contain car chases, and of course, the chase is a conventional narrative spectacle that has its origins at the beginning of cinema. In addition, many of the BMW films use melodrama as a conventional dramatic mode of Hollywood cinema, such as last-minute rescues and just-in-time escapes – a Tibetan boy leader-in-exile is saved from assassins (*Chosen*, Ang Lee, 2001); a successful dash to deliver a heart for a vital transplant keeps peace and defeats tyranny (*Ticker*, Joe Carnahan, 2002); pictures taken by a fatally wounded war photographer are transferred across a hostile border checkpoint in time to expose the truth (*Powder Keg*, Alejandro González-Iñárritu, 2001). Melodrama's rhetoric is to construct moral legibility in aesthetic form. Melodrama 'is structured upon the "dual recognition" of how things are and how they should be' (Williams, 1998, p. 48) – it is 'an allegory of human experience dramatically ordered, as it should be rather than as it is' (Booth, 1965, p. 14). Thus, melodrama is a form of dreaming about how society should be, and the BMW advermovies give new life to age-old desires, 'dream fetishes' and 'commodity fetishes' that become indistinguishable (Buck-Morss, 1989, pp. 117–118). Thus, in reality, democracy is crushed, tyrants prevail and the truth is repressed, but we dream of self-determination, peace and justice.

## DIY video and the Star Wars kid

The digital technology that is available to huge corporations such as BMW is also becoming widely accessible to individuals who can emulate the professionalism of commercial media. In theory, anyone is capable of producing a film that can be made available on the Web. Everyone does not have access to Hollywood budgets and cultural capital, but it is widely possible to make moving image commodities that can be distributed via Internet technology, with sufficient novelty or technical achievement to attract attention. Desktop media production facilitates the production of this 'DIY video' in the context of specific Web cultural activities such as the production and consumption of SWK videos.

I was virally infected by the SWK meme when the first, or original, clone video was sent to me as an e-mail attachment by one of my students. The SWK 'films' or clone videos usually fall well below the quality threshold set by BMW films, but then they don't need to achieve that level to work as an effective cinema of distraction in Web culture. The makers of SWK videos are prosumers of desktop video and Web technology who mimic the work of professional media industries. Whether through practical necessity to keep the websites running or through ambition to be commercial providers of media, SWK websites develop revenue streams such as merchandising, advertising and sales to pay for the hosting. As such it is just one of the many DIY participatory Web cultures that adopt the strategies developed in traditional media economies.

The fascination of SWK video culture is the shift from consumption to production that is encouraged by the use of Web technology in contrast to the more traditional technologies of mass media reception. The SWK has become a commodity-on-display through comedy and postmodern sampling. It is funny to see a video in which an overweight teenager imitates exaggerated Jedi warrior moves using a golf ball retriever pole as a light sabre. The use of special effects software to turn the pole into an actual light sabre in the original remix of Raza's video adds to the sense of comedy and validates both manipulation as a technical skill and the sampling of the moving image heritage as cultural capital. However, the symbolic value of the videos is extracted through exploitative and harmful imagery that raises questions about the basis upon which a democratic participatory cinema can be established.

Through viral e-mailing and the addition of hundreds more clone videos made available through hypertext links and networked websites, the SWK became an Internet icon, a 'Web celeb' and the focus of a memetic instruction to produce and distribute Web video. The meme, a small piece of cultural information, replicates itself by inviting the desktop video producer to manipulate the original SWK video as a new video that can then be passed on or made available to others.

A typical production strategy involves editing parts of the original SWK video into found footage such as in *Psycho Kid* (andrew@soundboards.myrmid.com), in which Anthony Perkins can be seen spying through a peephole at the SWK in a space that we would normally expect Janet Leigh to occupy (Figure 2.1). Other strategies include taking the figure of the SWK from the background of the original video shot in the school studio and compositing that into found footage with additional manipulation such as in *Star Wars Kid: A New Hope* ('Major Eiswater'; in association with *Starwarskid.com*), in which an astonished Mark Hamill and Alec Guinness appear to be watching a tiny hologram of the SWK performing to music from *Saturday Night Fever* (John Badham, 1977).

Thus, the SWK 'films' can be seen as a form of video graffiti involving the bricolage of pre-existing commoditized media belonging particularly to the cultural heritage of cinema. This Web culture is a form of distractive play amongst young, probably predominantly male, people where Internet fame and peer review and recognition are valued in Internet forums, discussion boards, websites and e-mail.

*Figure 2.1* Two 'frame grabs' from the SWK video *Psycho Kid*.

In terms of the dialectics of modernity, the Web constitutes a levelling of media access as a utopia of plenty in the contemporary mediascape. The technologies of desktop video and Internet connectivity and dispersion converge to allow unprecedented media production and personal creativity. Simultaneously, ideologies of consumption are at work, for instance, in the way that DIY video practices emulate media professionalism and fame and turn private moments into public properties. In this way very different circumstances of production are brought into early Web cinema's system of on-demand video culture.

This deployment of technology allows new dimensions to traditional roles of the moving image, from teenagers in bedrooms to the commodification of execution videos by terrorists who turn the camcorder on themselves as news journalists.

As novelty, SWK videos represent the continued expansion of the materialization of moving image media as transformation and re-presentation. These short moving image texts are difficult to categorize with precedence. Personal expression through video in the public domain has reached previously unattainable levels. Yet, although many SWK videos can contain material that has originated with the video-maker, they are mostly assembled from existing media as a cultural heritage to be sampled and montaged largely as parody. In a similar way to that in which Hollywood cultural capital makes the BMW films interesting, it is the presence of the SWK as a commodity-on-display among the cultural heritage of cinema and television that gives this Web cultural practice its significance. However, there is a neat reversal that justifies juxtaposing these two disparate examples. Whereas 'The Hire' is a series of adverts that are commodified as films, SWK videos are films that are fetishized as adverts. SWK parodies are advertisement that advertise the love of film as a cultural heritage, and the vanity of self-promotion of the people who make these videos for the fame of media production. SWK videos are 'dream fetishes' that chase the logic of late modernity as the personalization of media and the validation of individualism.

## Conclusion

Technology has been used to materialize the use-value of film – film as an aesthetic experience commodified. *BMWFilms.com* is an example of how we engage with expanded cinema as viewers and collectors of new forms, new genres that are at the same time old forms – the 'new as the ever-same' of modernity as conceived by Benjamin. SWK culture demonstrates participation in production as imitation of the strategies of traditional media. The Web via the Internet is a gateway and a delivery system for film as material digital files that can be seen as resonant cultural objects, 'fetishes-on-display' in the Web arcades. The Web is also a 'cinema of distractions' and 'attractions', a digital playground allowing playful enchantment of utopian non-work and the hybrid work-leisure of user-generated content achieved through proximity to electronic machines, and this is where our hopes and fears for Web cinema are made material, where our love of film is tested.

The two fragments of Web cinema brought together in this chapter provide evidence that we should be fearful about the exhibitionism of this online audio-visual culture. The BMW Films advermovies mobilize Hollywood resources to Web short film production, bringing viewers into new relationships with advertisers. The ability to make films available to others is greatly extended, but participatory film production is not inherently progressive. One might hope that participant production will bring progressive forms of more democratic media, and certainly there are interesting experiments such as *A Swarm of Angels*, a 'groundbreaking project to create a £1 million film and give it away to over 1 million people using the Internet and a global community of members' (http://aswarmofangels.com). So, there is still the possibility that we might become trained in good habits.

## Notes

1. Little attention has so far been given to definitions or histories of 'Web cinema'. Barry (2003) suggests that Web cinema consists of moving pictures made specifically for the Internet, but this seems quite narrow, given the origins and usages of moving image material that can be accessed on the Web.
2. The term 'prosumer' is attributed to futurologist Alvin Toffler in *Future Shock* (1970) and in particular *The Third Wave* (1980) and refers to the process of closing the gap between producers and consumers, facilitated by the technologies of the 'post-industrial' age.
3. Everett (2003) combines 'digital' and 'intertextuality' to refer to the sensory plenitude of representation and end-user practices of interactive digital media that use 'clicking apparatuses'.
4. Atom Entertainment, a company that provides 'short-form, on-demand' games and videos, has trademarked the phrase 'Entertainment Snacking' to describe how its sites (brands) such as *AtomFilms* provide quick, instant gratification through 'atomized' content that delivers Web users to advertisers.
5. Between 1927 and his death in 1940, Benjamin worked on what subsequently became known as *The Arcades Project*, published in 1982 as *Das Passagen-Werk* and translated as an English version by Eiland and McLaughlin (1999). For a consideration of the philosophical coherence behind the project's fragments, see Buck-Morss (1999) and refer to *new formations* 54 (Burrow, Farnell & Jardine, 2004/2005) for an examination of the impact of the project on cultural and Benjamin studies more generally.
6. 'Carlos Soto' was a pseudonym used for the film's actual director, Spike Jonze, as part of the playful strategy of the advertising campaign designed to blur reality and fiction.
7. An 'alternate reality game' (ARG) is a cross-media game that attempts to blur the experience of being in and out of the game world. ARGs use mainly online resources, and typically involve the player with a story and puzzles to be solved for prizes. The first well-known ARG was a game developed to

promote the movie *A.I.* (Steven Spielberg, 2001), created by Microsoft and referred to as 'The Beast'.
8. Jan Wentz also directed *The Porter* (2004) for Mercedes-Benz, an equally mysterious, but non-interactive narrative starring Max Beesley and featuring a theme song by Bryan Ferry.
9. A weblog (Web log or 'blog') is a type of online journal that has been described as 'push button publishing for the people' (*Blogger.com*). 'Tagline' (http://www.tagliners.org) is the name of this particular blog that is dedicated to film culture, and it is run by brothers Stephen and Alistair Reid.
10. Unusual, but not without precedence. For example, Ford of Britain sponsored Free Cinema documentaries in a series called 'Look at Britain'. Titles included *Every Day Except Christmas* (Lindsay Anderson, 1957), *We Are the Lambeth Boys* (Karel Reisz, 1959) and *The Saturday Men* (John Fletcher, 1962).

# 3
# On Some Limits to Film Theory (Mainly from Science)

*James Elkins*

This chapter is an informal elaboration of a PowerPoint presentation and comments on stills and QuickTime movies rather than making a continuous argument.[1] I hope that the heuristic purpose of the original will make this version useful.

The presentation was a look at some ways that recent film-making technologies, especially those developed in science (and some specifically in the military), should make it difficult to keep using concepts such as *still, film, motion,* and *picture* in the ways they are used in film criticism. It was a speculative presentation, proposing that films made outside art can contribute to current theorizing in film studies. I presented several kinds of scientific films, arranged according to the trouble they might cause for conceptualizations of the instant, the frame, temporality, the movement-image, mimetic representation, the gaze, and the spectator's role. Looking back on the material used to construct this chapter, I notice that a more general provocation was simply the existence of an enormous body of filmic work that has nothing explicitly to do with the human body, with narrative, or with social interactions. But that is not how the presentation was structured.

The first topic was the erosion of the concept of the instant (and of the 24 frames per second (fps) orthodoxy) by scientific films that take millions of fps. Then I mentioned, in telegraphic fashion, four other topics: (1) films constructed from nonvisual data, (2) excesses of the visual (when there is too much to see), (3) films in which light itself is a convention, and (4) films in which objects themselves are conventions. The presentation ended with a second look at the erosion of the instant.

*Figure 3.1* Plasma event.

## The end of the instant

My opening example was several films of plasma events, made with a Kodak fast-framing camera called an EF1012, running at 1,000 to 2,000 fps (Figure 3.1).[2] The films are negatives of plasma events; in the positive, the plasma would have appeared as a bright flash against a black background. The scientists were studying the effects of injecting elements like lithium into the plasma stream, but that is not important here. What counts is the extremely short duration of the frames. Each frame in such films is about 200 microseconds, or 0.0002 seconds: more like an "instant" than the typical frame of a 24-fps film camera.

As a second example, I offered Sam Edgerton's images of atomic explosions, made with his magneto-optical camera called a Rapatronic. These pictures, which have only recently been published in any quantity, revealed a moment in the detonation of an atomic bomb that had only been surmised before Edgerton invented his camera.[3] The phenomenology of an above-ground atomic explosion used to be described as a bright flash, followed by an expanding fireball, which in turn gave way to the familiar mushroom cloud. That is how Oppenheimer and other early observers described it. Edgerton's camera revealed a phase before the bright flash, which passed by too rapidly for the human eye or for ordinary mechanical-shutter cameras. The Rapatronic camera captured uncanny images of enormous, soft-looking spheres expanding over the desert (Figure 3.2).[4]

In this image, the explosion is expanding outward from the bomb, which was placed on top of a tower in the desert in the southwestern United States. Three jets of fire travel down the guy wires that support

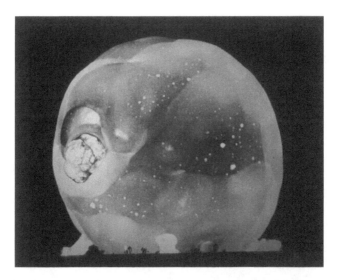

*Figure 3.2* Rapatronic photograph of atomic explosion, Sam Edgerton.

the tower, crashing into the desert floor. Joshua trees (desert plants, which are about 10 feet tall) are silhouetted against the swelling explosion. These images were largely unknown until they were published a few years ago, and even now most have no dates or locations. (Researching these, I came to the firm impression that the Department of Energy, Livermore Laboratories, and other government-funded institutions have many more of these photographs, but that can't be proven.) There is at least one film of these explosions, pieced together from individual frames made by Rapatronic cameras set up in banks. (The cameras could not be wound fast enough to make a film, so Edgerton had to make many cameras to produce on film.)

For me, the interest of these images is their sheer strangeness and the way they make the mushroom cloud seem almost benign and familiar by comparison. Here, I want to point to their unprecedented approach to instantaneity: each Rapatronic image captures just a millionth of a second – a thousand times closer to an "instant" than the typical one-thousandth-of-a-second digital camera snapshot.

I prepared this table to indicate some of the possibilities.[5] I gave an example of the picosecond range, a film – not very interesting to view, perhaps – recording 90-femtosecond (90 quadrillionths of a second) laser pulses striking a silicon surface (Figure 3.3).[6] The film is recorded in frames labelled in picoseconds and nanoseconds (trillionths of a second

Table 3.1: The erosion of the filmic instant.

| Millisecond | One-thousandth sec | $10^{-3}$ sec | Ordinary cameras |
|---|---|---|---|
| Microsecond | One-millionth sec | $10^{-6}$ sec | Edgerton's Rapatronic cameras; multiple image-capture framing cameras (1,000 to 100,000,000 fps) |
| Nanosecond | One-billionth sec | $10^{-6}$ sec | Gated still-video cameras (image intensifier + CCD); resolve down to 100 ns |
| Picosecond | One-trillionth sec | $10^{-9}$ sec | (no cameras specific to this range) |
| Femtosecond | One-quadrillionth sec | $10^{-12}$ sec | Smear or streak cameras (optical oscilloscopes); resolve down to 300 fs = 0.00000000003 sec |
| Attosecond | One-quintillionth sec | $10^{-15}$ sec | (not yet resolved) |

and billionths of a second). As the film plays, a shadow shifts across the disk; it's the laser, carving out a concavity in the surface. In the resulting reconstruction, which I am not reproducing here, the spatial axes are in nanometres. Distances and temporalities this size aren't available to intuition, as Kant said, using the distinction between *Zusammenfassung* and *Auffassung*; but the point here does not concern the disputable division between what can be taken in phenomenologically and what cannot. Rather I am interested that we are seeing here something wholly other than the "instant" or "still" familiar in film criticism. As I gave the presentation, I suggested that film criticism does not have a way of *excluding* such examples – they cannot be irrelevant, for example, just because they are not meant to function as art.

(Incidentally, in regard to Table 3.1, all of the advances were funded by the government of the United States, and all of them were at least partly for military uses. Nanosecond gated still-video cameras were developed to study the effect of high-impact projectiles on tank armour.)

I drew two conclusions from these materials:

(i) Ordinary film stills are not still: they are samples of enormous stretches of time (1/500th second, as opposed to 1/5,000,000,000 seconds). Movie stills are more like Lessing's idea of temporal accumulations, and perhaps they should be theorized in those terms.

(ii) The ordinary 24 fps "flow" of cinema can be reconceived as an indefinitely prolonged sequence of these "stills." The apparent unity of

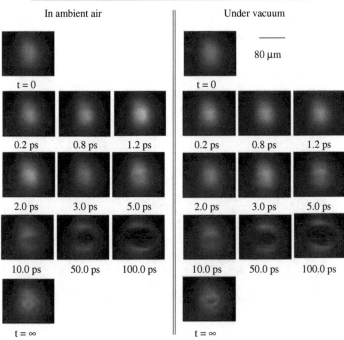

*Figure 3.3* Frames from two films showing 90-femtosecond (90 quadrillionths of a second) laser pulses striking a silicon surface.

the frame – its function as an irreducible sign or morpheme – can come to seem artificial. The sense of instantaneity, of the momentary, of excerpts from the "flow of time" alters.

## Pictures constructed from non-pictorial data

My example here was a wonderful brief film made by astronomers, showing what appears for all the world as an orange pinwheel spinning in outer space (Figure 3.4). (It has been reproduced many times on the Internet and is worth looking up. All the scientific films in this chapter are on the Internet, and ideally this chapter should be read with a browser.)[7] The object is a binary star system; the two stars revolve around one another, and one of them throws off a streamer of gas as it revolves.

58  *On Some Limits to Film Theory*

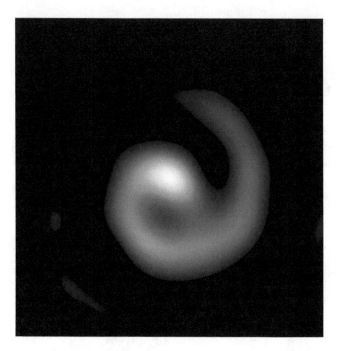

*Figure 3.4* Binary star system.

The little film appears to be a movie made through a telescope, but actually it is elaborately constructed out of several kinds of nonvisual information. The arts do not have anything like this, so I will describe it briefly.

Each single frame of the movie began with data from three telescopes. The resulting frame was not an ordinary photo for at least four reasons:

(i) Each frame represented infrared wavelengths (used to cut through interstellar dust), so the star system would not have been visible to unaided eyes, to begin with.
(ii) It was false coloured, which is typical of many astronomical images.
(iii) To generate the frames the astronomers used *heterodyne detection*. That means that slightly different signals from two telescopes were combined, creating a lower frequency. The frames of the movie were made with radio waves carried in wires.
(iv) Most interesting (and counterintuitive), each frame was generated using an interferometer array. In interferometry, each telescope

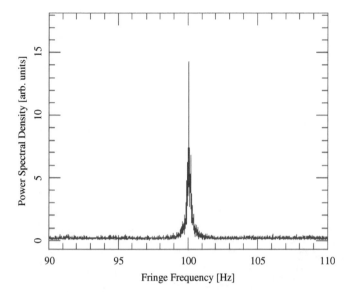

*Figure 3.5* Interference pattern.

captures a single bit of data, not a full image. The combined information from two telescopes is a "one-dimensional" interference pattern like this (Figure 3.5).[8]

It takes three telescopes to make a "two-dimensional" picture. (I am using dimensions loosely here, to underscore the fact that no telescope generated any image.)

In regard to this kind of film, I proposed three things:

(i) In cases like these the concept of *picture*, and therefore of *film*, does not depend on the act of looking, or the problematics of the gaze. It is constructed *to appear as if it did*.
(ii) The real is differently elusive than it is in Lacan: the actual object is unimaginable as an object of visual attention and so is not approximated by the film.
(iii) The fact that the image itself is built out of what is not visible (several times over: wavelength, interferometry, heterodyne reduction . . .) has a significant corollary, because the film itself serves non-visible ends – and by that I mean that it's the astrophysics that counts, not the film itself, which was made just as a curiosity.

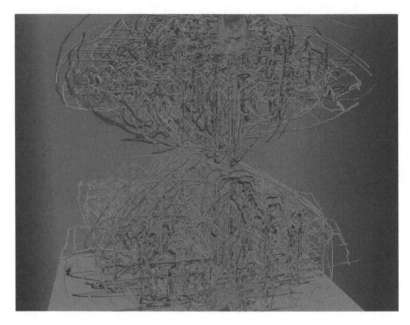

*Figure 3.6* Dislocation dynamics with a billion copper atoms.

## Excesses of the visual

Another wonderful film is the distributed-computing simulation of one billion atoms in a block of copper (Figure 3.6).[9]

The film shows a block of copper, with channels cut at the top and bottom. When metal is stressed, atoms shift position, causing the material to harden (provided the force is not sufficient to break it). The rendering routines omit any atoms that haven't moved – that is why the first frame looks like an empty box – and show only atoms at dislocations, demonstrating the "zippering action" of crystal deformation. The film is the result of a prodigious calculation, since the interactions of all one billion atoms had to be calculated to produce each frame in the film.

Before I draw a conclusion about that film, I will give another example, which represents a common kind of film in science: a rendering of the folding of a protein molecule (Figure 3.7).[10]

This is the way a protein naturally folds itself, from a more-or-less straight form to a tight curl. In the original film the effect is squiggly and

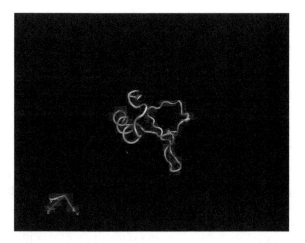

*Figure 3.7* Protein folding.

nervous looking, not at all the way I imagined molecules in my body moving. This kind of film is increasingly common in biochemistry, because computers now allow scientists to calculate all the forces that act on every atom in a protein (simplified in this film into a single thread, but actually a forest of atoms). The Internet is full of such films, some of them odd enough to rival anything produced in arts animation.[11]

Regarding films that are the products of intense, often distributed computing, power, I drew two conclusions:

(i) These are *sums* of individual images, or *averages* of them, not individual images or montaged images, as in the arts. This phenomenon has not been studied in the arts, as far as I know, but it has been theorized by the historian of physics Peter Galison, who sees "logic tradition images" like these as a different kind of image from "image tradition" pictures made in the conventional way.[12] Twentieth-century physics, he argues, mixed the two: the arts have remained largely only on one side of the equation.

(ii) These films contain too much information to be seen: they are effectively available only as tokens or samples of an excess of visual information. In that special sense, they cannot be seen, and their partial (or predominant) invisibility is different from the invisibility of complex or fast-moving scenes in the arts. These are a new possibility in the current interest in the unrepresentable.[13]

## Films in which light itself is a convention

Images of individual atoms have been common in surface chemistry and atomic physics since the invention of the electron microscope. It is not as widely known that movies of atoms have been made. They can be entrancing: the atoms shuttle back and forth as if they were restless, or they fly around one another like dancers in fast motion. One of the virtuosi of such movies is Jan-Olov Bovin at Lund University, Sweden. For a number of years he has been producing films of atoms precipitating into the surfaces of crystals (Figure 3.8).[14]

Here the top row of atoms in a gold crystal changes shape as individual atoms settle in place. In other films, atoms can be seen in the vacuum surrounding the crystal. Researchers at IBM have made films in which pairs of atoms spin around one another, attracted and repulsed in turns (Figure 3.9).[15] The scientist's description of this film reads like a romance. "When two atoms approach," he says,

> they feel an attractive force. As they approach closer, this attractive force turns into a repulsive force. This can be seen in real time: summarized by the frames labelled by time. In this case, two atoms approach, circling one another (indicated by the arrows). Then one of the atoms moves rapidly away to a spot about 0.5 nanometres distance away. Finally the other atom follows.

In these examples light is a convention in the sense that the light that enables us to perceive these films and their still was not involved in their production. The images are electron microscope images, meaning that electrons were the "illumination." Electron microscopy has a long history of imaging techniques that make the contrasts generated by electron transmission (or reflection) *look like* the behaviour of visible light. In the case of films of individual atoms, light is also conventional because the objects themselves are near the wavelength of the illumination (the electrons), and so by the laws of physics there is no way to make the atoms sharper, to bring them into focus. Nothing lies beyond these pixellated blurs, although it's a convention of ordinary digital film and photography that blur is inherent in the camera and not the object.

Here I drew two conclusions:

(i) The object is present but cannot be seen *with light*. There is a question regarding how to understand the expression "seeing" in this

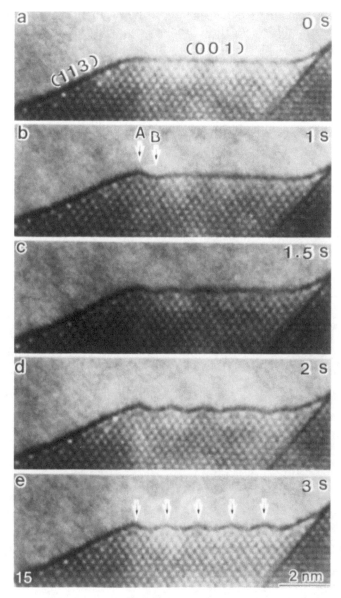

*Figure 3.8* Gold atoms in a crystal.

case: we do not see these objects, with or without the aid of instruments; rather we use the technology to produce images that *look like* they were made with light.

(ii) The creation of visibility is distinct from the creation of time, which is unaffected by these substitutions. Notice that the film excerpted in Figure 3.9 is in real time – unlike the films of molecules, these atoms are moving at a "human" scale and can be captured using frames of a duration commensurate with ordinary film.

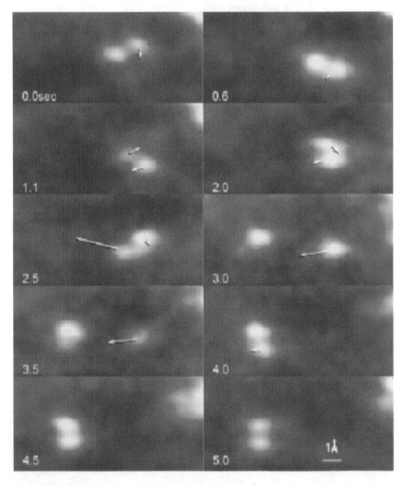

*Figure 3.9* Two gold atoms interacting.

## Films in which objects themselves are conventions

It is possible to go even further from everyday experience, because it is possible to make a film of something that is *itself* a pictorial convention. Quantum mechanics provides the classic example. Discussions about whether quantum mechanical phenomena can be visualized are a conventional part of the discipline, and have been since its inception. Paul Dirac is famous in this regard: he chose not to illustrate his writing, claiming that the subject is inherently beyond human intuition. (This has also been studied by Peter Galison.) Other physicists have taken the opposite point of view and have tried to make quantum mechanical phenomena visible. An example is the contemporary physicist Bernd Thaller, who has made part of a career out of colourful visualizations of quantum phenomena (Figure 3.10).[16]

In this particular film, a particle – say an electron – approaches a barrier with two holes. As the particle passes through the holes, it interferes with itself like water waves, instantiating the famous wave-particle duality. Thaller also colours the particle in stripes, encoding more information

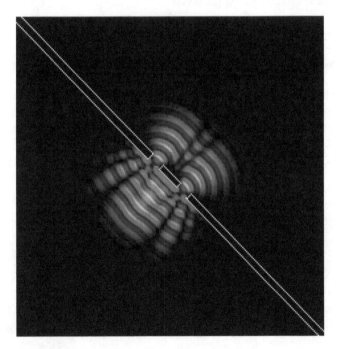

*Figure 3.10* Electron crossing a barrier with two holes.

about it than he could with just black and white. (The colours represent the phase of the wave equation mapped on the imaginary plane.) Much more could be visualized, and these images aren't enough to reproduce the wave equation, but they are a determined effort to visualize what many people consider outside of visualization.

Regarding these films in which objects are conventions, I suggested these three points:

(i) The objects are invented by the choice of parameters: they do not preexist the choice of constants, variables, and conventions, in the way that a tree could be said to preexist its iconic representation in a photograph.[17]
(ii) The objects' absence from films like these is also different from their absence in fields such as astrophysics, where objects can be simply *inaccessible* to vision. This is structural absence, not absence contingent on technology.
(iii) The creation of objects like the striped particle in Thaller's film is again distinct from the creation of time; time is generated within these image-making protocols.

## The end of the instant, revisited

I ended my presentation by returning to the first topic, the dissection or atomization of the instant, as it is configured in film theory. (I thought it would be prudent to return to art.) I showed two frames from an interactive video by the artist David Claerbout, a piece called *Untitled (Carl and Julie)*.[18] Claerbout's video appears to be a still image, but when the viewer enters the space, a motion detector triggers a video sequence in which the little girl (Julie) turns and looks out at the viewer (Figure 3.11, left frame).

*Figure 3.11*   David Claerbout, *Untitled* (Carl and Julie).

After a moment, she turns back (Figure 3.11, right frame). The piece is a lovely example of how issues *somewhat* like the ones I have raised occur in art. Claerbout's video is a "still," except for one portion, which is a video "in" the "still." The concept of an instant is questioned here, and the relation of still photograph to moving image is also rethought.

Another example of contemporary art that approaches the issues I have been exploring is Jaume Plensa's installation in Chicago's Millennium Park, called *Crown Fountain* (Figure 3.12).[19]

*Figure 3.12* The Crown Fountain by Jaume Plensa.

The work consists of two glass-brick towers, with videos on their facing surfaces and a shallow pool between them. The fronts of the towers show mainly faces – other images are involved, but they aren't relevant to what interests me. The faces are shown in four-minute segments, and there are a total of 1,000 faces that appear to cycle randomly. Frequently the images seem to be *almost* stills, because the faces don't change expression very quickly. (Other times, the faces do change expression, and most dramatically some of them pout, and a real cascade of water pours from their mouths.) One reason the faces seem to be almost still is that they were slowed down; the technical preparation of each video involved finding an optimal 40-second stretch from a longer tape, and copying it in reverse, to make an 80-second sequence that ran forward and then backward. Those 80 seconds were then dilated to four minutes. Blinks become especially odd, almost bovine, and gradual changes of expression can become nearly imperceptible.[20]

These two examples of artworks that play with the distinction between the still (or the instant) and the motion might have several consequences for the conceptualization of the instant. In the presentation I mentioned Deleuze's "movement-image," which could be altered by bringing examples like Plensa and Claerbout into consideration. Without narrative (as in Plensa) and without "stills" (as in Claerbout), the distinction between temporal change and the instant would itself become unfocused. But my larger purpose in introducing art examples was to propose that such reconceptualizations would not be as challenging, or as fundamental, as the kinds of things that are taking places in the sciences.

I am not particularly interested in the distinction between science and art (not to mention the distinction between art and the military!), and my presentation was not meant to suggest that non-art films might harbour some *different* kind of film theory.[21] If we agree not to worry about the distinction between art and science – which involves, among other things, declining to discuss why films like the ones I have shown here might be less "interesting" or "relevant" for film studies – then the erosion of some of film theory's crucial concepts may become a pressing interest.

I ended the presentation with another heuristic list, this time of selected themes in film theory, that might recede into a critical background in relation to the kinds of films I had been showing:

(i) Distinctions between film and photography, or film and stills, that depend on presence (as in André Bazin or Garrett Stewart)

(ii) Themes of memory, *he-has-been-there*, loss, and death (as in Roland Barthes; Jay Prosser, or Laura Mulvey's *Death Twenty-Four times a Second*)
(iii) The filmic mirroring of memory and experience (Deleuze), or the anxiety of the experiential lag (Régis Durand)
(iv) Theories of time peculiar to film (Mary Ann Doane, and again Deleuze).

All these, and doubtless many more, lose some of their urgency when they are seen against the backdrop of the astonishing and disorienting achievements of recent science and technology. That was really my only point in the presentation, and I'll make it my only point here: we, in the humanities, should look as widely and eclectically as possible, before we try to theorize what film might be.

## Notes

1. Actually, an Apple Keynote presentation. Unfortunately, all the ostensible upscape design features of that software, in comparison with the stultifying capitalist interface of PowerPoint, are lost here.
2. Tokamak Fusion Test Reactor (TFTR), from J. D. Strachan et al., (1997) pp. B103–114.
3. See my "Harold Edgerton's Rapatronic Photographs of Atomic Tests," (Elkins, 2004).
4. Courtesy of Palm Press, Concord MA, www.palmpress.com
5. See Bowley, Honour and Speyer, 1997.
6. The film is available from the Mechanical Engineering Department at Berkeley: www.me.berkeley.edu/ltl/research/fs.html.
7. Courtesy www.physics.usyd.edu.au/~gekko/wr104.html. To find copies of the movie, Google "WR104."
8. isi.ssl.berkeley.edu/system_overview.htm#optics.
9. Farid Abraham of IBM Almaden Research, in collaboration with LLNL personal Mark Duchaineau and Tomas Diaz De La Rubia; www.llnl.gov/largevis/atoms/ductile-failure/
10. Courtesy University of California at Davis, Process Systems Engineering; see www.chms.ucdavis.edu/research/web/pse/research_areas/protein_folding_dynamics/protein_dynamics.php.
11. For example, a film made by Kay Hamacher, on www.kay-hamacher.de.
12. See Galison, *Image and Logic* (1997). See also my "Logic and Images in Art History," response to Galison's *Image and Logic*, in *Perspectives on Science* (Elkins, 1999b).
13. This is pursued in my "Einige Gedanken über der Unbestimmtheit der Darstellung," in G. Gramm and E. Schürmann (eds), *Das unendliche Kunstwerk: Von der Bestimmtheit des Unbestimmten in der ästhetischen Erfahrung* (Elkins, 2006).

14. Courtesy Jan-Olov Bovin, http://www.jan-olov.bovin.nu
15. IBM research page: "Imaging Atoms at Sub-Angstrom Resolution with a Corrected Electron Microscope," at domino.research.ibm.com/Comm/bios.nsf/pages/sub-a.html
16. These are archived on Bernd Thaller's website, http://www.kfunigraz.ac.at/imawww/thaller/. There is also a book and CD: Thaller, *Advanced Visual Quantum Mechanics* (2005).
17. For problems with iconicity, see *Photography Theory*, in J. Elkins (ed.), *The Art Seminar*, vol. 2 (2007a).
18. David Claerbout, *Untitled (Carl and Julie)*, courtesy of Yvon-Lambert Gallery.
19. Jaume Plensa, *Crown Fountain*. Millennium Park, Chicago, 2004. Two glass-brick towers, fountains, one thousand video loops. Photo: author.
20. There is more involved in *Crown Fountain* in terms of temporality; see my "What Do We Want Photography to Be? [a reply to Michael Fried's "Barthes's *Punctum*, also in *Critical Inquiry*]," *Critical Inquiry* (Elkins, 2005).
21. The reasons for *not* attending to the distinction will be set out in detail in my *Visual Practices Across the University* (Elkins, 2007b). I have also argued this in *The Domain of Images* (Elkins, 1999a).

# II
# Norms

There are substantial difficulties in saying what properly counts as cinema technology. Are the institutions, forms of regulation and, above all, the norms of perception functions of technology? So often does the focus remain on what is seen (and to a lesser extent, what is heard) that other technological dimensions of cinema remain blurred. The chapters in this section address the question of how norms and forms arise in, on, around and alongside cinema technology. What is a norm? A norm in the strict sense is biological. It describes the stable conditions and states of an organism. It is a norm of the human body that the pulse beats between 40–100 times per minute. A norm is not given once and for all. It is established through repetition, practice and habit (eat well, exercise regularly and the heart rate will be lower). After a heart attack, for example, new norms may regulate circulation. Life is no mere metaphor for cinematic technology. Something living or alive in cinema depends on norms. What norms apply in cinema?

Norms have an equivocal status for living things. They belong neither solely to the living nor to its milieu, but express a relation between the two. They arise contingently, instituted in the course of events. The French philosopher of science and medicine Georges Canguilhem wrote that 'normative in the fullest sense of the word is that which establishes norms'. Several of the chapters in this section address the appearance of the normative character of cinema technologies (Canguilhem 1989, p. 127). In his chapter on early twentieth-century film theatres in Toronto, Paul Moore discusses the combustible character of early film stocks and the gradual weaving of different relations of social, legal, technical, architectural fire prevention around the assemblage of screen, projector, film reels and theatre. Here, the norms span boundaries and differences between materials (celluloid nitrate) and social groups ('mobs', 'crowds', 'strangers'). A norm may take the (visible/public?) form of a law describing the width of aisles or exits in the nickelodeon. Crucially, Moore suggests that a technical specificity such as the flammability of filmstock in close proximity to an electric arc-lamp project often serves to anchor an extensive set of norms that expand relations between technology and institutions. Here, norms of the apparatus begin to look like Michel Foucault's notion of governmentality: a whole substructure of procedures, regulations, protocols, designs and institutions that remain largely invisible but that frame events and position individuals and groups. Any account of cinema and technology ignores this governmentality and its normativity at its peril.

In his account of normativity, Canguilhem described how accidents and disease give rise to new norms that emerge as adaptations to changed internal or external environments. Has cinema undergone more 'heart attacks' than other media? Is it because it powerfully normalizes the already heavily sensory fields of vision and hearing? A more complex exploration of the relation between life and (cinema) technology could address this question. Inadvertent visualization of cinema's own technical processes lies at the core of Jan Harris' chapter. Drawing on and differentiating two important cinema theorists (Gilles Deleuze and Friedrich Kittler) in terms of their treatment of shock, Harris' chapter examines the recurrent figure of the double in cinema. In Kittler's work, the cinematic double represents the way the medium severs perception, memory and thought. The form of the double on-screen encapsulates the recognition of that loss in front of the scene, wounding any narcissism of the subject. In Deleuze's account too, the figure of the double, particularly the automaton, shocks the thinking subject. However, Deleuze conceives this shock differently. For him, the double figures not only how cinema exteriorizes thought in certain dangerously technological and normative ways, but how it frees up thought in certain respects to think differently. The externalizing of thinking on screen permits certain renewals.

In Kate O'Riordan's chapter on genomic science and cinema, this governmental, even biopolitical life of cinema technology appears starkly. Genomic science represents one of the most concerted scientific attempts ever undertaken to render the norms of living things visible. Not only seeing, but changing norms of life lies at the heart of genomics. Genomic science's normative efforts (in Canguilhem's sense), its capacity to establish norms through technological action, are the object of many recent (science fiction and horror) films. Norms of cinema rely on the disappearance of the technological apparatus and artifices into the background. Any attempt to call attention to them begins to unsettle the distributions of power they enact. As O'Riordan suggests, every time that cinema explores technological action on the living, it cannot help but call attention to its own technical investment in life, liveness and living (with) images. Genomic science is implicated in the normativity of living bodies just as cinematographic production is implicated in the normativity of seeing and hearing.

Every technology brings with it a complicated mixture of norms, forms and institutions. Where does all of this leave technology? Film and media studies have paid close attention to the formal properties of cinema (in cinematography especially). However, from the perspective of the work done by the chapters in this section, we could say that cinema's formal technical properties derive from the accretion of norms and normativity. Norms generate forms. Forms of life can be seen as the aggregate results of the normativity of life, as adaptations to certain kinds of accident and injury in environments. Specific forms (the double or the clone) are frozen results of the invention or maintenance of norms. Norms require active maintenance to sustain the apparently constant attributes of forms.

# 4
# Socially Combustible: Panicky People, Flammable Films and the Dangerous New Technology of the Nickelodeon

*Paul S. Moore*

On 16 January 1908, a 15-year-old projectionist died of burns after the film he was showing caught fire at the Hippodrome Theatorium in St. Catharines, Ontario, a small city between Toronto and Niagara Falls (*World*, 1908). Just a day later came news of another celluloid fire and panicky picture show audience in another Ontario town, Ingersoll (*Telegram*, 1908). Both incidents followed on the heels of a theatre disaster in Boyertown, Pennsylvania, where 170 people died in a panicked rush to flee a fire reportedly resulting from the explosion of a moving picture projector. Although moving pictures were ultimately cleared of culpability in Boyertown, the tragedy remains associated with the dangers of early movie-going (Smither, 2002, p. 433). Horrific details from Pennsylvania filled the front pages of newspapers across the continent including Toronto (for example, *Globe* 1908; *News* 1908), but the death in St. Catharines brought close to home the dangers of a relatively new gathering-place: the nickelodeon five-cent show, or theatorium (Figure 4.1). Reporters drew the readers' attention to the long history of theatre fires, and newspapers reviewed several tragedies of the past, most recently the Chicago Iroquois Theatre fire in 1903, which had led many cities throughout North America to enforce new fire safety bylaws for theatres (Brandt, 2003). But this time around, the cinematograph machine was singled out as the culprit, with its electric arc lamp and its combustible reels of cellulose nitrate films. Justifiably or not, the still-novel technology seemed to escape the bounds of even the most stringent requirements in the construction of theatres. Safety designs for exits, escapes, stairwells, doorways and asbestos stage curtains could not contain the explosive mix of celluloid, electricity and hot projection lamps. The *chemical combustibility* of moving picture technology only reinforced nascent notions about nickelodeon audiences being excitable

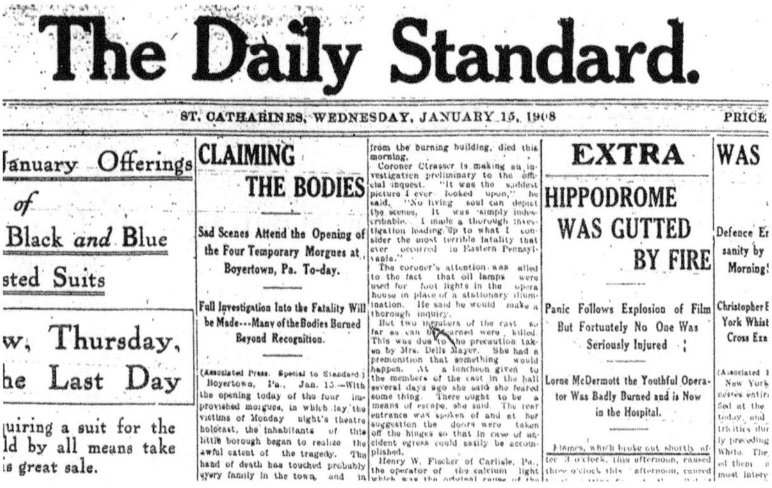

**The Daily Standard.**

ST. CATHARINES, WEDNESDAY, JANUARY 15, 1908 PRICE

January Offerings of Black and Blue ...sted Suits

...w, Thursday, ...he Last Day

...uiring a suit for the ...ld by all means take ...is great sale.

**CLAIMING THE BODIES**

Sad Scenes Attend the Opening of the Four Temporary Morgues at Boyertown, Pa. To-day.

Full Investigation Into the Fatality Will be Made---Many of the Bodies Burned Beyond Recognition.

(Associated Press. Special to Standard.) Boyertown, Pa., Jan. 15.—With the opening today of the four improvished morgues, in which lay the victims of Monday night's theatre holocast, the inhabitants of this little borough began to realize the awful extent of the tragedy. The hand of death has touched probably every family in the town, and in

from the burning building, died this morning.

Coroner Ctrasser is making an investigation preliminary to the official inquest. "It was the saddest picture I ever looked upon," he said. "No living soul can depict the scenes. It was simply indescribable. I made a thorough investigation leading up to what I consider the most terrible fatality that ever occurred in Eastern Pennsylvania."

The coroner's attention was alled to the fact that oil lamps were used for foot lights in the opera house in place of a stationary illumination. He said he would make a thorough inquiry.

But two members of the cast so far as can be learned were killed. This was due to the precaution taken by Mrs. Della Mayer. She had a premonition that something would happen. At a luncheon given to the members of the cast in the hall several days ago she said she feared some thing. There ought to be a means of escape, she said. The rear entrance was spoken of and at her suggestion the doors were taken off the hinges so that in case of accident egress could easily be accomplished.

Henry W. Fischer of Carlisle, Pa., the operator of the calcium light

**EXTRA**

**HIPPODROME WAS GUTTED BY FIRE**

Panic Follows Explosion of Film But Fortunately No One Was Seriously Injured

Lorne McDermott the Youthful Operator Was Badly Burned and is Now in the Hospital.

**WAS**

Defence Er... sanity by Morning!

Christopher ... York Whit... Cross Exa...

*Figure 4.1* News of the disastrous theatre fire in Boyertown, Pennsylvania, appeared next to details of a local fire and death in St. Catharines, Ontario, in January 1908.

and panicky, in part because they were disproportionately juvenile, female, foreign-born and working class, an important point I will return to shortly.

Within months of the Boyertown incident came a rush of laws specifically addressing the cinematograph and its flammable celluloid films. In Ontario, Massachusetts, and other places throughout North America, legislators gave cinema its first legal definition. Film was identified as a hazardous substance needing careful, bureaucratic inspection and licensing. This spate of legislation early in 1908 marked the moment when film technology achieved a broad, public persona. In North America, there had already been an entrepreneurial boom of nickel show openings around 1906, followed swiftly by public debates over their social role. Reformers, police, parents and politicians, each and all together, questioned the maturity of nickelodeon audiences and the effects of easy access to filmed depictions of crime and immoral acts. On this cultural and moral plane, there remained plenty of room for disagreement and deliberation over the commercial merits of the picture show, the moral effects of its pictures and the need to censor and supervise audiences. However, the 1908 explosion and catastrophe in Boyertown, and its many echoes worldwide, such as the death in St. Catharines, finally made one aspect of cinema indisputable: the five-cent show was a hazardous place. The volatile combination of flammable celluloid films and panicky people crowded into nickelodeons meant movie-going was *socially combustible*. A century later, decades after the urgency of the problem dissipated, it is easy to assume that fire safety regulations are merely dampers on the energy and potential of exciting, crowded gatherings in public, urban space. The police and governments, of course, could use safety codes and bylaws to discriminate or harass supposedly bothersome or indecent activities. Building codes and inspections were indeed introduced largely at the insistence of business interests and insurance companies to prevent property damage and protect land values. However, politicized efforts and abuses do not automatically turn fire safety into an ideological tool of urban governance. Following Bruno Latour (2005), we can treat celluloid *itself* as a social actor in the networks of film regulation. Respect should be paid to the *material properties of film technology* at the nickelodeon in order to understand fully the central importance safety played in guiding decisions about the best fit between this novel technology and existing local cultures. I argue that safety measures achieved perhaps the earliest consensus over regulation because of the clear benefits for the public good made stark after disastrous fire panics. Such licensing codes do not tend to ban things outright, but instead police indirectly by stipulating conditions of consumption – who can take part, when and where things can happen. For public welfare and safety, licensed and inspected businesses like picture shows became responsible for policing their own customers (Valverde, 2003). Characterizing the picture show as a socially combustible place emphasizes how fire safety instigated some of the earliest film-specific laws. These fire safety laws were soon extended into elaborate film bureaucracies encompassing inspection, censorship, taxation and restricted admissions (barring unaccompanied children from attending films, for example). The frame of social combustibility thus signifies how material safety laws, by defining the technology itself as hazardous, were simply the flashpoint for regulating a range of aspects of movie-going.

Toronto makes a widely relevant case study in this respect (Figure 4.2). Economically and commercially, this Canadian metropolis was largely integrated into a continental market. For cinema in particular, Toronto and Canada were effectively just another region in the American *domestic* mass market. Like larger American cities, at the turn of the last century, Toronto was a bustling centre of commerce and manufacturing, doubling its population through mass immigration to 400,000 in the first decade of the twentieth century. Unlike American cities, however, those immigrants were overwhelmingly from Britain and Ireland,

78  *Socially Combustible*

*Figure 4.2* The cinematic spectacle of electricity began with the bright lights of the sidewalk marquee. Crystal Palace, Toronto. Photograph courtesy of the Archives of Ontario.

although there were still highly visible and important Jewish and other ethnic subcultures (Harris, 1996, pp. 23–32). Such minorities, even in a culturally British city, showed Toronto's urbanization shared much with American cities, especially when it came to moral reform issues and the 'social purity' movement (Valverde, 1991). In their legal institutions and more traditional daily routines, Toronto and other Canadian cities had a deliberately British character, or distinctly colonial at any rate (Isin, 1992). However, even as I delve momentarily into details about Toronto, this look at early film regulation applies more widely to the emergent place of cinema in urban life. Taken as a sketch, even the legislative aspects apply to municipalities in almost any part of North America, as well as Britain and its former colonies. Focusing on a specific case allows a detailed analysis of the local impact of cinema and how it was policed and regulated. This is especially important, almost necessary, as a means of understanding the character and infrastructure of early cinema before the industry became vertically integrated and known as Hollywood.

Responding to the death in St. Catharines and the disaster in Boyertown, the first Ontario law addressing the cinematograph in any way was based on a similar piece of legislation introduced to Massachusetts weeks earlier. The April 1908 law amended the existing regulation of safety exits in public buildings, which had previously meant churches and theatres, but now applied to 'all places of amusement' as well (Ontario, 1908). The amendment went further than its nominal interest in exits, however, with additional clauses specifically addressing celluloid film. There were provisions for a provincial licence of all moving picture machines and also their projectionists, still known as 'operators' – both instituted a year later in 1909. But the law *immediately* required the inspection and approval by municipal police of every 'cinematograph or similar apparatus' and all locations handling or storing 'combustible film more than ten inches in length'. From this time forward in Toronto, moving picture machines would be strictly regulated as part of urban policing. Promptly in May 1908, John Griffin, the showman who then controlled a majority of Toronto's picture shows, wrote to the city's chief constable, inviting inspections for his new amusement licences (Letterbooks, 1908).

By 1908, cinema had already existed in Toronto for over a decade, but the fire safety issue was hardly the first attempt at regulation. Debates over the morality of cinematic images occurred within a year of the apparatus's debut on 31 August 1896 (Bossin, 1951). Some aldermen on city council in August 1897 tried to prohibit 'Veriscope' moving pictures of the Corbett-Fitzsimmons prize-fight that took place in Nevada in March that year (Craik, 1961; Gutteridge, 2000, pp. 73–74). The argument was simply that the films should be banned because professional boxing matches were themselves prohibited (*Telegram*, 1897). At this point, however, the attempt to censor cinema failed and there was no easy consensus over how to regulate and police the content of moving pictures (*Star*, 1897). Despite continuing debates over the moral and social problems arising from cinematic technology, long-established licensing procedures and laws policing indecency sufficed for another decade. The rapid proliferation of nickel shows upset the balance of regulation, prompting governments to replace policing on the beat with a modern, bureaucratic system to match the modernity of cinema.

The social apparatus of cinema, the exhibition site and its network of commerce, regulation and sociability is as important as the optical apparatus in defining the technology. Within even the first months of the first projected moving image in 1896 (in Canada), there were already several places to see films: in the context of the industrial exhibition, as part of a variety show programme in an established theatre downtown and on their own in the temporary space of a leased store on the main shopping street (Morris, 1978, pp. 1–13). As elsewhere, films soon became a daily part of the vaudeville bill. Had film remained peripheral to existing, already instituted practices, it might have been treated as unproblematic, as a secondary device, an instrument without ends in itself. However, beginning in 1906 in Toronto, and more or less simultaneously everywhere else in North America, thousands of entrepreneurs opened five-cent picture theatres. They built an institution around the technology. Nickelodeon, theatorium, penny gaff: the picture show gave the technology of cinema a social institution of its own in movie-going. Before long came concerns about its social regulation.

Conventionally, film histories began with the debut of the apparatus: August 1896 for Toronto. Such origins are rarely cultural epiphanies, however. An early account of cinema's debut in Toronto joked that 'in those days X-rays were more popular' (Bossin, 1963). Perhaps the best measure of how 1896 was a moment of social continuity, rather than rupture, can be found in the city licence schedule, the primary municipal device for managing and monitoring business operations. The division where movie theatres eventually ended up was the general category for entertainments charging admission, which were subject to an annual licence fee of $50 long before cinema arrived (for example, Toronto, 1890). This licence category – the fee itself – was well defined decades before the first nickel show.

Nickelodeons made moving pictures more affordable than prior public amusements and thus accessible especially to children and the working class. Greater access did not stop there, as picture shows happened every day and spread rapidly to every shopping street in cities like Toronto. No longer were they merely commercial amusements limited to special carnival occasions, nor were they corralled downtown. Nickelodeons became part of domestic neighbourhood life; they were the amusement equivalent of corner stores. Their appeal to children, and their profit *from* children, brought nickel shows quickly to the attention of progressive reformers urging stricter and more transparent policing and regulation. In Chicago, the matter flared into public view in April 1907, in newspapers and among reform agencies like Jane Addams' Hull House (Grieveson, 1999). Simultaneously in Toronto, police confiscated a film called *The Unwritten Law*, a semi-fictionalized depiction of the well-known Thaw-White murder trial (*News*, 1907). This sparked several weeks of debate in daily newspapers over the censorship of plays and pictures, the licensing procedures for nickel shows and the police reports of children who were stealing to get nickels to see shows (for example, *Star*, 1907; *World*, 1907). It became evident that picture showmen were treading on the spatial and demographic terrain of churches, schools and families. Nonetheless, at this point city politicians and the police claimed the legal status quo was sufficient. One newspaper echoed this official restraint in its headline about an investigation of the city's theatoriums: 'Five Cent Theatre Harmless Here; Merely Creates Taste for an Entertainment' (*Mail and Empire*, 1907).

As I have already shown, the issue of fire safety shifted the terms of these debates over cinema's effects from the individuated morality of particular persons in the audience to the specific idea of a *mass* audience. By foregrounding the scenario of a theatre fire, it was evident that nickelodeon audiences could act as a crowd – panic. Fire safety issues highlighted panic as a possible audience effect of movie-going. In a sense, the chemical combustibility of celluloid films dramatically crystallized the problem: the picture show audience was a mass audience, and the picture theatre was a socially combustible space.

### Safety tames the social whirl

Just as the Ontario legislature was debating the April 1908 fire safety law regulating cinema, a new roller coaster called the Social Whirl was operating in Chicago and being promoted for sale to fairground operators in the show business magazine *Billboard*: 'This is not a dream, but a real live one; occupying space, 60 × 150 ft'. Although as a roller coaster the Social Whirl might have been constrained to occupying just 9000 square feet, urban space more generally was a type of social whirl, one that, in the view of the authorities, required as careful an installation and management as any amusement park ride. A constant problem for urban order was the threat of a major conflagration, as great city fires levelled acres of built urban real estate throughout the nineteenth century (Rosen, 1986; Novak, 1996). In 1904, a large part of the centre of Toronto had been destroyed in a major fire, and proper supervision of the material construction of buildings in the central area of the city was a key part of the plan to ensure such a disaster did not recur. The well-being and livelihood of the city, in all of their aspects from real estate value to the very life of each person, were seen to depend in no small part on fire safety. The particular form that this concern took in theatres, churches and public halls addressed the additional prospect of deaths caused not by any material danger but the social danger of a fire panic.

Urban everyday life could never be experienced as a pleasurable social whirl as long as the threat of everyday combustibility was foregrounded. All novel materials deemed hazardous because of their flammability required adjustments to routine fire safety measures, not least those suggested by insurance adjustors and fire chiefs (Novak, 1996, pp. 56–59; McSwain, 2002). But along with flammable industrial materials, there was a sense that certain practices were inherently combustible as well, that in certain contexts people themselves could collectively burst into panic. Fire safety was as much about managing what was seen as a social combustibility in practices like film-going as it was about securing the explosive materials that were involved in creating the scene of gathering. Put simply, fire safety legislation was an important public educational measure, instructions for the public on how to inhabit the order of the act by acting orderly should a fire actually erupt in a public building. A fine line seemed to separate amusement from panic.

Many thorough social histories of the nickelodeon, however, are practically befuddled by the persistence of fire safety as a key concern at the time. I risk exaggerating the significance of passing comments, but my point is that the issue of fire safety in my study of Toronto cannot be merely a passing comment. Consider, for example, how Richard Abel (1999, pp. 32–33) notes with surprise how *Billboard* magazine kept harping on the dangers of moving picture fires even as it reported all the new and profitable storefront shows. Fire safety issues are elsewhere seen as an ideological mask on the part of authorities wishing to control ethnic or working-class social gatherings. Urrichio and Pearson (1993, p. 31) point out that keeping buildings up to code was a costly venture that surely drove out of business marginal, immigrant showmen whose nickelodeons were cast as most offensive. While in the same passage they grant that 'many physical hazards' were part of going to the nickel shows, Urrichio and Pearson still call zoning and safety codes 'thinly veiled attempts at suppression' with an 'ideological agenda'. It is admittedly important to note that safety codes had unequal effects, but I would be gravely misrepresenting the situation in Toronto if I accounted for discriminatory judgments against working-class and ethnic audiences without taking seriously the validity of concerns for the material conditions of film-going. In other words, sympathies with marginal audiences can have the unfortunate and unintended consequence of assuming physical safety was of no concern to anyone but the propertied class. The effect is to continue subscribing to an oversimplified and condescending image of early audiences, dating back to at least Lewis Jacobs' (1967, p. 56) comment that working-class families did not mind the crowded, unsanitary and hazardous conditions.

Mark Jancovich (2003, p. 38) argues that the safety regulations of the 1909 Cinematograph Act in Britain effectively set up a way of zoning amusement, while downplaying the explicit goal of fire prevention because fire hazards were often exaggerated. 'Even when fires did break out, few people were killed by the fires themselves, but rather by the panic which ensued'. Fire safety regulations, however, were *intended* to prevent the problem of theatre panic as well as fires. This is ultimately key to a full understanding of how the regulation of the space and its materials also ordered the audiences, such as when Pearson and Urrichio quote an investigation by New York's fire commissioner: 'It is a panicky crowd which patronizes the moving-pictures houses of our city – mothers and children in the predominance – many of them foreign born' (Pearson and Urrichio, 1999, p. 66). The argument that the nickelodeon audience was perceived as immature and uncivilized, feminine, juvenile and foreign is important, and it provides an opportunity to more strongly consider how fire safety might be more than merely a matter of physical safety. It begins to reveal why fire safety in moving picture shows would be essential, because the immature audience was seen as easily panicked. Such aspersions against the early movie audience were hardly restricted to moralistic reformers. Andreas Huyssen (1986) reminds us that cultural critics, too, have regularly revealed an elitist streak by associating mass culture with women and minorities. The idea that moving picture audiences were especially panicky is hardly restricted to fire hazards – the 'train effect' where some rube runs, startled, away from the oncoming animated locomotive has been called the 'founding myth of cinema' (Bottomore, 1999).

A fire panic in a public building only implied the chaos of a crowd suddenly threatened, experiencing fear. The cause of mass death in theatre panics was not fear but the uniquely social danger that came from the peculiar mass behaviour of a panicking crowd. Investigations following the Iroquois Theatre fire in Chicago discovered with horror that most deaths were caused by people rushing *as a crowd* in a confined space. The modern problem of crowds in urban space, let alone a panicking crowd in a confined urban space, is key to understanding why theatre and film audiences would be cast as immature. Indeed, immaturity was literal in the worst theatre disasters. As in Boyertown's Sunday family show, most of the victims at Chicago's Iroquois were children and women because the fire broke out during a holiday matinee. Bodies were piled ten feet high from the rush of the fire panic. While some died from blindly following the rush of the crowd, unable to find their own way in the fire panic, others died because of their inability to avoid that rush: people were trampled and crushed (Brandt, 2003, pp. 52–58). If the thought of burning to death or dying from smoke inhalation was not bad enough, the spectre of death caused by mass panic invoked the fragility of civilized, sociable public conduct on which the modern city ordered its everyday life. The very possibility of this type of irrational social behaviour called attention to the need for regulation.

Georg Simmel provides a key sociological theory of the fragility of sociable public conduct in modern civil society. The tenuousness of modern, urban sociability among crowds of strangers is distinct from political theories of the social contract (Macpherson, 1962). Simmel's particular contribution to knowledge of the social character of modernity proposed there was a danger of sociability leading to overly formal and rationalized, and thus dispiriting, conduct. Sociable modernity mismatched the formality of actions and the need to feel like an active participant (Simmel, 1950, pp. 40–57). On the other hand, Simmel's characterization of the modern metropolis and the modernity of his day, as noted by David Frisby (1986), emphasized the fleeting and transitory contingency of everyday urban life. Despite being at odds with a subjective sense of self, sociable routines and a blasé attitude helped make sense of a modern, urban environment that barraged the senses with constant change. Altogether, the mental life of the metropolis was at odds with its built situation, at the nickelodeon just like anywhere else. The juxtaposition of amusement and hazard at the nickelodeon was not exceptional, nor was the effort to manage the hazard once it came to attention.

The conduct of an audience as a group of strangers in a confined space is a prime example of the tenuous balancing act of sociability. If the norms that made being part of an audience enjoyable were so brittle that alienation could be a result, then a corresponding danger was the easy way sociable spaces could be abandoned altogether. The instability of crowds led to disaster when sociability dissipated all together in a panic. It was similar, but contrasted in effect, to the way a mob could result from a mass political gathering. But a panicking crowd in a theatre was not even as understandable and ordered as a mob incited by a charismatic speech to riot. Advertising for nickel shows emphasized how people could come and go as they pleased. In Toronto, a high-class nickel show affiliated with B. F. Keith's in January 1908 used the phrase 'Come when you like, Stay as long as you like' in ads run in all of the city's daily newspapers. In the early days of continuous shows, film showmen nurtured the audience's urge to enter and leave at will. However, the urge to leave happened all at once and involuntarily in a fire panic. The problem was how to make exiting in case of fire a rationalized act, something an audience did collectively rather than in a rush as an irrational crowd. This required people to retain sociable, mannered control of their bodies, even in the event of a hasty exit during a fire. Norbert Elias (2000) embeds his understanding of state formation in a history of manners, explaining that sociable citizenship is rooted in the ideal of continually being in control of bodily functions. Civilized interaction depends on embodied discipline and self-regulation, strongly linked to the awareness of *becoming* civilized and in turn the process of civilization (Quilley and Loyal, 2004). In this sense, one small part of state formation could be fire safety at moving picture shows, or at least conversely the possibility of panic in a theatre fire could undermine, in a small way, the very basis of the protective authority of the state. Again, the prospect of losing all sense of mannerism, acting with fear and panic, is the looming shadow of the civilizing process, frighteningly cogent in the prospect of a fire in a crowded, confined space.

Theories of crowd psychology from the late nineteenth and early twentieth centuries, most famously Gustave LeBon's theory (2002), proposed how group action could be both collective and irrational at the same time, but nevertheless, all too predictable even when reacting to a moment of surprise. This informed Robert Park's (1972) sociological definition of the crowd as a directed, engaged collective temporarily sharing space, whether or not composed of strangers. Indeed, a collective focus is what distinguished the crowd from the masses (for example, of workers and shoppers) populating public urban space in American downtowns. Park's description of the crowd is remarkable for how it applies to audiences, perhaps more than any other crowd. But then it is all the more troubling that an audience has its attention held by an illusion, by projected moving images, engaged through only a technological apparatus. The focus of a modern, urban crowd could be instituted without a charismatic authority figure and no longer depended on embodied leadership. This space, after all, was commercial, and the congregated people were largely strangers to each other: a temporary, voluntary crowd of people paying nickels and dimes to see a show. In a sense their commitment was *to the show*, not to each other. Add to this the darkness of the auditorium. Heap on top, finally, the electricity used to operate the picture machine, often supplied by a portable gas generator, and finally the chemically unstable celluloid film.

The chemical combustibility of celluloid can thus be a flashpoint igniting wider recognition of the social combustibility of film-going crowds. The material part of the fire hazard could be handled through protocols designating jurisdictions to supervise handling film. The public act of legislating supervision also worked towards handling theatre panic – the social part of the fire hazard – by supporting the sociability of the film-going crowd, which was seen as fragile. Proper policing of fire safety in public buildings, including the expert advice of the city architect and the professional wisdom of the chief of the fire brigade, openly exhibited how actions were taken to make these establishments safe. This exhibition of safety was as important as any safety code for managing the threat of panic, not just the possibility of fire in itself. Regulation was needed for social psychological reasons as well, to assure the public at a theatre that smoke did not necessarily mean fire and further that fire did not require panic. Rational measures could replace irrational fear and prompt a rational response to fire instead of panic. Cleared aisles and conspicuous exits were thus soon required in moving picture theatres just as they were in large playhouses, churches, schools and office buildings. The regulation of theatres had to ensure not just that fires did not start, but also that panic did not result if one did take hold. In the years following 1908, there are scattered stories of panics averted and audiences calmly clearing picture theatres as the projectionist controlled a fire in his booth. At times, the pianist even played a march to give rhythm to the emergency exit (for example, *World*, 1911; *Billboard*, 1910; *American*, 1913).

Once the Ontario law regulating moving pictures was enacted in April 1908, municipal police forces were mandated to inspect every operation of a moving picture machine and storage of films. In Toronto these police duties were extended to municipal licensing as well, and the letters of the chief constable show that the Board of Police Commissioners proceeded with complete autonomy over the decision to licence shows. The novelty of cinematographic vision was coming to require a complex rational-legal supervision as it took on a place of its own in the range of urban practices of amusement and shopping. The way that fire safety, of all the possible aspects of film technology, precipitated clarity in regulations only highlights how the meaning of film was articulated iteratively through social conditions, through efforts to assign film an order as problems arose. Film-going came into view as something problematic and hazardous, but at every point was treated as something within the means and jurisdiction of governments. Every additional layer of regulation – censorship, taxation, the exclusion of children – responded to a slightly different but still problematic social effect of film technology. Treated in this way, the technology of cinema includes its local regulation and showmanship as equals with the invention and distribution of the apparatus itself. All were necessary to manage filmgoing as a social practice, to bring it into being and make it meaningful and understandable as a mass medium that gathered all of the public within its practice.

## Acknowledgements

Research was completed while I was a postdoctoral fellow in Cinema and Media Studies at the University of Chicago, funded by the Social Sciences and Humanities Research Council of Canada.

# 5
# Cinema and Its Doubles: Kittler v. Deleuze

*Jan Harris*

## Introduction

This chapter explores the parallels between Gilles Deleuze and Friedrich Kittler's respective accounts of cinema via an exploration of their analysis of the theme of the double, or doppelgänger, in particular as it emerges in German expressionist cinema. Both thinkers concur in the belief that the double is not a theme that accidentally befalls cinema, but is rather the narratological registration of the medium's technical conditions. In this respect, both will been seen to distance themselves (to varying degrees) from Siegfried Kracauer's sociocultural reading of early German cinema, *From Caligari to Hitler* (Kracauer, 2004 (1947)). However, this consonance will serve simply as a prelude to an exploration of a more profound divergence regarding cinema's ontological status, which reflects a differing assessment of the relation between the human and technics.

There are several reasons for staging such a confrontation under the sign of the double. Firstly, we might note the increasing influence of both theorists' bodies of work within film and cultural studies. In Deleuze's case there has been a considerable growth of interest in his two-volume study of cinema (Deleuze, 1986 (1983), 1989 (1985)), despite its distance from regnant theoretical positions and its Bergsonian provenance (a philosopher whose own estimation of cinema was the embodiment of the very error he sought to overturn) (Bergson, 1911 (1907)). Although his project has yet to attract the sustained engagement that it warrants, Kittler's star in Anglo-American media studies also appears to be in the ascendant (see Winthrop-Young, 2002), and references to his work are increasingly common (for example, Chun and Keenan, 2006; Gane,

2005). The turn to these thinkers has, to a greater or lesser extent, been commensurate with a growing awareness of the role of 'the question of technology' in debates regarding old and new media and their attended cultural forms. Within the context of film theory this has taken the form of a concern with the impact of the digital image and its challenge to the presupposition of indexicality. Thus the growing appeal of these thinkers resides in part in the possibility that therein may be sourced elements of a post-digital theory of film (for example, Cubbit, 2004). And in this respect, an exploration of the divergence that exists between Kittler and Deleuze's readings of the double may serve to draw attention to the wider implications for film and media theory of the inimical ontologies that subtend their respective accounts.

Before outlining these, however, it may be useful to provide an indication, in the most general terms, of precisely what is meant by the double in this context. The double (as here understood) can be approached through Freud's comments on the uncanny (1964 (1919)), a sensation often aroused by amongst others 'waxwork figures, ingeniously constructed dolls and automata', which precipitate an ontological crisis wherein one is unsure if an 'apparently animate being is really alive; or conversely, whether a lifeless object might not be in fact animate' (1964, p. 217). Freud, drawing on Otto Rank, argues the uncanny has its origin in the early stages of individual and collective psychogenesis, where a 'double' (for instance that of the body's 'soul', or the individual superego) served as a means of consolidating identity.

In the course of maturation such phantasms are renounced, but their vestigial forms haunt the psyche, and individual and collective traumata trigger their return as the uncanny. Our concern here will be the confusion of the living and the technical, the autonomous and the automatic that Freud regards as symptomatic. However, this confusion will be seen in terms of cause, and the discourses that treat it as symptoms.

The emergence of the uncanny and the double within a Germanic context is of course significant, as Titford notes, 'the German language, by its very syntax ... is anthropomorphic ... anthropomorphism is inherent in the German consciousness (1973, p. 19), and this tendency, coupled with more immediate influences of German Romanticism and history, provides a means of accounting for this genesis. However, the irresistible and international spell the theme has cast over the medium, as even a cursory inventory of the doubles (for example, the golem, vampire, zombie, the wives of Stepford and various sci-fi automata and cyborgs) that stalk film's imaginary confirms, is likewise significant and cannot be resolved by appealing to the cultural conditions that account for its inception. Consequently, what is offered below takes its direction from Titford's prescient observation that 'German expressionist cinema is significant in the first instance, not because it offers a penetrating analysis of society, nor because of what it has learned from the . . . psychology of its age. What gives its special quality is its concern directly and indirectly, with the filmic process itself' (1973, p. 18), and argues that this proposition finds its fullest theoretical elaboration in the film theory of Kittler and Deleuze.

Thus Kittler and Deleuze's commitment (though of differing degrees) to a 'media materialist' reading of this motif, such that the double is revealed as a narratological registration of cinema's technological conditions, represents a radical, though ultimately persuasive, account that breaks with established psycho-social readings (while recognizing the value of the latter in illuminating why, in Deleuze's words, 'German cinema . . . was perhaps best placed to announce something new which was to change cinema') (1989, p. 263) and in so doing offers an explanation for its enduring appeal.

### Kittler: Film as imaginary

Kittler's analysis of cinema is presented in his *Gramophone, Film, Typewriter* (1999 (1986)) – a kind of technical addendum to his opus *Discourse Networks 1800/1900* (1990 (1985)) and the media science established therein. Discourse networks are 'scriptorial' or 'notation systems' (Wellbury, in Kittler, 1990, p. xii) comprised of 'the network of technologies and institutions that allow a given culture to select, store, and produce relevant data' (Kittler, 1990, p. 369). They are at once overarching systems that encompass entire eras and societies, and at the same time only articulated through local practices. Consequently, they must be traced, assembled through the investigation and collation of apparently insignificant scriptorial 'events', and the conditions that Kittler establishes for their excavation constitutes an index of the constellation of thinkers whose singular synthesis provides the foundations of his project. Thus like the epistemes of the 'archaeological' Foucault, within which statements cannot be attributed to individual or a collective intention but instead located within an 'anonymous field whose configuration defines the possible position of the speaking subject' (Foucault, 1972 (1969), p. 122), discourse networks are radically extrinsic. And like Foucault's epistemes, Kittler argues that these networks can only be described retroactively; the nature of a given network can only be understood when it has been supplanted by its successor. This reflects a second feature, that of mediality, which can be understood as a radicalization of McLuhan's equation of medium and message. For Kittler any historical formulation of the human, meaning or society is to be rigorously returned to the conditions of its inscription, in other words the reigning assemblage of media technologies. Every term is to be sacrificed to this mediality: there are only historically specific constellations of media technologies, performing at different scales with disparate materials what Kittler believes to be the core functions of all media: storage, processing and transmission.

Having abnegated the subject and its intentions, as well as the explanatory power of the 'social' and 'cultural', Kittler elects the body as the locus of discourse networks. Thus, like the 'genealogical' Foucault, Kittler views the body as a field of forces from which a subject is extracted, and as a surface on which a network is inscribed. The subject, or rather the illusion of a subject (which Kittler contemptuously dubs the 'so-called man' – *der sogenannte Mensch*), is simply a determinate variable of a given network's distribution of components as articulated on the body. Kittler has addressed two major networks, those of 1800 and 1900, and via their analysis he has cautiously outlined the characteristics of a third network, that of 2000. These have been exhumed through the patient analysis, and systematic juxtaposition, of coeval but otherwise disparate texts and artefacts. A procedure seeking to bypass their manifest content in order to uncover something 'spoken without being said, thought without being thought . . . written and simultaneously erased . . .' (Derrida, 1978 (1967), p. 229). The specific context of Kittler's treatment of cinema is the exposition of network 1900, inaugurated by the holy trinity of technical media: the gramophone, film and typewriter. In keeping with the equation of the subject with its media matrix, the disparate technical conditions of the storage media of 1900 leads Kittler to map them onto the Lacanian categories of the real (gramophone), imaginary (cinema) and symbolic (typewriter). This transposition dictates the terms of Kittler's film theory. The gramophone's status as the 'real' arises from its ability to trace the amplitude of its input data – put simply, the grooves cut on wax are a direct, continuous transcription of their sonic event. In contrast the cinema begins with deception: a series of static images are projected in rapid succession, fooling the eye, exploiting the nerves temporal threshold and inducing the illusion of continuous movement. To capture the visual as a direct trace in the manner of phonography's isomorphic 'real' was beyond the capacities of the technologies of 1900 since 'optical data flows are two-dimensional' and 'consist of high frequencies . . . thousands of units of light per unit of time must be transmitted in order to present the eye with a two- or even three-dimensional image' (1999, p. 118). Given the impossibility of the direct storage of optical data, as 'a medium that is unable to trace the amplitude of its input data', cinema necessarily owed its existence to cuts, samples and selections. All the forms of moving image that constitute mass media, from cinema to television to the digital technologies of today, are comprised of excerpts and segues, whether the 24 frames per second of traditional celluloid or the various bit/time ratios of the animated electronic image (Kittler, 2001).

Film is imaginary because it is founded on 'the film trick preceding all film tricks' – the illusion of continuous movement. Kittler consolidates the Lacanian dimension of this description by reference to the 'mirror stage'. This, in keeping with his reading of Lacanian psychoanalysis as the 'historical effect' of its ambient network, becomes 'quite simply, cinema': its *spaltung* and the moving image's illusion are in terms of their mechanics analogous:

> On the one side we have the real of a prematurely born body, whose sensory neurons in the first months of life . . . are myelogenetically to immature . . . not to [result in a perception of] a fragmented body. On the other side of this fragmentation – a fragmentation similar to the 24 discrete film stills which comprise one second of a motion picture – we have a purely sensorial feedback of the mirror image which transmits optical illusions of unity to the infant, exactly as the film feed . . . appears to the eye as an imaginary continuum.
> (Kittler, 1997, p. 139)

Cinema both enacts and undermines our collective imaginary identity – it haunts and is haunted by the scene of the mirror: 'chopping or cutting in the real, fusion or flow in the imaginary-the entire history of cinema revolves around this paradox' (1999, p. 122); its origin is as much a matter of arrest and decomposition (that is, photography) as it is one of motion or synthesis: *the animated image is always a reanimated image.*

Cinema is an effacement of the discontinuity of images through the exploitation of the potential this very discontinuity affords (that is, montage), and that permits the grander syntheses of time and space that are its hallmark and freedom. The spectator becomes the site of a double 'imaginary' synthesis, firstly at the level of the image itself (in that it appears imbued with constant motion), and secondly at a narratological level (where multiple takes are spliced together to synthesize an imagined duration), and Kittler's reading implies that this paradox is inescapable, and thus that cinema as a medium and an aesthetic is its exploration, or doubling. Moreover, this paradox is for Kittler the reason for the 'shock effect of the film' as described by Benjamin and others (Benjamin, 1973, p. 240). Liquidating 'the fund of stored images in . . . [the] psychic apparatus', the illusion of the moving image is the ruin of the mirror stage (as illusion), and in exploding 'the narcissism of one's own conception of the body' (Kittler, 1997, p. 93) the (re) animated image communicates to its spectators the shocking fact that an apparently unified sensorium can be replicated by discrete technical media. Just as one's recorded voice sounds unfamiliar when played back, so on celluloid the reanimated body returns as uncanny: when first encountered on the silver screen, 'all gesticulations appear . . . ridiculous'. The media of 1900 present a cluster of disparate traces that are only with effort subsumed under the sign of a single self. They preclude the particular form of interiority or inner life that preceded them (in Kittler's system the 'double' engineered by the network of 1800). The silver screen holds a mirror up to 'nature', in which we behold not an ideal, integrated body but rather an incondite Golem born of techno-medial 'trace detection'. In this manner '. . . doppelgängers or their iterations celebrate the unconscious as the technology of cinematic cutting, and vice versa' (Kittler, 1999, p. 153).

## Film films filming: The Doppelgänger boom

In the course of developing his thesis Kittler traces the 'doppelgänger boom' that marks early cinema from Edison's 1910 *Frankenstein* onwards and that finds its clearest articulation in German expressionist cinema, as evidenced in works such as Ewer's *Der Student von Prague* (1913), Wegener's *Der Golem* series, Mack's *Der Anderer* (1913) and Wiene's *Das Cabinet des Dr. Caligari* (1920) – a constellation of films whose influence permeates the cinema of the fantastic. Elsaesser (1990) in his own treatment of this tradition identifies some of the shortcomings of the canonical readings of these films. For example, Lotte Eisner's declaration in *The Haunted Screen* (1963 (1952)) that 'German cinema is . . . a development of German Romanticism' in which 'modern technique merely lends a form to Romantic fancies' (Eisner, in Elsaesser, 1990, p. 172) presupposes 'that a different technology does not affect . . . the function of themes that the new medium appropriates' (1990, p. 172), while Kracauer's 'tautologous' equation of Caligari and Hitler effects a double reduction: German history is identified with cinematic narrative, while cinematic narrative is revealed as nothing but historical allegory. However, in Kittler the 'doppelgänger motif films the act of filming itself' (Kittler, 1990, p. 277), and in these works 'film doubles to the first degree [are] ... joined by film doubles to the second degree' (1999, p. 96). The double of the first degree (that of the cinematographic illusion) is recapitulated at the second degree (in the form of the double as theme or subject); thus the doppelgängers 'double doubling itself'. Consequently, Kittler rejects Kracauer's 'simplified sociological' account of expressionist cinema in which the somnambulistic automaton of *Caligari* is seen as a mantic synecdoche of the hypnotized masses that supported the Reich.

Kracauer credited *The Student of Prague* with introducing 'to the screen a theme that was to become an obsession of the German cinema: a deep and fearful concern with the foundations of the self'. Baldwin's (the eponymous student) struggle with his doppelgänger dramatizes 'the difference between the ruling set and the middle class – differences deeply resented by the latter' (2004, p. 30). For Kracauer this displacement of the conflict between the 'two Germanys' in the imaginary realm of film reflects the Weimer bourgeoisie's reluctance to address the material conditions of their unease. The doppelgänger motif is a retreat to psychological complications and inner dualities in the face of outer uncertainty. Otto Rank, Freud's 'historical case worker' (Kittler, 1997, p. 86), in his *The Double: A Psychoanalytic Study* (1971 (1914)), granted *The Student of Prague* the honour of the first film to be psychoanalysed. Like Kracauer, he saw it as testimony to the fragility of the self but in the face of a resurgent id, rather than class conflict. For Kittler, *The Double* betrays cinema even as it inaugurates its psychoanalysis. In conflating the double on the screen with that of Ewer's screenplay and in eliding the latter with those of German Romanticism, it ignores the transition from text (1800) to technical media (1900). Rank's fidelity to Freud's 'psychic apparatus obstructs any understanding of the technical' (1997, p. 95), and so he fails to recognize the figures that will haunt Weimer cinema for what they are: the messengers of their medium.

*The Student of Prague* is 'pure' media allegory dramatizing that 'cinema is what kills the soul', wherein the initial *shock* of the moving image becomes a prolonged assault. Baldwin is a man suicided by cinema, subjected to an extended exposure to the double – he can only find integration in dissolution and death. McLuhan spoke of how each medium had as it content the form of a pre-existing medium: in conformity to this mediatic cannibalism, cinema consumes the 'so-called man' as formulated under by an earlier network.

Similarly, while Kracauer's account of *Caligari* approaches the film as a meditation on power and authoritarianism, and as 'an outward projection of psychological events ... staging ... that general retreat into a shell which occurred in post-war Germany' (2004, p. 71), for Kittler it is an object lesson in how 'doubles double doubling itself': from its narrative structure, doubled in the form of a frame narrative in which is embedded the core plot, to the doubling of Caligari himself. Apropos of the latter Clément has observed, 'Cesare is nothing but Caligari's young double; Caligari is himself nothing but the double, and many times redoubled: double of his eighteenth century Italian model, and maleficent double of the beneficent psychiatrist whose restored shape concludes the story' (Clément, 1990, p. 200), and argues that in this fashion *Caligari* enacts through 'the huge and magnified forms of expressionism the phantasmic figures of the era in which psychoanalysis could begin', and in particular the 'divisions' and 'aggressive fragmentations' that attend abrupt exposure of the mirror stage's mechanics (1990, p. 193). Kittler grounds Clément's reading (1999, p. 148, n. 105) in the materiality of media: instead of abject and defensive splitting 'with celluloid and cuts ... Dr. Caligari or his official doppelgänger emerges victorious' and in this bears witness to the logic of the wider discourse network.

Thus the substitution of a 'life-size puppet' for Cesare allows Caligari's double to carry out his will and raises questions of mediums and media. Drawing on the observation that in early cinema life-size mannequins were used for those functions later fulfilled by stuntmen, Kittler argues that 'Cesare is always already a silent movie medium, and it is for this reason alone that he can be a somnambulistic and murderous medium' (1999, p. 148). Here Kittler plays on the various senses of 'medium'; Cesare the medium (that is a sideshow prophet) functions as Caligari's medium (that is, a means of acting by proxy) within the frame of a novel (technical) medium. Cesare is 'the weapon of Caligari the artist. Psychiatrists created the first cruise missile systems, reusable to boot' (1999, p. 149): as a medium he channels the future logic of network 1900, from discerption and storage to implementation and recombination.

Likewise, where Kracauer sees the theme of hypnotism (as found, for instance, in *Caligari* and Lang's *Dr Mabuse* (1922)) as 'a technique foreshadowing ... that manipulation that Hitler was ... to practice on a gigantic scale' (2004, p. 73), Kittler sees yet more media allegory. The ensorcellment of sinister anti-heroes dramatizes cinema's installation of a direct neurological data flow. The marriage of media hardware and human wetware places class and politics in abeyance. Thus (in implicit rejection of Kracauer's two Germanys thesis), 'Whether part of the ruling classes . . . or part of the classes being ruled . . . everyone's retina is on the screen. The spectator . . . reacts to the film screen as if to an external retina that is telecommunication with his own' (Kittler, 1997, p. 98). In this manner Kittler's media materialism leads to a break with the hermeneutic circle of psycho-social parallelism. Refusing to subordinate technology to culture (the doppelgänger as an upgrade of the 'fancies' of Romanticism), psychology (the double as psychoanalysis's nativity play) or history, it avers the absolute priority of the discourse network over these terms. While resolving certain problems, such a manoeuvre is itself problematic, as the following discussion of Deleuze's explorations of these issues will hopefully demonstrate.

## Deleuze

Kittler's treatment of the double in cinema displays a certain proximity with Deleuze's invocation of the spiritual automaton as a symbol of the cinematic experience; like Kittler, Deleuze argues for the double as a figure that haunts cinema, and like Kittler Deleuze reads it as the narratological expression of the medium's technical conditions. While it is beyond the bounds of this chapter to address the nature and significance of Deleuze's two-volume study of cinema, a few brief comments may serve to provide some sense of the framework in which the observations explored here were originally presented.

In the preface to *Difference and Repetition* Deleuze adumbrates the grounds for a future confrontation of philosophy and cinema, arguing that the former has reached a climacteric beyond which philosophy in the 'old style' – the construction of synoptic systems borne of the labours of men (sic) of genius – will no longer be tenable. In confrontation with a world whose artifice grows exponentially, philosophy's future necessitates its suturing to new spheres of endeavour, not least cinema. The result would be no mere commentary but the creation of a 'double' with 'the maximal modification appropriate to a double' (1994 (1968), p. xxi). Deleuze's aim in engaging cinema is thus not to produce a philosophy *of* cinema, but to make of cinema an occasion for philosophy. This encounter is grounded in a re-presentation of Bergson's thought, whose purpose is to read the latter against its indictment of cinema as a concretization of those habits of the intellect that quantified time and so precluded an apprehension of time as *duration* – as an indivisible continuum known only to intuition.

Thus Bergson established an opposition between the time of chronometers (a spatialized time comprised of isolated, homogenous units) and duration (in which each instant is irreducibly related to a change in the whole). Deleuze seeks to equate duration with 'matter-flux', or the image qua movement (thus all temporal entities consist of relations between images – indeed, images are nothing but relations – and from this position confines Bergson's 'cinematographic illusion' to the technology of cinema (that 'imaginary' dimension explored above). Cinema, as cultural form and aesthetic experience, represents the introduction of an art of the movement-image to a universe of movement-images; it is the organon of duration. Deleuze identifies two major forms of cinematic duration – the movement-image and the time-image. Their contradistinction – primarily (though not exclusively) diachronic – provides the *Cinema* books' major axis, and its development results in a complex grammar of movement-images. In the simplest outline the movement-image is the first form of cinematic image; here images result from the relations and caesuras between perceptions and actions. Since its duration is the result of the transition from movement to movement, it presents as an 'indirect' image of time. In contrast the time-image, which Deleuze sees as characterising post-war cinema, offers a 'direct' image of time: no longer subordinate to movement/action, it reveals time as the *primum mobile* and movement/action as the consequence of its passage.

### The spiritual automata

These themes are developed in considerable detail by Deleuze, but within the present context the essential factor is the extension of cinema beyond its formal bounds – the co-implication of image, viewer and cinematic event in a whole. The movement of the moving image is thus double; it is both mechanical (originating in a discrete material technology) and psychological or 'spiritual', since it induces a movement within the viewer (indeed, it reveals the latter as nothing more than a nexus of movement-images): 'Cinema not only puts movement in the image, it also puts movement in the mind. Spiritual life is the movement of the mind' (2000, p. 366). Deleuze hypostatizes this double movement in the figure of the 'spiritual automaton'. This term is derived from Spinoza and Leibniz, the former proposing it as a means of refuting Cartesian dualism, and the latter as an inevitable corollary of his principles of compossibility and inherence. For both it reflects an involuntary, almost algorithmic dimension of cognition, revealing it as at once immaterial or 'spiritual', and automatic – mechanically determined by the dictates of external laws, in a manner analogous to the clockwork automata of the era. But whereas the spiritual automaton of seventeenth-century philosophy was confined within the subject, the Deleuzian spiritual automaton embodies cinema's putting into play of the distinctions between inside and outside, human and technics: 'the spiritual automaton is machinic thought' (Rodowick, 1997, p. 174), the latter understood not in terms of reflection but as the double movement of mind and image. The spiritual automaton is thus 'a limit, a membrane, which puts an inside and an outside in contact, . . . makes them clash' (Deleuze, 1989, p. 206).

The figure of the double or automaton is consequently not something that seizes cinema from the outside, but the inevitable expression of its conditions as a medium: 'cinema considered as psychomechanics . . . is reflected in its own content, . . . it confronts automata, not accidentally, but fundamentally'. This confrontation is evidenced by various doubles, automata and simulacra life forms that populate the history of the medium, not least in 'the procession of somnambulists, the hallucinators, hypnotizers-hypnotized in expressionism' (1989, p. 263). Like the Kittlerian doppelgänger, the Deleuzian spiritual automaton is both the movement of thought induced by the moving image and the movement of the body reconstituted on the screen. Bogue notes that while 'various figures might represent the spiritual automaton – the robot, computer brain, the zombie, the alien', Deleuze 'chooses the mummy' (Bogue, 2003, p. 177) (perhaps alluding to Bazin's belief that cinema is driven by a 'mummy complex' – the desire to create an imperishable double)[1], and the mummy, in its status as an uncanny, disintegrated body that moves upon the screen, offers a parallel to the 'othering' of the body by the cinematic image described by Kittler. Indeed, Deleuze talks of the 'regime of the "tear"' under which the body's putative cohesion is torn asunder such that 'the division of body and voice forms [an] . . . image "non-representable by a single individual"', in which the body 'constitutes neither a body or a whole, but the automaton . . . in the sense of a profoundly divided essence' (1989, p. 268).

As in Kittler, the automaton embodies the fundamental 'shock' induced by the cinematic image. Cinema qua movement-image is uncanny and delivers *'a shock to thought, communicating vibrations to the cortex, touching the nervous and cerebral system directly'* (Deleuze, 1989, p. 156; emphasis in original). Deleuze terms this the *nooshock*, understood as an insult to the thinking subject that discovers an external necessity in what appeared most free, and must adjust itself to this confusing redistribution of its capacities. Thought no longer designates an operation performed by the subject, but is introduced from outside, and the nooshock as a confusion of the automatic and the autonomous is inseparable from a technological augmentation of the subject:

> It is in fact [cinema's] material automatism that causes to surge forth from the interior of these images this new universe that imposes little by little on our intellectual automatism. Thus there appears, in a blinding light, the subordination of the human soul to the tools which it creates, and vice versa. It turns out that there is a constant reversibility between technical and affective nature.
>
> (Faure, in Deleuze, 1989, 308, n. 1)

The subordination of the toolmaker to its tools brings to mind network 1900's effraction of the subject, while proposing a reversibility conspicuously absent in Kittler's thought. This reversibility is an integral aspect of the spiritual automaton, and reflects Deleuze's particular understanding of the double:

> the double is never a projection of the interior; on the contrary, it is an internalisation of the outside ... It is never the other who is a double in the doubling process, it is a self that lives in me as the double of the other ...
>
> (1988, p. 98)

## The non-organic life of things

As a result, the automation of thought through technics holds out the potential of a considerable freedom and peril – a freedom, in that the 'great spiritual automaton' as the 'highest exercise of thought' introduces the subject to the forces of the outside, creating a brain-machine assemblage that enriches and extends, and perilous, because it threatens a subordination of the inside by an outside: the automaton no longer responds to *the* outside because it is pre-programmed by a (pseudo) outside – 'he is dispossessed of his own thought'. This darker formulation of the automata is that found in the doppelgängers of expressionism, and in this regard Deleuze is more sympathetic to Kracauer's reading than Kittler, arguing that in the hands of propagandists 'the spiritual automaton became fascist man'. However, like Kittler Deleuze believes that Kracauer's reading takes 'an external viewpoint' rather than setting 'itself inside cinema' and so recognizing the role of the technical conditions of the medium in determining its social impact (1989, p. 264).

The spiritual automaton's potential for liberation is best understood through the figure of Artaud and his own theory of cinema (see Artaud, 1972) as enthusiastically recounted by Deleuze. For Artaud the cinema is a 'matter of neuro-physiological vibrations', a 'nerve-wave' that assaults the brain, giving rise to a non-representational or machinic thought, experienced as the ever novel 'repetition of its own birth'. Artaud compares this dimension of cinema to automatic writing as practiced by spiritualists and surrealists, wherein 'a higher control' couples a conscious subject and an unconscious or supra-subjective thought (1989, p. 165). This brings to mind Duhamel's critique, namely that with cinema 'I can no longer think what I want, [since] the moving images are substituted for my thoughts' (Duhamel, in Deleuze, 1989, p. 166), and Deleuze observes that, presented thus, Artaud's theories do not take us beyond expressionism, which had already introduced the substitution of thought, hypnosis and the splintering of the subject as explicit themes. Artaud's originality resides in the saving grace he locates in the very condition that Duhamel laments: cinema is to be understood as a 'dissociative force' that introduces a 'hole in appearances', exposing the 'essential powerlessness at the heart of heart of thought' that is the spiritual automaton. Cinema dissolves our habitual relation to thought and the outside, and its theft of thoughts becomes for Deleuze–Artaud 'the dark glory and profundity' of the medium since 'we should make use of this powerlessness to believe in life, and to discover the identity of thought in life' (1989, p. 170). The powerlessness of thought suspends the metaphysic of the 'thinker' and the chimera of a thought that would be adequate to the entirety of life. In thought's impuissance we encounter, paradoxically, the power of a new mode of thought borne of a relation to an unthought outside that produces it. Cinema understood as spiritual automatism thus offers the possibility of a renewal of the relation between the human and the world. As a result the spiritual automaton, in its various guises, poses 'a question of the future' while at the same time invoking 'the most ancient powers'. This can be seen clearly in German expressionism, which establishes a link between what Eisner describes as 'the Germans . . . eerie gift for animating objects' and the moving image while formulating the question of the future – that of the passage from Caligari to Hitler, and the dream of a new, fascist man (1989, p. 263). We have already noted, however, that Deleuze does not straightforwardly subscribe to Kracauer's thesis, despite this embrace of the passage from doppelgänger to Reich, and this is a consequence of the particular conception of the 'outside' that quickens these figures. This outside, manifesting both as the tenebrous and as a futurity, must ultimately be understood in terms of the originary plenum of movement-matter – 'the material universe ... as the machine assemblage of movement-images' (1986, p. 59). This is the 'life' that Deleuze believes vivifies the doppelgängers of expressionism and their heirs, a:

> ... non-organic life of things, a frightful life, which is oblivious to the wisdom and limits of the organism, is the first principle of expressionism ... From this point of view natural substances and artificial creations, candelabras and tress, turbine and sun are no longer any different. Thus automata, robots and puppets are no longer [extrinsic] mechanisms ... but somnambulists, zombies or golems who express the intensity of non-organic life: not simply in Wegener's *The Golem*, but also in the Gothic horror film of around 1930, for example Whale's *Frankenstein* ... and Halperin's *White Zombie*'
>
> (Deleuze, 1986, pp. 52–3)

From this perspective the umbral, crepuscular *mise-en-scène* that characterizes these films, and the sundry automata and doubles that populate them, are congeneric. Kracauer's presentation of *Caligari* touches upon this coalescence of action and *mise-en-scène* when it speaks of 'a perfect transformation of material objects into emotional ornaments', such that Caligari emerges as a 'magician himself weaving the lines and shades through which he passes' and Cesare on his nocturnal prowls appears 'as if the wall exuded him' (2004, pp. 69–70). But this is read in terms of psycho-social parallelism – a deformation of the everyday born either of a surge of revolutionary energy that dissolves fixed forms or of the derangement of the individual psyche. In contrast, in Deleuze the doppelgänger is an encounter with the horror of the non-organic, which renders 'anthropomorphic urban surroundings [as] devils no less real than the Golems of Nordic legends' (Titford, 1973, p. 21) – a realm uncovered but not created by the convulsions of the individual or collective mind.

## Conclusion

It is apparent then that despite the points of contact outlined above, the theories of cinema and its doubles put forward by Deleuze and Kittler diverge in their basic assumptions. For Deleuze, as we have seen, the automaton constitutes both danger and freedom, and it is this latter possibility that sets his account of the double apart from Kittler's. Kittler sees cinema in terms of an invasion by an outside that expunges an illusory interiority. However, this offers no possibility for renewal because it merely reconfigures the capacities of the 'so-called man'. Thus automatic writing is figured in *Discourse Networks* as 'anything but freedom' – void of higher commands it 'says nothing of thought or . . . understanding; it speaks only of speech and glibness' (Kittler, 1990, p. 228). For Kittler, 'Golems constitute a danger: stupid Doubles of a humanity that has no longer existed since media were also able to substitute for central nervous systems' (1997, p. 97); the somnambulists of Caligari are precursors of 'the first cruise missile systems, reusable to boot'. This reflects Kittler belief that the cinema is inextricably bound to war, its serial images borne of a technology transfer from automatic firearms, such that 'the transport of pictures only repeats the transport of bullets' (1999, p. 14). The separation of man and media that defined 1900 and the reintegration of these media in the form of the universal medium of the digital ('the Golem made of Golems') is a process driven by war. Deleuze acknowledges this in his comments on *War and Cinema* (1989 (1984)):

> . . . the situation is still worse if we accept Virilio's thesis: there has been no diversion or alienation . . . on the contrary the movement-image was from the beginning linked to the organization of war . . . historically and essentially.
>
> (1989, p. 165)

Thus the 'photo and cinema pass through war and are coupled with arms', a trajectory that leads cinema 'beyond itself towards the electronic image' and transforms 'the whole of civil life . . . into the mode of the *mise-en-scene*' (1989, p. 309, n. 16). But while Kittler embraces Virilio's vision and extends it to the evolution of technical media in its entirety, Deleuze relegates it to a possible vector of the moving image's development. This bespeaks a fundamentally different assessment of the double, and by extension its components: not least, the human and technology. In Deleuze, doubling 'resembles exactly the invagination of a tissue in embryology' (1988, p. 98), and cinema as doubling offers the possibility of participating in a neo-vitalist or non-organic folding of humans and their life-world, while for Kittler there is simply the rearrangement of signs, bodies and media – the ratios between these will alter, *but their relation will remain partes extra partes*. Indeed, Kittler sees Bergsonism as a refusal of the 'real' of cinema in favour of the imaginary imago of *duree*: its 'philosophy of life thus became a kind of movie that . . . sacrificed its working principle, the cutting of images, to what was only a cunningly produced illusion in its viewer' (1990, p. 278).

In this manner the theme of the double and its articulation in German expressionist cinema offers a privileged point of access into the implications of digitization for their theories, and vice versa. In the case of Kittler, the emergence of the digital image as cinema's end is inscribed in his figuration of its beginnings. That is to say that the equation of film with the imaginary, as part of a process of diremption and implementation, is revealed only by its contrast with the grand convergence of media, that is, the computer. From this perspective Kittler's entire account of cinema is premised on digitization, despite its absence as an explicit theme (1999, pp. 1–19). While digitization is not granted the same centrality in Deleuze's *Cinema* books, his concluding comments on the advent of the 'electronic' or 'numerical' image, and its relation to the time- and movement-images as well as to theme of the spiritual automaton, demonstrate that his film theory is also in part a response to those 'images coming into being' that will 'either renew or destroy it'. Deleuze, in keeping with his commitment to doubling as a multiplication that bears witness to a reservoir of non-organic life exceeding the limits of the human and technics, argues that the numerical image was already anticipated in the experiments of the cinema of the time-image.

In this respect the time-image in its engagement with automata, and as a spiritual automaton in itself, posed the question of the future. This capacity to anticipate, to move in advance of technology, Deleuze identifies with a 'will to art, or . . . yet unknown aspect of the time-image'. This is not simply an appeal to a primordial aesthetic impulse, but rather the expression of the power proper to the assemblage, which, in conformity with Deleuze's conception of the double, is not defined by its technical component.

In stark contrast to this 'will to art', Kittler asserts that what underpins and unites disparate discourse networks is their status as information systems comprised of senders, transmitters, destinations and receivers, and that since 1900 these functions have become increasingly independent and interdependent. This position casts human communication and society in terms of a historical chrysalis that incubates informatics: a process whose motor is war – 'As a complex system war . . . engages in the continuous extraction of information, it uses that information . . . for the further gathering of information . . . War – has always fuelled media' (Winthrop-Young, 2002, p. 834) – and whose telos is sci-fi eschatology – 'Without . . . mankind, communication technologies will have overhauled each other until finally an artificial intelligence proceeds to the interception of possible intelligences in space' (Kittler, 1999, unpaginated).

Hansen (2002) argues that this overarching vision renders Kittler Deleuze's 'contemporary antitype'. Kittler comes not to praise but to bury cinema, announcing not only 'the obsolescence of the cinematic image in the age of digital, but the digital obsolescence of the image as such' (Hansen, 2002, p. 69). The doubling that we have explored in Kittler's work here concludes with the doubling of cinema in the digital image.

Thus, while for Kittler doubling implies media technology as a process of evacuation and simulation, Deleuze's account of the 'numerical image' stresses its potential for reinventing cinema, which as we've indicated is to be located in that which falls outside its technical conditions. The advent of the numerical image necessitates a renegotiation of the 'man-machine assemblage', and thus the question posed by these new technologies is that of 'cerebral creation, *or* deficiency of the cerebellum?'.

Information technology, and the digital image in particular, is 'useless' unless it is deployed against the sufficiency of informatics for itself, a gesture condensed in the question *'what is the source and what is the addressee'* (Deleuze, 1989, p. 269; emphasis in original). Following Hansen, we note that Deleuze's formulation of this question involves an appeal to the critique of the cybernetic model of information proposed by Raymond Ruyer, which exposes *'the profound intertwining of the technical and the organic in human being . . . a trajectory antithetical to that described by Kittler'* (Hansen, 2002, p. 79; emphasis in original). In emphasizing the essentially symbiotic or hybrid nature of information technologies, Deleuze rejects the implicit teleologism of discourse network theory, and affirms a vision of doubling as a multiplication, a continual overspilling of a non-organic life subtending technology, matter and the human.

## Notes

1. Although Deleuze explores this theme as it manifests in Dreyer's films rather than the mummies of Hollywood, there exist a number of interesting connections between this tradition and German expressionism. The mummy entered the cinematic imaginary in name, if not in form, with Lubitsch's 1915 *Die Mumie Ma/The Eyes of the Mummy*, a film that emerged from the same milieu as the doppelgänger boom, while the first Hollywood treatment, *The Mummy* (1932), was directed by Karl Freund (cinematographer for *Der Golem* and *Metropolis*), who introduced to it many of the motifs of German expressionism. Curiously, Freund's one appearance as an actor was under the directorship of Dreyer.

# 6
# Genomic Science in Contemporary Film: Institutions, Individuals and Genre

*Kate O'Riordan*

## Introduction: Genomics and film as technoscience

The intersections of human genomic science and contemporary film occur at several different levels, and this chapter starts with some notes towards an explanation of how genomic science can be understood, what these intersections are and why they are important. It then goes on to examine some of the detail of how genomics has been figured in recent contemporary film, using *Code 46* (2003) and *Godsend* (2004) as examples. Finally, it develops the argument, set out in the analysis of the films, that genre is central to the way in which genomics is understood, and the chapter ends by pointing to some ways in which such understandings are undergoing significant shifts, in contemporary filmic constitutions of the science.

Genomics is a technoscience (Latour, 1987) – as such it is a contested term that refers to a range of institutions and practices related to the study of whole organism genetics, or genomes, as in the human genome map. As other chapters in this book examine in more detail, film is also a technoscientific apparatus, and it reproduces itself, and other technologies, through its proliferating forms, texts and institutions. Film was developed through, and alongside, medical imaging practices (Cartwright, 1995), and panoptic processes of documenting, regulating and reproducing society through modes of visual knowledge production in the nineteenth century (Foucault, 1977).[1] These functions of recording, illuminating and regulating life continue to be important elements of film today; at the same time the materiality of film and the meaning of mediation are continually contested.

However, while film reached markets in the late nineteenth century, between 1894 and 1896 (Young, 2006, p. xxi), genomics is still on its way to finding and creating its markets. However, like nascent film applications such as Marey's imaging experiments of the late nineteenth century (Landecker, 2006) and the Mitchell and Keynon productions of the early twentieth century (Toulmin, Popple and Russell, 2004), nascent genomic audiences are also enrolled in projects of identifying themselves, and others, through highly technologized mediations. Current human genomic applications extend to DNA testing for ancestry and disease histories, for example, interpellating audiences into regulatory narratives, and forms of governance, about who they are through biotechnological identification. Early cinematic audiences were asked to come and see themselves on film (Toulmin et al., 2004 ), while uses of film in medical experimentation appeared to illuminate the movement of the human body, beyond the capability of the unaided eye, and thus contributed to new ways of identifying bodies (Cartwright, 1995).

Film, like genomics, can be thought of as a biotechnology in several senses of the formulation. It is part of a project of both mapping and reconfiguring life, representing what appears to exist in the world, and promising to intervene. Film and genomics discursively promise to reveal what already exists, showing us life, while disavowing the ways in which film and genomics are implicated in constructing what they purport to describe, or in other words, effecting their own structural transparency. However, they are both enrolled in high-tech mobilizations of technology as power, in which both technosciences are produced visually and spectacularly through promissory rhetorics about changing the world.

## Representation and reconfiguration in film and genomics

Two important strands of aesthetic filmic development – realism and illusion (Darley, 2000) – are also closely intertwined with two major strands of development in the biomedical sciences – mapping and intervention. On the one hand biology has been represented as an intellectual tradition of representing life, and projects such as the human genome map are part of this image. On the other hand contemporary biomedical sciences seek to reconfigure and re-imagine life, and they are represented as powerful in these capacities, primarily through the promises of genetic modification and regenerative medicine. Ian Wilmut, the scientist who led the team that created Dolly the sheep, claimed in the co-authored popular science book *After Dolly* that cloning showed that there is no such thing as a biological impossibility, that he was able to reverse cellular time and that in the future thousands of people would be cured through regenerative medicine (Highfield and Wilmut, 2006).[2]

The spectacular power of genomics to create and intervene in lives is crystallized in, and evoked through, icons such as Dolly (the clone) and the images of the late Christopher Reeve (the paralysed figure to be cured) – images that have been mobilized over and over again in the discourses of genomic reproductive power and regenerative medicine, produced by global networks of scientists, politicians, biotechnology companies, pressure and patient groups and media professionals. However, this spectacular power is also subsumed into the mundane and is perhaps more potent in this mode. Genomics constitutes a biopolitical mode of power that is embodied, and thus disappears as a spectacle, and this mode is explored in relation to *Code 46*.

In this exploration of power the chapter draws on a Foucauldian model of biopolitical governmentality, used by Nicolas Rose (2001) and also by Sarah Franklin (2000) when she claims that

> We are currently witnessing the emergence of a new genomic governmentality.
>
> (p. 188)

In her discussion of genomic governmentality and *Jurassic Park*, Sarah Franklin uses Lisa Cartwright's analysis (in *Screening the Body*) to create a link between the governance of life, and film.

> Using film as a literal 'biography' or inscription of life, another link connecting life not only to labour and language, but also to spectacle and animation, allows the question of life to be reframed.
>
> (2000, p. 197)

Cartwright examines cinema as a 'technology for configuring life' (1995, p. xi). Her object of study is medical film, not popular culture, and she locates her study clearly within the 'modernist culture of Western medical science' (1995, p. xi). Franklin uses this link to move into a discussion of *Jurassic Park*, implying that even film might be regarded as a genomic technology. Thus, Franklin maps Cartwright's work onto popular film and moves from governmentality (via Foucault and Canguilhem) to film, arguing that

> At once a book, a film, a theme park, and a global brand *Jurassic Park* is an ideal theatre in which to observe the new genetics as performance.
>
> (2000, p. 197)

Film both represents and re-imagines life, configuring it through complex oscillations across realism and illusion and through a continued preoccupation with technoscience. *Jurassic Park*, one of the most significant filmic examples of the technoscientific (genomic) imaginary (Franklin, 2000), attempts to beguile audiences with a spectacular vision of technology through special effects and thus represents the effects of genetic modification (the dinosaurs) as visually amazing and beautiful. At the same time the narrative and plot provide a morality tale warning against the use of genetic modification and the power of technoscience unleashed (Franklin, 2000; Stern, 2004; Wood, 2002). Such technophobic 'fence straddling' (Young, 2006, p. xi) entails a representation of the visual beauty and splendour of imagined technoscientific developments through visual special effects on the one hand, while drawing on the flexibility of existing narrative frameworks for constituting meaning about science (Turney, 1998) on the other. As Aylish Wood points out in her analysis of 'technoscience in contemporary American film', this borrowing across, of and between, film and technoscience allows film texts to draw on the high status of technoscience, to draw the audience into the pleasures of its consumption, while also deploying a more familiar narrative structure warning against such pleasures (Wood, 2002). One of the significant things about this move to both attract and disavow is that it contributes to an ambiguity in the way the technoscience is represented, where the high status of technoscience is used to sell films by drawing the audience into the pleasures of consuming that which the film plot ostensibly warns against. The contradictions of these pleasures, and their capacity to make narrative structure ambiguous and complex, are marked when they occur in mass market and hybrid genre films such as *Jurassic Park*, or its human corollary *The Island*.

Human genomics is a technoscience that brings these traditions of representation and reconfiguration, or description and intervention, together. As the study of whole organism genetics, developed as a global endeavour through the Human Genome Project in the 1980s and 1990s, it is constituted through genetic modification, genetic identification, gene therapies, regenerative medicine and cloning. Human genomics is the 'mediated science par excellence' (Haran et al., 2007), constituted and reconstituted through multiple media forms, and intersecting global discourses of art, film, TV, news, science fiction, advertising, scientific literature and popular science writing. It is an area in which the role of the media in its multiple forms, including film, in the making of science is perhaps more acute than any other.

Kate O'Riordan 109

It is not the aim of this chapter to collapse film into genomics, or to argue that film is a genomic technology, nor to follow Eugene Thacker's argument that genomics is entirely a medium (Thacker, 2004). In emphasizing the general parallels between, and intersections of, film and genomics as technoscientific media, it is my intention to highlight some of the similar conditions in which both forms are constructed and to emphasize the importance of these connections in thinking about film and genomics. It is the aim of the chapter to examine some of the specificity of the relationship between contemporary film and genomic science in the making of genomics as a global discourse. Film is an area of the media in which human genomics is contemporaneously and globally constituted, and it is an area in which meanings about human genomics are made and contested and are undergoing remaking and change.

## Genre and genomics: *Godsend* and *Code 46*

The two films examined in this chapter have human genomic themes expressed though genetic engineering and cloning. They both deal with reproduction, genetic similarity and geneticized kinship. Through a comparison of these two genre films, a science fiction (SF) film, *Code 46* (Winterbottom, 2003), and a horror film, *Godsend* (Hamm, 2004), the chapter examines the figures of science, and the scientist, in relation to genomics in contemporary cinema. Throughout this analysis I argue that in *Godsend* science becomes separated from society and figured through the individual scientist, while in *Code 46,* science is a mechanism of social power and subsumed through the body into the infrastructures of governance. Thus, the two films construct different versions of the 'genomic science' that produces the embodiment of the clone.

The chapter argues further that these different productions relate to the genre differences of the films; *Godsend* draws on and is inscribed by horror, while *Code 46* is a science fiction film. Thus, *Godsend* can be thought of as embedded in traditions that are partly structured through the representation of individualism and interiority, while *Code 46* is more clearly embedded in traditions of representation that locate individuals as subject to governmental systems of technoscience.

An analysis of the two films shows how meanings around genomics are constituted through narratives of both structural power and agency. Genre is a key framing element in the ways in which genomics can be explored in these films, and it is clear that the genre specificities of these films shape the way in which genomics can be made meaningful, while at the same time genomics contributes to a reworking of these genres

(Hills, 2004). The constitution of genomics in film oscillates, moving from genre fiction and niche markets (horror and SF) to broader and more flexible locations in the contemporary media imaginary as genomics and cloning are reconstituted as scientific practices (Haran et al., 2007; O'Riordan, 2008).

*Godsend* is a horror film directed by Nick Hamm, and *Code 46* is a science fiction film directed by Michael Winterbottom. The films were funded through production and distribution companies in the US, Canada and the UK, and were on theatrical release for a limited period in 2004 in the UK, before going to DVD. *Godsend* is the more mass market of the two films, in that it reached a larger audience share, but it was released in the UK, immediately prior to the release of *Spider-Man*, (another film with genomic themes), which then dominated the major cinemas, overshadowing other films in the same period. The theatrical admissions in the UK for *Godsend* in 2004 were recorded by Lumiere at around 358,000. *Code 46* was controversially unpopular with the studio and also had limited release in mainstream cinemas.[3] The admissions in the UK for *Code 46* were approximately one-tenth of those of *Godsend*, recorded at around 35,000.[4]

In these two films genomic science is causally linked to applied cloning techniques, through the process of reproductive cloning. In both films this is enacted as a reproductive process of control over the (social) body. Intersecting with public debates about reproductive and therapeutic cloning, stem cell research, genetic identification technologies, commodification, instrumentalization, eugenics and social control, the two films produce very different hypothetical scenarios about reproductive cloning.

*Godsend* represents the scenario that reproductive cloning is viable, and it simultaneously intersects with debates about 'playing with life' through a quasi-religious framing of reproductive cloning. The film suggests that the so-called Dolly technique (by which a mammal was cloned from an adult cell via cell nuclear transfer in 1997, UK) could be used in humans. This was a move made in several films produced after the cloning of Dolly, such as *The 6th Day* (2000). The narrative draws on the same argument used by 'maverick' scientists who have been represented in other media forms (mainly the press) as laying claim to human reproductive cloning (Severino Antonori, Richard Seed, Panos Zavos), namely that human reproductive cloning could provide a form of fertility treatment. The narrative reiterates religious and secular arguments surrounding human reproductive cloning, and it signifies the geneticized body of the clone by using the visual image of the twin.

Kate O'Riordan 111

In *Godsend* this geneticized body is manipulated to resurrect the dead, and cloning is imagined as an embodiment of evil. In *Code 46*, on the other hand, a future is imagined where such debates over the morality of reproductive cloning are redundant. In the highly technologized and highly regulated future of *Code 46*, cloning and bioengineering are normal aspects of the social control mechanisms in place. This analysis foregrounds the genre differences between individualistic narratives in horror film, in which science is constituted through the body of the scientist on the one hand, and science fiction film, in which genomics operates as a diffuse mechanism of governance on the other.

In thinking about these genre differences I find it useful to reflect on Barry Grant's (1999) analysis in *Alien Zone II* where he offers a set of defining characteristics as belonging to the genres of horror and science fiction respectively. Horror he defines as emotional, corporeal, contained, moral/naturalized, with a visual orientation down or in. In contrast, science fiction is defined as cognitive, of the mind, open, concerned with the social order and with a visual orientation upward and outward (Grant, 1999). This model of generic contrast is problematic, particularly in how it deals with the body, and it is important to note the capacity for individual films to travel across these genres. Science fiction and horror became central elements of mass market, hybrid genres from the 1980s onwards, and they often structure elements of the same film. However, Grant's (1999) analysis can also provide a model for thinking about the intersection of genomic themes in relation to both genre similarity and difference, in these two films. In this analysis the focus is on both the genre similarities and the differences between a moral body narrative contained within a framework of ethics and individuality (horror), and a narrative about the social ordering and governance of bodies framed through political tensions between structure and agency (science fiction).

## *Code 46*

*Code 46* is a science fiction film, described by one reviewer as one of the most perfect cyberpunk films ever made (Savlov, 2004). It draws both aesthetically and thematically on *Blade Runner* (Scott, 1982), *Twelve Monkeys* (Gilliam, 1995) and *Gattaca* (Niccol, 1997). As with all of these films, and post-cyberpunk film more generally, the subjective experiences of the main characters are the vehicles for exploring the representation of the future/present subject positions within technoscience. This is to say that in addition to an exploration of technological and scientific innovation, cyberpunk is about imagining identity as it intersects with, and is regulated through, technoscientific fields. The tropes of cyberpunk such as bioengineering, cyberspace, surveillance systems and artificial intelligence are already in place – assumed as part of the cultural disposition of the *mise-en-scène*, rather than reproduced as spectacular processes of discovery or disaster.

*Code 46*, the title of the film, refers to a law criminalizing a kind of postmodern incest. In the technoculture of the film, IVF, cloning and genetic engineering have become commonplace practices and traditional kinship structures such as the family have been reconfigured. This changes the conditions and understanding of incest. These conditions produce a social situation, in the film, where many people are genetically or biologically related but are unaware of this. Thus, knowledge is dislocated from the body as information. There are walk-in genetic screening centres where prospective couples must test for genetic compatibility, to *discover* their genetic identity. This relocates genealogical information as knowledge in the body that must be revealed through technological intervention. 'Code 46' is a piece of legislation that is used to separate genetic material as kinship groups, and other ritualized social structures no longer exist to do so. According to the narrative, William and Maria, although complete strangers who live on different continents, have genetic similarity in the 90 per cent plus range, diegetically meaning that they are clones, or clones of one of their parents. It is indicated that Maria is a clone of William's mother. Heterosexual contact with a genetically similar body is punishable through medical intervention (hence Maria's experience in the abortion clinic) if the act is unwitting, and punishable through exile to the wastelands outside of the urban centres of the film (Maria's fate), if performed knowingly.

Science and scientists are represented as part of a technoscientific apparatus in *Code 46*. Science is subsumed into a broader set of mechanisms that regulate society, where there are no distinctions between the technologized apparatuses of law, health, medicine and consumption. The abortion clinic and DNA testing kiosk, in which some of the scenes of the film are set, are part of the same monolithic and authoritarian infrastructure that regulates society. Likewise, the issuing of travel permits (required for any border crossing) is linked to legal, medical and economic criteria through a centralized structure of global regulation.

The figures that embody science in the film are regulators who 'enforce' science as a governing mechanism. Maria, one of the two central characters, has a non-consensual abortion and is detained in a clinic where this is performed on her; simultaneously her memory is erased, and a virus for conditioning is administered. The gatekeepers of the abortion clinic are women, represented in clinical dress, and Maria is held is a small, bright cell-like room. These processes and surroundings emphasize the role of the clinic in the regulation of society in this film in which the institutions of law and medicine operate together through DNA testing.

In addition to the abortion clinic, the walk-in genetic screening service also relates to how the scientist is positioned in this film. In this situation the scientist is a technician. This is a more mundane role than that invoked by the 'maverick scientist' and is similar to that of a technician in a photographic service or laboratory. Through this space, where the laboratory is made into an accessible place of popular consumption, the body of the scientist is reconstructed as mundane, and the 'science' of genetic testing is reproduced as a technique of everyday life, a 'technology of the self' and a mode of governmentality.[5] Thus 'the street' of the future/present of science fiction assimilates the high-tech space of the genetic testing lab and the process of sequencing, through reproducing the laboratory as a retail space for popular consumption. This positioning of the scientist represents both the scientist and non-scientists as subject to the discourses of genomics, emphasizing structure and reducing the agential subjectivity possible.

This assimilation process, where the products of technoscience are both structural regulatory mechanisms and popular retail spaces, is simultaneously a familiar fictional trope of cyberpunk (everything can be bought on the street) and a situation analogous to the incorporation of technologies in everyday life, for example, the nineteenth century's 'new technologies' of light, electricity and photography's incorporation into popular culture in the twentieth century. The women in the abortion clinic and the female technician at the genetic testing service are mundane bureaucrats in the administrative structure of the technoscientific regimes that orders life in the story world of *Code 46*. Thus, although cloning is a central theme and director Michael Winterbottom claimed that he wanted to explore an Oedipal love story through cloning, the film is not primarily about the spectacle of genomic science. It is about power – the regulation of space, the movement of bodies and the subsuming of technology into the everyday. In this context genomics is present but it is diffuse, structuring the text as an invisible but containing mechanism invoking self-regulation, and thus constitutes an apparatus of governmentality in which agency disappears. In this genre location, genomic science can disappear into the cultural forms of everyday life and is not produced as a high-tech spectacle for the viewer.

Part of the disappearance of genomics into the everyday is linked to the representation of subjectivity in *Code 46*. Cloning has already occurred before the action of the film begins, and is integral to the identity of the characters. In this film, reproduction is shown as already regulated through the clinical processes of IVF and cloning; thus the genomic theme is constituted through the subjectivity of the central characters. It is their shared genetic makeup that appears to drive their attraction and creates the sense of déjà vu that they experience upon meeting. This shared genome is constituted in Maria's recurring dreams and ongoing memory of William. Their experience as individuals in the world is determined by their genome, and genomic science is thus expressed through their subjectivity, permeating their body and psyche. Through this they are produced as subjects of a technoscientific apparatus. The expression of genomics through subjectivity also occurs in other films such as *The Hulk*, where Dr Banner (junior) has been genetically engineered before birth, and *Godsend*, in which the child is a clone. However, in both of these films the cloning or modification process occurs as a spectacle during the narrative and is not an a priori condition of all identity.

In *Code 46*, the geneticized body momentarily resists the regulatory mechanism of the law, and biological determinism is reproduced as fate through cloning. In other words the genome is destiny in this film. William and Maria cannot be together because of the similarity of their geneticized bodies, which are regulated through law. However, their desire for each other is figured as overwhelming, determined by the information of the genome, and while Code 46 operates to regulate the horror of 'sameness' in a heterosexual order (Stacey, 2003) through prohibition, their bodies momentarily resist the law by refusing the self-regulating mechanisms of governance. William rescues Maria from the abortion clinic, and they briefly escape the regimes of control. She recovers her memory of William, which is already 'hard wired' into her genome and manifest in her dreams. There is then a short sequence where Maria and William appear to escape both the biological and geographical structures of containment before being recaptured. Thus their genetic similarity appears to generate an attraction that resists and overrides the law, at least temporarily. However, their resistance causes the system to enforce that which has been refused, and after this transgression it is William who is reprogrammed through viral conditioning and Maria is exiled.

Through a spatial displacement of the lab onto the street and the representation of the body of the scientist as technician or nurse, genomics is represented as a pervasive mechanism of governmentality. Genomics operates through this mechanism because it is a productive force that regulates the everyday 'life' of bodies. Through the genomic determination carried in the bodies of the protagonists, this governmentality extends to the molecular, not just interfacing with bodies but permeating and constituting bodies. The differences between this kind of Foucauldian paradigm of science as structural regime in *Code 46*, and the modernist narratives of autonomous subjectivity in horror, are explored below.

## *Godsend*

*Godsend* is part of a set of genres that coalesce as 'horror'. One notable aspect of this film is the range of horror elements that it encompasses: it combines cloning-as-horror, with possession and the supernatural, and combines the serial killer with the monster in the shed/cellar/woods. Matt Hills and Eugene Thacker both discuss genomics in relation to horror, and the genres of horror, in far more detail than I do here (Hills, 2004; Thacker, 2002). *Godsend* draws strongly on the multiple conventions of horror films and ultimately positions the clone as an embodiment of evil. Adam is an eight-year-old boy killed in a car crash; his parents are offered the opportunity to clone him. The opportunity is offered to them by a Dr Wells (Robert de Niro) who comes to the church where they are preparing for the funeral. The cloning is performed in the guise of a 'normal' but high-risk IVF procedure, and the parents have a new baby who grows into a twin of the previous Adam. The familiar visual model of the clone as identical twin is deployed, but after the cloned Adam reaches his eighth birthday, he begins to 'change'. Thus, genomics is linked both to the image of the twin and also to genetic mutation, two of the most common tropes in genomic film repertoires. The film also deploys the image of the microscopic view of cell enucleation to visually cue the process of cloning. This image has been produced as a global icon, dominating the UK news media as the visual anchorage for a range of cloning and stem cell stories. This self-conscious claim to a realist temporality and aesthetic is developed throughout the film, which is set up as a vehicle for mobilizing ethical debates about genomics in the form of reproductive human cloning.

The initial premise offered by the clone's father, Paul, who is a biology teacher, is that the new Adam (through his cells) remembers his previous life. This is explained in the following analogy:

> DNA is like a fuse box, some genes are turned on, others are turned off, they are all present in each cell.
>
> *(Godsend)*

Paul develops a theory that some of Adam's genes are 'turned on' to the possibility of genetic memory. This explanation is used to account for Adam's sleepwalking and 'night terrors'. However, the plot is made much more complicated by the disclosure that Dr Wells has also tried to use the opportunity to bring back his own deceased son, through Adam, by 'reprogramming' Adam's DNA to have some of this other child's personality traits – this is an interesting departure, given the film's realist premise, and the implausibility of this aspect of the plot suggests that the film is at its weakest when it traverses genre boundaries.

As well as the 'biohorror' (Thacker, 2002) of the clone, Adam then also performs the evil/possessed child seen in other 'child horror' films such as the *Omen* (Donner, 1976) series and *Children of the Corn* (Kiersch, 1984). There are four alternate endings to the film on the DVD release, and these range from Adam killing one or both of his parents and the doctor to one of them killing him. In the version that saw theatrical release, the ending is left open with the parents and Adam moving to a new neighbourhood for a 'fresh start', while the clinician scientist disappears. In the new house Adam encounters someone in the wardrobe, indicating that the new start idea is doomed, and the film ends at this point.

Reproductive cloning is familiarly positioned here as a 'Faustian' bargain in which the parents have succumbed to temptation and eventually pay for their extra years with their son. The analogy of Pandora's box is used by Dr Wells, the geneticist/clinician. The boy is positioned as a Frankensteinian reanimated corpse-type freak of nature and as possessed. The grief and desperation of the parents (especially the mother) is seen to have driven them into an extreme position in which they have committed 'moral trespass'. Their behaviour is defined as such in a fight scene between Adam's father, Paul, and Dr Wells, in a church, which ends with Dr Wells leaving Paul for dead in the burning building.

Cloning is positioned as 'bad' (embodied as evil), and the character of the doctor is positioned as a Faustian 'Mephistopheles', intertextually linked to Robert de Niro's 1987 role as Loius Cyphre (Lucifer) in *Angel Heart*. Dr Wells is shown stalking around his dark study, shrouded by purple curtains, antique furniture and piles of books, with a fire always burning in the grate. He is depicted as having some kind of psychic connection to the Adam clone, and this is conveyed through the use of sound in a scene where Adam kills another child while geographically some distance away from Dr Wells. Images of Dr Wells and Adam are juxtaposed in succession, throughout the murder, and the diegetic sound of Dr Wells clicking two yin/yang worry balls together in his study also plays though the murder scene in the woods, psychically linking the two characters and retrospectively implicating Dr Wells in his own son's murderous acts. Paul's character is anxious to create some distance in the moral ground between himself and Dr Wells, and the dialogue between Wells and Paul is used to create a moral framework about the ethics of reproductive cloning, termed as 'experimenting with life'. Paul positions Dr Wells as a scientist, not a doctor, as he 'pretends'. In this dialogue, and in a previous scene between Paul and the ex-nanny to Dr Wells' son, a strong distinction is made between being a doctor (coded as good) and being a scientist (coded as bad). This film uses the character of Paul to provide an ethical structure as he articulates an opposition to Dr Wells. Paul is also set up early in the film as representing rational moral principles. This is played through his reluctance to take a well-paid job in the private sector over his existing state sector job. The character of the mother, Jesse, is used to articulate a contrasting emotional framework in relation to the mother/child bond. As she says early on in the film

> This is about Adam, sometimes ethics have to take a back seat.
> *(Godsend)*

Dr Wells embodies power and flawed genius in the film. His characterization alternates from his representation as a humane genius with an amoral vision, to that of a corrupt megalomaniac with an immoral secret agenda. However, the introduction of a plot element linking the clone to Dr Wells' dead son complicates any reading of the film as about reproductive cloning per se. This added element links more closely with 'possession' narratives, and the use of dream sequences and the multiple personalities of Adam contribute to this supernatural composition.

This constitution of a genetic narrative through a supernatural is examined in Paul Rabinow's (1999) discussion of genetics, spirituality and the supernatural. Sarah Kember notes in her discussion of Rabinow's (1999) work that

> The problem with (geneticised) life is that it exceeds both natural and philosophical classification. It is diffuse, abject, unrecognisable, anxiety-provoking.
> (Kember, 2003, p. 147)

The film is an exploration of that which is assumed to be scientifically possible (post-Dolly), but has been assumed until very recently, in the US context, to be morally reprehensible and illegal – 'abject ( . . . ) anxiety-provoking'. The film draws on horror conventions such as the image of the dark cellar, an old shack in the woods, long shots, shadows, dream sequences and jump cuts, in the context of a realist aesthetic. The film conveys an incoherence and exceeds clarity in that it mixes cloning with possession and has four alternate endings on the DVD. There is a shot of a spiral staircase that exemplifies this incoherence; it could connote the double helix, as spiral staircases appear symbolically across films with genetic themes; it could also signal horror through the human vulnerability to the long drop. However the image is not picked up again, and it is neither clarified nor developed.

This film explores the interiority of the characters through their feelings, emotions and psyche. It simultaneously evokes the sovereign subject and causal agent, while science is linked to the body and the psyche. The interiority of the spectator is also called upon through this address to consider the personalized ethics of this version of the masculine corporeality of reproductive cloning.

### Genomic governmentality

Governmentality according to Judith Butler's reading of Foucault can be understood as

> A mode of power concerned with the maintenance and control of bodies and persons, the production and regulation of persons and populations, and the circulation of goods insofar as they maintain and restrict the life of the population.
>
> (2004, p. 52)

This model, like those of Foucault (1990) and Rose (2001), extends governmentality beyond ideological and state apparatuses to the practices of everyday life and to the care of the body and the self. Genomic governance is constituted through genetic testing in health, genealogy and forensics, in individual decision-making in relation to testing and diagnosis (Bunton and Petersen, 2005) and a 'eugenics of risk' (Lemke, 2002).

*Code 46* can be read as imagining what regimes of genomic instrumentality might enact. It appears as a text in the dramatic mediation of technoscience and provides a visualization of a technoscientific future/present. This dystopic vision of manipulation and totalitarian governance operates not through the nation state, but through a diffuse globalized infrastructure. Genomics is one 'mode of power concerned with the maintenance and control of bodies and persons' in this film that is primarily concerned with extrapolating from the multiple and diffuse mechanisms of power that currently regulate bodies. This dramatization of diffuse regulatory structures constitutes a vision of genomics in which individual agency disappears, a disappearance reflected in Winterbottom's references to Oedipus. The forms of governmentality in *Code 46* highlight the tensions between the individual and genomic governance, which at once settles on the body but at the same time disavows its agency. Thus, the body is represented as the unit of power in terms of its effects, while simultaneously losing the agential capacity to produce effects of power. This fatalistic constitution of power is a dystopic vision, at once corporeal and diffuse, which contrasts with narratives about individual agency that figure embodiment and corporality in relation to agency.

## Genomic individuals

Individual characters are an integral part of narrative, and the figure of the scientist has a long history of narrative mobilization (Frayling, 2003; Haynes, 1994). The figure of the scientist is used to mobilize plots and to explore different meanings for science across multiple media forms. In storytelling about science, individual scientists are positioned as discoverers of scientific theories, and inventors of technological applications and practices. Popular representations of genomics have deployed scientists to tell stories, through the characterization of Francis Crick and James Watson as the 'discoverers' of the double helix in the 1950s, to John Sulston and Craig Ventnor as 'racing' to find the map of the human genome in the 1990s. Throughout the development of the Human Genome Initiative (which became the 'map'), related stories about the mapping process in the 1990s were delivered in the press, and in many scientific papers, through a simplistic 'discovery of a gene for X' formula (Van Dijck, 1998). Fears about reproductive cloning technologies continue to be narrativized in the news through the dramatization of claims by individual scientists, such as Dr Zavos's failed clone implantation in 2004.

In film, representations of science have been constituted through the body of the individual scientist, as well as the individual clone. The characterization of such figures of the scientist in film has often drawn on literary precursors such as Prometheus, Dr Frankenstein and Dr Faustus (Haynes, 1994; Turney, 1998; Van Dijck, 1998; Kember, 2003; Wiengart et al., 2003). Although a range of characters are drawn on to different ends, many contemporary cloning or genetic engineering narratives position genomic scientists as mavericks, or misguided men who have lost their way or are sometimes just evil. Often they are figured through these negative inflections precisely because they are involved in genomic science (*The 6th Day*). Although scientists are often portrayed negatively (Frayling, 2003; Haynes, 2003), genomic scientists have been figured as particularly dubious, through their appearance as characters in SF and horror, and genomics has been portrayed as a dark form of science through these locations.

The academic framework of public understanding and public engagement of science (PUS/PEST) has instantiated the individual scientist as the pivotal figure that needs to communicate with publics. Instrumental or deficit models of science communication tend towards the idea that individual scientists should convey their knowledge more effectively and more accessibly. Other models imply that scientific research agendas should be subject to, and partly shaped by, public consultation processes. This model still involves individual scientists communicating with 'lay' groups in order to make such groups understand the benefits of science. Thus individual scientists carry the responsibility for, and embody, scientific research. In these models science is seen as a process mobilized by agential scientists who 'cause' it to happen and the 'effects' as something that other individuals are free to adopt or refuse, in a neo-liberal model of agential choice.

The use of individual characters to embody and 'cause' science in film means that, on the one hand, concepts of science are removed from a structural context and understood as expressions of individual genius. On the other hand, fears and fantasies about science can be exorcized through plot resolutions in which the individual scientist is disempowered or stopped or goes through a process of self-realization. The practice of science is thus represented as a mode of self-regulation and a matter of personal ethics. The institutions of science and the applications of technology are represented as transparent and distinct from other spheres of life, through the figuration of science, through scientists, as a set of individuated single, agential actors who 'cause it'.

## Mechanisms of science and genre: institutions and individuals

In *Godsend* genre conventions of horror are drawn on and reworked to produce a causal narrative about genomic science in which Dr Wells appears as the responsible agent. The fact that he misinforms the parents involved in his cloning experiment and approaches them when they are still in shock from their bereavement undermines any reading of this responsibility being shared across the characters. Dr Wells is dislocated from medical establishments through his maverick and secretive behaviour. Genomic science, and its offspring, the clone, are thus embodied as evil through the figures of Dr Wells and the cloned child, who are both constituted through the paradigms of horror.

Although the dialogues between Paul and other characters in the film set up a moral framework to explore a range of bioethical positions, the film locates these arguments as individual instances of moral decision-making and informed consent. Genomic science is represented as 'playing with life' in a Christian framework and as 'bad' science. It is thus punishable through horrific consequence. However, the use of the figure of the maverick scientist opens up an ambiguity that leaves the institutions of science unquestioned, through the individualized narrative that produces Dr Wells as a scapegoat. In other words, the preoccupation with individual morality disavows any political implications of biotechnology.

Through conventions of science fiction *Code 46* reproduces genomic science as an aspect of governmentality within the horizons of technoscience in which familial genetic knowledge is no longer available and genetic information is at once embodied but dislocated, requiring testing to bring information about genealogy back to the individual and invest information as knowledge. Such a configuration of genomics allows it to disappear within the horizons of technoscience, reproducing genomics as omnipotent. This also potentially closes up the space to critique genomic science through a reading of it as already assumed as inevitable. Both films thus leave broader questions about genomic science ultimately unquestioned by representing this inevitability. This relates to a trend in contemporary film, where genomics has moved from a historically more prevalent location in niche-market genre film such as SF and horror (and SF/horror hybrids) and is now becoming a theme in an increasing number of mass-market multi-genre Hollywood action films (*Jurassic Park, The 6th Day, The Island*).

However, although both films ultimately leave genomics unquestioned by figuring it as inevitable, *Code 46* offers a critique of power. Through the figuring of genomics as subsumed into the everyday practices of the 'near future' self, genomics loses a relation to individual agency and operates as a corporeal mode of governmentality, and in doing so provides a vision of how power might be operating in the present. Thus, the tension between the individual and forms of governmentality opens up a space to question genomics as a mode of power.

This contrasts with the de-politicization of the spectacle of genomics, figured as a radical science culminating in the corporeal horror of the clone in *Godsend*. Arguably *Godsend* is a less convincing text because the horror of the figure of the clone on which it tries to draw has been destabilized and undermined by contemporary discourses of cloning as therapeutic. *Code 46* on the other hand draws on the contemporary constitution of cloning as a technoscientific process and the ways in which genomics operates as corporeal inscription reconstituting the mundane and the everyday.

In the two films examined in this chapter, genomics is represented as science fictional on the one hand and horrific on the other. Within these framings two different types of dystopic visions are evoked, one about the loss of human agency in the face of structural power and the other about the power of human agency to do evil. Representing genomics through these generic framings means that genomics is inscribed with, and can be explored within, the terms of those conventions. It also means that the genre expectations are reshaped by the discourses of genomics, and some of the tensions in these films are relational to extra-diegetic factors such as the mediation of human genomics though other sites (such as news media, policy documents, and popular science writing). One of the responses to the release of *Godsend* was that it was irresponsible to portray genomics in terms of horror, in a time when the contestation between hope and fear is so central to the capacity for contemporary genomics to secure markets through therapeutic cloning and stem cell research. However, such markets for genomics are still being formed, and audiences' expectations of genomics are undergoing constant revision in relation to hopes, expectations and experiences of genomics as it moves beyond SF and horror.

## Acknowledgements

Many grateful thanks to Dr Joan Haran, Prof. Jenny Kitzinger, Prof. Maureen McNeil, Prof. Jackie Stacey, Dr Matt Hills and the editors of this collection, for their generous contributions to the development of this chapter.

## Notes

1. A detailed history of film, the changes in this medium and its relationship to other forms and an examination of the relationship between the medium of film and the industries of cinema are beyond the scope of this chapter. These

issues are dealt with by many other scholars such as Christian Metz, David Bordwell, Andrew Darley, Lisa Cartwright, Andre Bazin and Janet Wasko, to mention just a few contributors to this diverse and rich literature.
2. Dolly was the first live-born cloned mammal in the UK, and the announcement of her birth in 1997 at the Roslin Institute in Scotland led to the creation or revision of policies on human cloning in many countries.
3. Tim Robbins was reported in an interview with Ashley Smith on Cinema Confidential as saying that MGM didn't like the film. 'TIM: I wish someone at MGM liked the film as much as I do. Q: What's the MGM comment? TIM: Well its being released in two theaters. Right there, I mean, c'mon we're not dumb are we? [laughs]' (Smith, 2004).
4. Figures recorded by the European Audio Visual Observatory, in the Lumiere Database.
5. I return to governmentality in greater detail in the later sections of this chapter.

# III
# Scanning

The four chapters in this section are concerned with thinking differently about the way films are viewed. They are concerned both with the technology of cinema spectatorship – the body of discourses and theorizing upon film-viewing – and with the particular viewing requirements of films in varied contexts. The shared premise of these chapters is that critical analysis of cinema should recognize the significance of cinema's technological character (at different stages of its development) upon the affective experience and practices of viewing films. The practice of looking at films usually involves the cognitive and emotional work of following stories, identifying with characters, studying performances and immersing ourselves in the *mise-en-scène*. At the same time it also usually requires the strange (in-)activity of sitting or standing in obscure rooms, remaining relatively quiet and immobile while staring at screens, gazing at the technical apparatus of cinema. The title of this section refers to the way that our eyes move across (and into the illusory depths of) the screen, and each of these chapters addresses the mobility of our gaze as we watch different types of film, often refusing the hierarchical ordering of the image as our gaze slides away from those areas of the image that are coded as narratively significant, towards the 'peripheral detail' at the edges of the frame (Cardinal, 1986). However, the scanning eye is also an analytical and interpretative eye, searching for intensities and significant patterns as it probes and traverses the surface of the image. The term 'scanning' also implies a close relationship between the way we view screens (and are positioned by and in front of them) and the image-processing technologies and mediating practices that generate the images that surround us – the scanning electron beam in the cathode ray tube of a conventional television set, barcode, flatbed and iris scanners, the scanning electron microscope, the remediation of cinema by TV as the images are cropped, 'panned and scanned' to correspond to the aspect ratio and formal conventions of television. Eschewing a critical framework that privileges or essentializes narrative, each of these chapters is concerned with films, as well as works in other media, that employ a variety of non-narrative or unconventional narrative strategies. However, the approaches suggested by these chapters are as appropriate for thinking about the way we look at gallery art, as they are for thinking about the way we watch mainstream narrative cinema.

Aylish Wood argues that in a contemporary cultural context, in which our attention is constantly dispersed across a vast constellatory field of media objects, we are required to process and interpret audio-visual texts that can be understood as consisting of 'competing elements'. Through a discussion of television drama, installation art, video games and digital cinema, Wood's essay explores the characteristic features of this interaction with technology and suggests that, rather than disrupting the spectator's subjectivity, the active distribution of attention functions to produce a subject position for the spectator. Rather than understanding film spectatorship in the conventional restrictive terms of a viewer's absorptive identification with a coherent narrative, Wood, like Walter Benjamin, invokes architecture as a model for understanding the viewer's relationship with an object of scrutiny (see Benjamin, 1973). In these terms, the spectator doesn't experience an audio-visual text from the secure, uni-focal position of subjective mastery – as something that is discrete, coherent, narrativized and temporally linear. Instead the spectator occupies mobile, provisional subject positions and is engaged in the process of making meaning from a dynamic, incoherent signifying environment. For Wood, this mode of engagement is necessarily constitutive as the spectator 'has to generate a position' from which the technologized sensory environment will be meaningful. Thus, rather than arguing that spectacular digital culture produces subjects that are radically and sensationally disembodied, dispersed and disengaged from their surroundings, Wood attempts to explore the ways in which we engage with our changing media environment.

Maja Manojlovic's essay is concerned more specifically with the ways in which digital cinema – that is, cinema that incorporates an 'aesthetics of the digital', rather than mainstream digital effects cinema – is watched. Through a consideration of Olivier Assayas' excessive film, *Demonlover*, Manojlovic explores the way that narrative time and space are reconfigured through this digital aesthetics in a way that requires a different mode of viewing. The unconventional organization and depiction of space in the film, Manojlovic proposes, demands a 'new form of attention, appropriate to the orientation of supermodern urban environments'. In particular, Manojlovic suggests, *Demonlover*'s diegetic architecture displaces feelings from their conventional attachment to characters and human bodies onto the spaces they inhabit. *Demonlover* explores and *foregrounds* the dematerializing effects of digital technology through an emphasis on *backgrounds*, 'an aesthetic intensification of spatiality'. What the film requires of a spectator, then, is a different mode of attention, not solely a narrative engagement – especially with such a narratively disjointed text – but the capacity to scan and read spaces and screens responding haptically to affective intensities and dislocations. Manojlovic's reading of *Demonlover* makes visible the ways in which cinema, representational space and ways of viewing films are being reconfigured by the digital shift.

Taking a broad historical overview, Christopher Rodrigues' chapter argues that the technological transformations that appear to characterize 'the new digital world' are in fact nothing new. Rather, cinema has always been preoccupied with a tension between transparency and opacity, representation and mechanism. From early cinema onwards, high-tech visual spectacle has been a central attraction of cinema, offering distracting, pleasurable images that mean our attention is (at least) divided between the narrative means and the narratives themselves. Focusing upon several film-makers whose work is preoccupied with cinematic technology, Rodrigues argues that through an unconventional manipulation of the relationship between background and foreground within the frame, their films solicit a complex play of attention and distraction from viewers. Directors like Jean-Marie Straub, Danièle Huillet, Jean-Luc Godard and Atom Egoyan structure their films so that the spectator's gaze is permitted to scan the film frame for meaning and incident. Rodrigues suggests that film theorists have tended to overlook the importance of décor, architecture, landscape and visual noise because of a critical preoccupation with the way that classical cinema directs the spectator's attention through hierarchically ordered on-screen space. However, Rodrigues suggests that the concept of a distracted mode of spectatorship in which our attention wanders offers a useful account of the way that mainstream cinema, as well as experimental films, is viewed.

In different ways, then, these chapters conceive of technology not just as a mediating device, a transparent interface or window between spectator and image, but rather as the opaque object of the spectator's gaze. The robot enters through Bennett's chapter as an embodiment of a cinematic apparatus manifested as spectacular technology. Based on a reading of a selection of science fiction films such as *Terminator 2: Judgment Day*

(Cameron, 1991) that feature children's intensely affective and interactive exchanges with robots, the chapter suggests that children are figured as ideal cinematic spectators. Rendered as techno-cinephiles, they embody a fantasy for the mainstream film industry of uncritical consumption. The problem with the child-robot relationships is that they usually cover over the ways in which technology is always-already physically and psychically incorporated in everyday experience. The films typically misrecognize technology as alien or futural. These chapters – and the films and other objects that they examine – invite us to see film spectatorship differently, and to see films differently – to recognize that it is cinema technology that we are gazing upon when we watch films.

# 7
# Cinema as Technology: Encounters with an Interface

*Aylish Wood*

In the current era of proliferating media technologies, from the various moving image devices we place in our homes to the numerous mobile gadgets we carry around with us, the world is increasingly framed through a multiplicity of interfaces. Our more long-standing moving image technologies such as television and cinema are also marked by this proliferation and so stand as indices for our experience of the expanding media terrain. For instance, *24*, the American television drama premised on 'real-time' action, periodically interrupts its flow with a countdown segment in which different narrative threads simultaneously appear on the screen in a split-screen arrangement. In watching such a split-screen framing of multiple events, viewers engage with the text in a way that is quite different to their viewing of the more conventional action sequences. Instead of being involved in a process of watching and interpretation centred on a singular flow of action, viewers have to spread their attention between the competing images, each of which carry a flow of action. In the following chapter I give an account of the impact of competing images, or competing elements, on viewing, and articulate it as an engagement with technology, one that resonates with broader changes in the landscape of moving image technologies. First, I explore the extent to which competing elements appear across different media, including gallery installations, digital games and digital effects cinema. Secondly, I argue that our experience of competing elements reveals the particular spatio-temporal conditions of an encounter between a human viewer and a technological system. In so doing, I claim such encounters as sites of emergent human agency.

## Digital inscriptions and embodied viewing

Central to my argument about an emergent agency is that the competing elements constituting audio-visual images establish a ground for embodied viewing. It follows that the quality of such an embodied experience depends on the detail of the ground through which this experience occurs. In cinema studies, seamless and non-seamless interfaces are familiar terms, and each represents different kinds of encounters for a viewer. All images are composed of elements, and typically these include actors, set design, costume and lighting. In seamless interfaces characterizing much mainstream cinema, such elements work together to favour a singular centre of attention for the viewer. Frequently, emphasis is placed on a character and its actions, with the other elements serving to support the character's representative and expressive aspects. By contrast, when competing elements exist in an image, a viewer's 'eye' is drawn in more than one direction. Sometimes this capacity to split a viewer's focus is obvious, as in the countdown segments of *24*. Other examples include the Windows interface on Internet pages, which is constructed around a set of elements that, often quite emphatically, compete for a viewer's attention. Words, still and moving imagery, pop-up inserts and occasionally sound, as well as a series of hyperlinks into other sites, co-exist on the pages, each seeking to catch the viewer's eye. In this multi-format and non-seamless interface, viewers can be understood as being placed in the position of having to distribute their attention across the competing elements in order to make sense of the information. As this involves taking up an orientation within the spatio-temporal organization of the window, we can understand this process of viewing as an embodied encounter between a human and a technological system.

This view of an embodied encounter contrasts with approaches within cultural and media studies that see the proliferation of moving image media as generating another instance of a dispersed subject, as, in watching the audio-visual world through a multiplicity of interfaces, we engage in a process of dispersal and distraction instead of attending to and so experiencing the world before us (Crary, 1999; Sobchack, 2004). In this chapter, I take an alternative position, arguing that the proliferating landscape offers not dispersal and distraction, but rather the propagation of a particular mode of human-technological interaction, in which a human viewers of competing technological interfaces have to generate a position from which they synthesize meaning. I take for granted that some aspects of our engagement with the world before us are set aside, but rather than only seeing this as symptomatic of some kind of loss, see it instead as something from which we can build a different means of thinking about technological experience. In making sense of the world through the interfaces of moving imagery, we directly experience the spatio-temporal incursions of technologies. These incursions take us to places we could never otherwise go, but in so doing also deny us the ability to exert full control over that experience. This is the compromise at the heart of our engagements with technologies.

The idea of competing elements provides a way of understanding this compromise as a process of synthesis rather than dispersal. But in order to do so, we first need to also consider how competing elements reconfigure textual organizations, and then move towards seeing texts as complex spatio-temporal organizations that reveal aspects of our encounters with moving image technologies as technologies. In cinema studies, the most prevalent means of understanding textual organization has been through the linearity of narrative. The notion of competing elements necessitates a revisiting of this understanding of a text. As I argue below, initially through installations, digital games and finally digital effects cinema, another way of thinking about the organization of competing elements is through the idea of architecture. Architecture is usually taken to be an arrangement of buildings within a given space. A temporal dimension can be added when considering how people inhabit the spaces, or the ways in which that space transforms over time. This spatio-temporal understanding of architecture lends itself to conceptualizing moving imagery constructed around a series of competing elements. For instance, Bill Viola's multi-screen installations, *The Five Angels for the Millennium* and *Going Forth By Day*, can be spatially described as installations based on five screens arranged within the exhibition space, usually a rectangular room. Although spatially accurate, this description only has a minimal purchase on a viewer's experience of the installations, which are also organized around temporal relationships that impinge on a viewer's freedom of engagement. A more full account of the architecture of these installations describes their existence as audio-visual competing elements arranged in space, but any experience of an installation requires that its temporal dimensions be included, and these are complex. One component of the temporal dimension is the relationships between the elements, and these are constantly transforming. A second, and complicating, temporal dimension is added by the presence of a viewer. If a viewer's experience is to be articulated, it needs to be understood in terms of a viewer's locatedness within the spatio-temporal organization of an architecture, and while this involves an orientation within the spatial arrangement of the five projections, it also involves an orientation determined by temporal relations between the textual elements themselves as well as between the textual elements and the viewer. Within this architectural organization viewers are unable to exert visual and aural control over what they see and hear; rather, they co-operate with the spatio-temporal restraints of the architecture. Although this encounter might well be taken as one of dispersal, such a perspective equates to allowing oneself to be lost to the system, and this is not the way we effectively interact with installations, or competing elements more generally. Instead, we are embodied as we locate ourselves by actively distributing our attention across competing elements with the aim of making a meaning. Through this process, viewers of complex audio-visual architectures gain agency.

## Digital effects cinema, digital games and competing elements

Before moving onto thinking about agency, I first want to expand the idea of competing elements to digital effects cinema and digital games. Although they are less obvious than those of Web pages or installations, competing elements also exist in digital effects cinema. As I discussed above, all film-making involves a number of elements coming together, and in effects cinema, both digital and optical, effects co-exist on the screen with human or live-action figures. With the introduction of digital effects there is an increasing tendency to create images in which effects and figures form competing elements. In the film *Minority Report*, during the sequences where John Anderton sifts through images on a transparent screen, two elements compete with each other. The movement of the mobile segments running horizontally across the transparent screen catch our attention, and have the potential to draw attention away from the figure of Anderton, and we may wonder which is more important.

Digital games also contain elements that compete for a viewer's attention. The most obvious of these are information bars that usually sit on the margins of a screen. Although not explicitly involved in the action of a game, the information they contain can be consequential. In *Half-Life 2*, for instance, the Freeman avatar's health bar has an impact on a gamer's strategy if the gamer is in a hazardous zone or under water, and playing involves cycling attention between the action and the information bars. Although less obvious, since they are not signalled as bars on the margins of the screen, the game space is also marked by different kinds of spatio-temporal organizations. In moments of play where there are no AI-avatars forcing a defensive reaction from the gamer, control over the avatar's spatio-temporal orientation is under minimal temporal pressure. The gamer is able to explore terrain or buildings without concern for any encroaching enemy. By contrast, when an AI-avatar intervenes in Freeman's progress, the gamer has to react. As a consequence, the gamer's spatio-temporal orientation is driven by the temporal pressure exerted by the AI-avatar, as the gamer has to respond to the AI-avatar's influence. Overall, the architecture of a digital game can be understood to be constructed from a number of competing spatio-temporal elements: the information bars, AI-avatar-controlled engagement and also an engagement controlled by the gamer.

Although digital cinema and digital games are very different kinds of texts to an installation, when they each include competing elements they share a distinctive spatio-temporal relationship between the viewer and text. Where approaches to the moving image, whether of cinema or games, have often taken the image to offer uni-focal interface to a viewer, the presence of competing elements complicates the spatio-temporal arrangement of the interface, and it follows that a viewer is offered a multi-focal engagement with the text. Central to the remainder of this discussion is my claim that competing elements, as they produce a multi-focal image, distribute a viewer's attention across the image.

## Competing elements and distributed attention

Digital sounds and imagery are experienced at the interface of the screen. And when they are inscribed with competing elements, a viewer has to make sense of them by distributing attention across the elements. By attention I mean the process by which we look towards some parts of the screen, and not others. Typically in continuity-based cinema the character is the main point of focus. All the cueing of a film – the editing, lighting, framing, costume, sound – point towards the character and how their actions fill and give meaning to the spaces associated with the screen. With competing elements, the cueing does not straightforwardly follow to a single point of focus, as two or more may co-exist. As such, digital effects can expand the narrative space in which characters compete for our attention with digital effects. Non-expanded and expanded narrative spaces often co-exist in different segments of a film, and a shift between the two is especially visible in *Minority Report*.

*Minority Report* opens with a double articulation of technology, as it shows both the fictional pre-cognitive technology of the story world and also one of the central digital constructions of the film: the transparent viewing interface overlaid with mobile images. Following the mistaken identification of the victim's address, Anderton has to return to again sort through the moving images from the pre-cognitives. When Anderton initially takes his position at the transparent screen, he is flanked by four other male figures, standing in a slight v-shape, with Anderton at the tip, looking at a single image. At this moment the architectural organization of the image is uni-focal, all the figures look towards a single point and their bodies are framed to underline this orientation. In addition, the *mise-en-scène* does little to distract a viewer from following this line of sight. This unusually rigorous uni-focal regime quickly gives way to a multi-focal one as the moving images begin to cross the screen, drawing attention away from Anderton, so that a viewer is looking between Anderton and the details of the moving image. The depth perspective is also flattened in these later shots, drawing attention away from the figures in the background and towards the competing elements of Anderton and the mobile elements. At such a moment, the textual organization reconfigures from a linear sequence of uni-focal imagery to a linear sequence of multi-focal imagery, which can also be understood in terms of a spatio-temporal architecture. Viewers not only distribute their attention spatially, but also across dispersed elements that are organized within a temporal flow.

Other films that have similar spatio-temporal architectures structured around competing elements include *Titanic, Dark City* and *The Matrix*, where the effects operate as vehicles for the narrative. In each film the effects, created by combinations of models and computer-generated imagery, make contributions to the narrative. The ship in *Titanic* is not simply the location of the romance between Jack and Rose, but has a narrative strand of technological hubris brought down by overconfidence and chance. In *Dark City* the mutability of the buildings during the tuning sequences acts as 'agents' of change, while in *The Matrix*, the strange distortions of time and space created by the effects add another layer to a narrative centred on a conflict for the control of time and space. Competing elements also exist in other ways within films. For instance, in *Hulk* split-screen elements frequently appear on the screen, while in *Pleasantville* some of the moments of colour transformation act as competing elements, while the more experimental extended split-screen work of *Timecode* generates competing elements that co-exist for the duration of the film (Wood, 2007).

Thinking about digital games, digital effects film or installations in terms of competing elements organized into a spatio-temporal architecture brings me to a broader point. By stepping back from the world of the film, digital game or installation, it is possible to instead stage an encounter with the screen and to present it as an important interface where technologies of image construction and viewers come into contact. The inscriptions of digital technologies are becoming increasingly apparent on screens through the appearance of competing elements. The spatio-temporal organization of these elements is central to processes of viewing, playing a part in enabling and orchestrating engagements and identifications. The idea of competing elements invokes something that we have always known about cinema, but quite often forget. Cinema is a technology, and the screen, or the multiplicity of screens that we have in the early twenty-first century, is a technological interface that influences not only what we see, but how we see it. To generate a model for thinking about the ways in which competing elements influence how we see, I draw on an idea explored by N. Katherine Hayles in her book, *How We Became Post Human* (Hayles, 1999). To counteract some of the more abandoned approaches to human and technological interactions, especially the idea of disembodiment, where the human body is left behind as everything else dissipates across a matrix, she mobilizes the idea of distribution as outlined in the work of Edwin Hutchins (Hutchins, 1995). According to Hutchins, in a network involving human and technological interfaces, the capacity to exert control is distributed across the two interfaces, with neither in full control nor fully determining. For instance, if we use a search engine on the Internet, we can set the parameters of the search, but the engine in turn searches according to a keyword recognition criteria. What we end up with emerges in the intersection between the user and the interface. Such a process is also in play in *Minority Report*. The detectives can only know what they think they know, because of the technological interface of the pre-cognitives. The complex system of humans (police and pre-cogs), plus all the visualizing technologies, distributes the capacity for seeing across those different elements. Of particular interest in Hutchins model is the way a human sense of being in the world is modified by an interaction with technology. This interaction is not taken to be a lessening of experience, but a reconfiguration of it through a technological interface. Hayles draws on this position as she argues that technologies more fully distribute the spatial parameters of the human body through extensions of the cognitive system: 'In this model, it is not a question of leaving the body behind but rather of extending embodied awareness in highly specific, local and material ways that would be impossible without electronic prosthesis' (Hayles, 1999, pp. 290–91). Viewing through the interface of a screen does not operate in the same way, as it is not an encounter in real time with activities and events occurring elsewhere, and the spatial distributions are more imaginative than actual. Nevertheless, this perspective is relevant to my model, as when different kinds of cinematic technologies create screens as interfaces with multi-focal elements competing for a viewer's attention, the viewer's initial means of engagement – attention – is distributed across the different elements of the image. The activity of viewing emerges in the context of an attention that is distributed, but rather than occurring across a network of technologies, it occurs across a set of elements embedded within spatio-temporal architectures created by the organizing capacities of moving image technologies.

Within cognitive science attention is understood as a process by which individuals attend to particular elements within their perceptive field (Pashler, 1998). Since this process involves selection – choosing to pay attention to something – it is an active one, but because it is selective it also involves establishing a compromise on what is attended to. As attention is paid to spatial and temporal elements in the perceptive field, cueing occurs, a kind of 'pointing to', which draws the attendee towards particular aspects of the perceptual field while at the same time pulling the attendee away from others. Although approaches to attention refer to visual acuity in the actual world, the idea of attention and cueing is relevant to the cinema. Cinema technologies organize time and space, whatever the kind of film. Taken straightforwardly, all cinema cues attention, disposing a viewer in different ways to what is occurring on the screen as the tactics of textual organization determine the viewing experience, intercepting engagements with characters, genres and so on. The two main competing elements in the *Minority Report* images discussed above are the mobile segments and John Anderton, as the background of the set is not cued, and these competing elements structure where we distribute our attention. A split-screen film such as *Timecode*, the information bars of games interfaces or the multiple screens in an installation offer different kinds of interfaces with a range of organizations and structures. *Timecode*'s four-way split-screen organization cues and distributes attention. The opening sequence of *Timecode*, because it builds from relative simplicity to a more complex organization, demonstrates the generation of the higher order of cueing that I mean by distributed attention. The shifting sound and image scapes of the first quadrant show the simple yet effective cueing of a single screen. But as the images and sounds build across the four segments, as camera movements catch the eye, as dramatic tension builds within a frame, attention is not simply cued but distributed across a range of competing elements. In each case, making sense of the elements requires a viewer to synthesize a meaning, and the freedom offered to a viewer to make this synthesis is a site of potential agency.

## Agency and choice

The formulation of freedom given by Maurice Merleau-Ponty is a useful starting point in thinking about such an agency:

> The world is already constituted, but also never completely constituted; in the first case we are acted upon, in the second we are open to an infinite number of possibilities. But this analysis is still abstract, for we exist in both ways at once. There is, therefore, never determinism and never absolute choice.
> 
> (Merleau-Ponty, p. 527)

Following on from this, I want to argue that engagements with interfaces constructed around competing elements can be characterized as an encounter between determinism and absolute choice, and that diverse spatio-temporal architectures offer different kinds of encounters. In watching *Timecode*, though the soundscape is limiting, viewers can perceptually fade in and out according to how their attention is engaged by the flow of images. This apparent freedom of engagement is qualified by varying degrees of determinism as the relationship between the four screens motivates the ways in which the flow is tracked. How viewers make sense of the different panels in *Timecode* is based on the ways the viewers distribute their attention across the panels, but the viewers are neither fully determined by the digital technologies nor offered absolute choice. What one sees finally emerges in the combination of the embodied attention of individual viewers, their orientation within the spatio-temporal architecture of the text, as they encounter the interface of the four-way screen, taking up an orientation that moves between the determinism of the pre-established organizations of the text and individual choices. The distribution of attention enabled by *Timecode's* formal experimentation has the potential to be a generative one, in that it opens the viewing interface to a diversity of possible viewing positions. It is in negotiating these diverse viewing positions that agency begins to become apparent. A similar argument may be made for Paul Driessen's split-screen animations. *The End of the World in Four Seasons* (1995) is constructed around eight rectangular sections arranged within the larger rectangle of the screen. The first experience of watching these images is of being confronted with a series of panels where there are numerous actions taking place. Initially, it seems that there is too much information and not enough sense. Gradually, however, sense can be made of the narrative threads by the choices through which panels are given attention, and the possibility for choice in paying attention establishes a degree of agency for the viewer.

To say more about this notion of agency I turn briefly to work in sociology on social agency. While the argument presented in this chapter does not involve agency in the same way as a fully articulated social agency, the latter does have purchase here. In *Gender and Agency* Lois McNay presents a view of generative agency (McNay, 2000). She takes to task versions of agency remaining grounded in what she calls negative agency or where the possibility for action is thought only 'through the residual categories of resistance to or dislocation of dominant norms' (McNay, 2000, p. 4). Instead, McNay seeks ways of thinking about agency where there is generative potential, and gives this idea more substance by citing the increasing movement of women into social fields previously confined to men. The potential for different kinds of agency exists not in resistant strategies but in the dialogical relationships emerging from the intersections between the particularities of gender norms (for women and men) and the particularities of the social fields. In developing her argument about agency McNay emphasizes the combination of Pierre Bourdieu's models of habitus and field (Bourdieu, 1990). Habitus expresses the idea that bodily identity is not natural but involves the inscription of dominant social norms, a process that includes both the establishment of the norms and a living through of those norms. The habitus is the site of the constitution of the person-in-action, a system of dispositions that is both objective and subjective. It is the dynamic intersection of structure and action, society and the individual. In developing the more delimited agency involved in the process of embodied viewing, I make an analogy between Bourdieu's description of the habitus and the interface established by competing elements. The competing elements are objective in the sense that they pre-exist and are visible to any viewer, but equally they are subjective, in that individual viewers, through the embodiment of distributed attention, make sense of the images through their own framework. The synthesis of meaning through the process of distributed attention also bears some comparison to Bourdieu's notion of the field. The field expresses the idea that individuals exist within an array of intersecting influences so that a category set up in the habitus can be reconfigured or deformed as lived through within any given field. The field is a frame for relational analysis, a multi-dimensional space of positions and the position-taking of agents. As the logic of one set of influences intersects with the logic of another, the two are transformed. Thus, as a viewer makes a synthesis of meaning across a series of elements, the relationships between the elements become transformed by an individual's viewing. The diversity of transformation varies with the organization of the text, in that some offer more or less opportunities for viewing differences than others. Agency emerges between structure and action in the habitus, just as it emerges between the organization of the texts and the viewer's synthesis of meaning.

Lois McNay, through Pierre Bourdieu, locates social agency in the interplay between the social player and social organizations. This kind of agency is relevant, although much more limited in scope, to a viewer making sense of a text. As the viewer's attention is distributed across the competing elements, the viewer is put in the position of synthesizing meaning across those elements. The extent of this agency varies according to the kind of structure in which the elements are embedded. For instance, an action-driven plot such as in *Minority Report* has a very tight organization of elements, giving less potential for making choices in interpretation. Overall, there is relatively little agency in viewing the competing elements. This contrasts with the more fulsome opportunities available to a viewer of *Timecode* and *The End of the World in Four Seasons*. A gamer's encounter with digital game architectures offer a range of agencies as the gamer engages with the distinct spatio-temporalities offered by a game world under the control of the AI-avatar or those under the control of the gamer.

Installations too offer degrees of agency in viewing. Viola's multi-screen installations offer viewers the choice of five screens at which to experience the audio-visual works, but claim their attention through bursts of sound that distract the viewers, placing them in the position of having to choose between one screen or another. Olafur Eliasson's *Your Double Lighthouse Projection* also reveals the relays of agency open to a viewer. The installation consists of two circular roofless 'rooms' placed within a larger gallery space. In the larger room, a computer-controlled system shifts the colour spectrum, while the second room is bathed in white light. As the larger room is sequentially illuminated with blues, greens, yellows, reds and so forth, the light changes what a viewer sees. My own experience was of firstly looking at the changing colours of the walls, and then noticing how the different light appeared to alter the skin tones of the other people present. One of the green tones was especially effective in giving a rather un-lifelike 'veiny' quality to the skin.

These two observations were followed by my oscillating between looking at the skin of my friends' faces and that of my hands, to try and see what effect all this light was having on my own skin. The immersive potential of being bathed in different coloured light is broken by the competing elements of seeing the effect of the light on oneself and others. Making sense of the whole installation, however, requires further work. While the playfulness of being in the colour-changing room is engaging, it is only part of the installation. The second part involves entering the smaller room bathed in white light and having the retinal memory of the first room affecting how the second room is seen.

The competing elements, either on the interface of a screen or generated by the elements of the installation, do not simply give access to a story world, play space or artwork, but are technological interfaces interceding in how we see what is on the screen. This becomes especially evident in *Your Double Lighthouse Projection*. The changing light of the larger room is computer controlled so that technology controls the colours seen. Furthermore, this colour in turn literally influences how the second room is seen. The technology of light display in one space generates a reaction in a viewer, which through the temporality of retinal memory has an impact on a second space. The installation generates a fascinating example of embodied viewing. Not only is the viewer immersed in the light space, the viewer's body is essential to the effect of the installation.

## Becoming embodied

Digital technologies have generated interfaces where the presence of technologies is inscribed through the evidence of competing elements, whether that is on traditional screens, monitors, televisions or the more expanded space of an installation in a gallery. By taking competing elements into account, we can begin to see these different texts as technological interfaces that reveal the ways in which technologies influence not only what we see, but also how it is seen.

*Your Double Lighthouse Projection* also brings into focus the question of embodiment, by which I mean the ways in which viewers are oriented by or in relation to the audio-visual materials around them. Installations, and certainly digital effects cinema and digital games, rarely embody as distinctively as *Your Double Lighthouse Projection*, but when structured around competing elements they do generate spatio-temporal architectures, and the viewers' experience emerges through their locatedness within the organization generated by this technological interface.

A particular feature of this interface is not simply that technology alters spatial orientations within the world, but also exerts a series of temporal pressures. In watching a film, playing a games or standing within an installation structured around competing elements, the viewers must locate themselves in order to generate any understanding of the moving imagery. The kind of embodiment and agency that this engenders varies with the architecture of the text. When speaking of the loss inherent in such an experience, the reference is often to the diminution of the human subjects' engagement with the world around them, as they turn instead to face technology (Crary, 1999). When speaking of the gains of such an experience, the reference is often to the new conditions created by or made visible through the technology (Hansen, 2004). What we miss in either of these descriptions is an understanding of the nature of the engagement between a viewer and the technological interface.

In our encounters with moving imagery we engage with an organization whose architecture places us in a different spatio-temporal environment. Technologies alter our spatio-temporal familiarity with the world, and an interface constructed around competing elements presents a perspective in which we can find evidence of technologies' potential to transform. An outcome of this experience is the exposure of both the possibilities and the limits of the agency technologies offer to us. In our relational negotiations within the spatio-temporal architecture of a system, we are confronted by both opportunities and also limitations. A facet of digital technologies, and of technologies more generally, is not that they disconnect us from the world, but rather that they create within it distinct kinds of engagements. In the current circumstance of continuing technological innovation, moving image interfaces provide us with representations not only of other worlds, but of articulations of the impact of ever-changing networks of interactions between humans and technologies.

# 8
# *Demonlover*: Interval, Affect and the Aesthetics of Digital Dislocation

*Maja Manojlovic*

Olivier Assayas has said that with his film *Demonlover* (2002) he was seeking to 'establish a post-Hitchcockian thriller mood and then just blow the whole thing up' (quoted in Peranson, 2003, p. 32). Indeed, Assayas bursts through the parameters of the conventional narrative with the aesthetics of the digital, which dislocate familiar referential, sensory and interpretive networks. Discontinuities in *Demonlover*'s narrative logic create *intervals* in the habitual process of signifying, allowing the characters to be 'manipulated by their own inner logic, or absence of logic' (Peranson, 2003, p. 33). Less tied to rationality, their body postures and faces become more readily available for urban space filled with digital screen technologies to simultaneously inscribe itself and be reflected in them. This dynamic of *absorption* and *reflection* creates complex structures of *affect*, which emerge from the 'framings' of the characters within the multiple and varied screens and reflective surfaces that fill the film. Driven by this digital aesthetic, *Demonlover*'s affectivity thus redirects spectatorial attention, Assayas insists, 'below the surface of narrative, where it [meaning] can radiate in much more powerful ways. Like some kind of drug-induced mood' (Peranson, 2003, p. 33).

Disrupting both visual and narrative logic, *Demonlover*'s digital aesthetics of reflections and refractions imbues the film's representations of corporate power, multinational commerce, espionage, the Internet and drugs with an intensity equal to the complexity and uncertainty of its world. Manifest in the reflective surfaces of screens and buildings, combined with the pornographic display of techno-fetishes that shape the contemporary idea of 'success' (private jets, limos and various hi-tech gadgets[1]), this intense spatiality sets the film's visual tone from the beginning. The opening scene in the first-class cabin on a flight from Tokyo to Paris establishes the glamour of jet-set multinational commerce and the cut-throat competitiveness of its players. How high the stakes are becomes evident when the main character Diane (Connie Nielsen) secretly tranquilizes Karen (Dominique Reymond), her immediate superior at the powerful conglomerate VolfGroup. After landing, Karen is kidnapped and thrown into the trunk of her sexy jet-black sports car by two young men. Quickly promoted to Karen's position by Volf (Jean-Baptiste Malartre), the director of the VolfGroup, Diane is revealed as a corporate spy, reporting to one of the VolfGroup's main competitors, an Internet company Mangatronics. At this point, the narrative suggests a Hitchcockian thriller, its action spreading along the complicated web of global commerce and espionage. Here, though, we may begin to see how Assayas undertakes to 'blow the whole thing up'.

He lets the intensity of the urban spatial aesthetics and the affective dynamics generated by the competing corporations and the pervasiveness of digital communication technologies direct the characters' actions. The film follows Diane as she attempts to sabotage VolfGroup's success in the acquisition of the exclusive rights to TokyoAnimé's revolutionary pornographic 3D mangas for the Internet. Her efforts to destroy VolfGroup are threatened when a U.S. Internet company, Demonlover, wants to join Volf as his conglomerate takes over the multinational distribution of the Internet porn. Mangatronics therefore orders Diane to torpedo Demonlover. Diane's investigation into the company reveals a connection between Demonlover and 'The Hellfire Club', an interactive porn and torture Web site. While apparently in complete control, her investigation places her in jeopardy. Suddenly made vulnerable, Diane is eventually completely subordinated, and ends up in thrall to 'The Hellfire Club'. Once Diane's status is in decline, the narrative continuity disperses and the causal logic breaks up, thus subordinating the narrative flow to the aesthetic and affective dynamics that shape it.

This narrative is, like the corporate hierarchies of power, mobile, and its players, the characters, are depersonalized to the point of being interchangeable. Like virtual capital, both characters and imagery circulate according to the whims of the market, the control and power governing them similarly decentred and faceless, abstract and fluid. This dislocation of the characters' power, affect and desire[2] generates intervals in the signifying process and constructs several overlapping threads of narrative, which become discernible only as the movie progresses, or upon second viewing. One such instance is the case of Elise (Chloë Sevigny), Karen's secretary, who becomes Diane's secretary when Diane takes over Karen's position at VolfGroup. Later in the film, it appears as if Elise, and not Diane, replaced Karen. Elise eventually takes over Diane's corporate position and Diane becomes *her* secretary. Hervé (Charles Berling), once Diane's colleague at VolfGroup and her lover, turns out to be working for Elise as well. By the film's end, Diane has been completely absorbed by the 'The Hellfire Club'. The final image of her is the one we see lingering on a computer screen, looking out at us from within 'The Hellfire Club' website, as if pleading for the restoration of her bodily materiality. This loss of materiality is correlative with the reconfigured sense of individuality and subjectivity that has been shaped by corporate power networks. *Demonlover* thus reveals the transformative power of transnational capitalism, which is capable of simultaneously reconfiguring both affective and spatio-temporal economies.

*Demonlover's* digital aesthetics reproduces the complex and disorienting spatiality, temporality and affectivity of a world governed by the logic of transnational capital. It is an aesthetic of *affect*, which *dislocates*[3] the human body onto the abstract urban space of contemporary transnational capitalism. I suggest that in the context of *Demonlover*, this dislocation of affect generates a different form and placement of spectatorial attention and corporeal sensitivity that focuses on and responds to the dynamic *interrelatedness* of the body with a spatial aesthetics. This dynamic relationship of the body to a spatial aesthetics emerges less from the cinematic use of digital effects than from the cultural assimilation of digital technology.

Assayas represents this dynamic interrelatedness of the corporeal and spatial through an optical and acoustical exploration of the process of transformations of urban space that is more sensual than cognitive, and generated by the pervasiveness of digital technology. In order to represent this process and the challenges it poses to conventional forms of spectatorial attention, the director uses aesthetic strategies borrowed from computer-generated imaging and experimental cinema. The non-linear narrative, abstract images of reflective glass surfaces and façades of postmodern architecture, intervals created by a black screen or blurred focus on supermodern urban neon designs, video-game-like action sequences and a meticulously crafted and eerie sound design by *Sonic Youth*, all generate a new kind of spectatorial experience that emphasizes corporeality and the *haptic* instead of conventionally predominant optic apprehension. Indeed, the expansive quality of the sound and music reverberating 'through' the images, stretching them or giving them a pulsating electric quality, contributes greatly to the creation of the haptic sensation. Assayas's cinematic strategies thus reveal the haptic not only as corporeal sensitivity but also as a new form of attention, appropriate to the orientation and apprehension of supermodern urban environments such as Tokyo, Paris and Los Angeles. The spaces of these environments are reflected in and absorbed by digital technology, represented by different kinds of screens and monitoring devices: computer screens, surveillance screens, large outdoor screens constituting a part of the architectural design and various hi-tech devices, from elaborate cellphones to microchips used for spying, as well as the standard electronic equipment used in corporate offices.

The dislocation and spatialization of affect in *Demonlover* is illuminated by the concept of affect developed by Gilles Deleuze. Deleuze's understanding of affect[4] is influenced by his collaborations with Félix Guattari, as well as by Baruch Spinoza's *Ethics*,[5] and, most prominently, by Henri Bergson's definition of affect as 'a motor tendency on a sensitive nerve', or 'a series of micro-movements on an immobilized plate of nerve' (Deleuze, 1986, p. 87). Such affect comes into effect 'when a part of the body has to sacrifice most of its motoricity in order to become the support for organs of reception', like the eye (Deleuze, 1986, p. 87). The moving body thus loses its movement of extension, and its movement becomes primarily the intensive movement of expression. These 'tendencies to movement or micro-movements ... are capable of entering into intensive series, for a single organ or from one organ to another' (Deleuze, 1986, p. 87). According to Deleuze, 'this combination of a reflecting, immobile unity and of intensive expressive movements' is what constitutes affect (1986, p. 87). For him, the paradigmatic instance is the face, which is itself a form of affect, an 'affection-image'.[6] Thus Deleuze suggests that 'each time we discover these two poles in something – reflecting surface and intensive micro-movements – we can say that this thing has been treated as a face (visage): it has been "envisaged" or "faceified" (*visageifiée*) and in turn stares at us (*devisagé*), it looks at us ... even if it does not resemble a face' (1986, p. 87). In this regard, we could consider a screen envisaged as affect, as the face or expression of micro-pulsating image(s) on a receptive immobile surface. This quality of reflecting and reflected unity – the visage/façade that is itself affect – is an intrinsic part of the surfaces of *Demonlover's* super-modern architectural design and the pulsating rhythm of its urban environment, both permeated by digital technology. Using Deleuze's conceptualization of affect, I consider its consequences in relation to the dynamics of *Demonlover* to the affective 'inside'/'outside', both of the screen and of the filmic spaces determined by electronic technology.

Assayas's film visualizes the interrelatedness of the body and contemporary spatial aesthetics as an increased *fluidity* between the 'inside' (characters occupying the space 'behind' the screen) of its computer-generated images and the 'outside' (characters occupying the space 'in front of' the screen), as well as the *absorption* of the 'outside' by the 'inside' and vice versa. This reversibility of the of 'inside' and 'outside' constitutes the elementary dynamics of the interrelatedness of body and spatiality, not only in instances in the film when digital technology is directly represented, such as in the visible presence of electronic screens, but also in the characters' everyday activities, such as riding the metro or driving a car. For example, when Diane rides the metro to meet her boss from Mangatronics, the scene ends with the camera focusing on the glass surface of the train window, rhythmically passing by the underground walls and stations, and then blurring them once the metro speeds up. As the image becomes increasingly abstract, superimposed coloured lights indicating fast movement, the spectator's attention shifts from predominantly visual recognition to haptic sensation, indicating a reorientation of the senses from primarily outward (visual) to primarily inward (feeling and sensation). To a great degree, this awakening of haptic sensation is also achieved with the amplified soundtrack created by *Sonic Youth*: the reverberating, screechy ambient sounds of the metro layered with screams from 'The Hellfire Club', which features only later in the story, and where Diane is ultimately imprisoned. Although these screams may not be immediately recognizable, the thickness of the soundscape, the speeding of the metro, the blurriness of the image superimposed with Diane's face, create a sense that she inhabits multiple places simultaneously: she is sitting in the train, seemingly in control of her actions, while money is being wired to her Swiss bank account, yet her subjectivity and her body are simultaneously being enveloped within another spatial layer in the electronic domain, 'The Hellfire Club'. At this point in the film, this layer is not visible; it is only sensible as an overall spatio-temporal affect. However, although immaterial, it nonetheless thickens into a very hermetic, fishbowl-like space, foreshadowing Diane's electronic imprisonment. Diane's embodied present is therefore already engulfed by this invisible, yet sensible presence of her dematerialized future 'behind' the computer screen: her present, past and future are being absorbed by and reflective of one another, just as the façades, glass surfaces and computer screens in her physical environment form multiple spatial layers, dispersing her embodied subjectivity into a series of spatially disjunctive images.

This fluid spatial dynamics generates an aesthetic strategy of multiplications and reflections through which a character is simultaneously framed by the film camera, surveillance camera, computer screen, or reflected and distorted by the multiple glass surfaces of postmodern architectural design. This *multiple framing and imaging* disperses the character's physical presence, which results in the *phenomenology of affect being expressed in and as its spatial counterpart*: the body absorbs and is absorbed by spatiality, and the intensities and locations of body and space become interchangeable. As Diane rides the metro, leaning into the seat, the glass surface of the train windows reflects the fast-paced, rhythmically pulsating light on her body and face: the micro-movements of the pulsating rhythmic movements of the train windows are reflected on her immobile body and face, which then dissolve into the abstract colours on the windows. Not only is Diane's face an affective surface, so are her body and the train windows. In other words, the *dynamics of extension and expression are dislocated*: the body sometimes loses its motor agency and becomes purely expressive, or intensive, as the space with which it has commerce – in this case the train windows – gains the capacity for the movement of extension. At the same time, the visible constituents of that space, such as architecture designed with multiple electronic screens, are reflective, also immobile, and yet intensely expressive. These spatializing properties facilitate the multi-layered dialectics of a new affective dynamics. Here, affect is dislocated from its traditional referential network centred in the human body and subjectivity onto the aesthetic intensification of space.

By varying and multiplying the body/space dynamics described above, *Demonlover* creates an *excess of space* (Augé, 1995) to constitute a diegesis whose dominant signifying aspect relies on the *non-linguistic*[7] and affective plasticity of its images and aesthetically exploits the contemporary cultural assimilation of the digital. Indeed, I suggest that it is precisely by exploring the modalities of the processes of spatialization as visualized by contemporary films such as *Demonlover* that we can understand the workings of the novel digital imagination that permeates our contemporary culture.

*Demonlover* unfolds in the contemporary space of supermodernity, which Marc Augé characterizes through three *figures of excess*: the overabundance of events, spatial overabundance and the individualization of references (1995, pp. 21–41). In relation to the first figure – the overabundance of events – Augé suggests that the contemporary world makes it difficult for us to apprehend the *whole* of the present or the recent past in its entirety. In the context of *Demonlover's* multiple narrative layers it is very apparent that Diane only imagines having control over events and their causality, when in fact she has none. Despite the action-packed storyline, her conscious activity and physical movement do not have an actual effect – everything she does is already pre-orchestrated by invisible powers. Failing to comprehend or influence the events, Diane is eventually subjugated to their course, effectively 'containing' her subjectivity. Although her face functions as an image of affect, a display of (in)tense expression, less of (e)motion, this intensity pulsates within and without. Most of the time her only relation to other characters is in competition. Thus her 'display' screens the affect absorbed from the contemporary corporate environment, dominated by electronic devices and a disassociated social order that determine its disjunctive temporality and spatiality. *Demonlover* shows how the intensity of such 'contained' affect of the digitally mediated transnational corporate environments, continuously generating and multiplying events, disrupts (the illusion of having) the capacity to apprehend such an overabundance of events as 'whole'.

Augé also suggests that the overabundance of coexistent events creates an *excess of time*, which in *Demonlover's* narrative manifests itself in temporally discrete narrative units (scenes), punctuated by *interval*s (black screen), as well as a dispersed temporality, which, in Vivian Sobchack's analysis of electronic presence, 'finds resolution not in the intelligibility of narrative coherence or in the stream of interior consciousness that used to temporally cohere as one's subjective identity but rather in a literal network of instants and instances' (2004, pp. 155–6). Thus Assayas's film explores the processes by which cognitive apprehension of constancy or 'the whole' is replaced by a discontinuous network of instants and instances. In order to represent these processes, Assayas employs the aesthetics of the digital and its spatializing properties, which he cinematically represents through the use of the interval interwoven with the 'ludologics' of repetition borrowed from video games. One such instance is a scene at a hotel in Paris, where Elaine (Gina Gershon), a Demonlover representative from the U.S., finds Diane spying in her room. There is a violent and bloody confrontation between the two women, who end their fight in the adjacent janitorial room. Diane seemingly asphyxiates her opponent with a pillow and exits the janitorial room. When she returns, however, there's no body there. Suddenly, Elaine appears behind the door and attacks Diane. Ultimately, both women are shown bloody and unconscious. A black screen, the interval, follows. The next scene shows Diane waking up on the hotel room floor. She checks out the janitorial room where the confrontation took place the night before: it is spotless. The rhythm and aesthetics of this sequence are very similar to those of video games in which animated characters have to move through different spatial and game levels that repeat as long as the characters get defeated. After a character gets killed, the game ends with a black screen and then reloads for the character to continue unharmed where it had previously been shot down. The black screen – the interval – operates as game software rebooting and marks the potential for a repetitive loop, signifying an interruption.

Nonetheless, the intervals also have a *connective* function, acting, in Deleuze's words, as 'a membrane which puts an outside and an inside into contact, makes them present to each other, confronts them or makes them clash' (1989, p. 206). An example occurs in a rainy night scene, when Elise confronts Diane with a pistol as the latter enters her car. Within the car, they can barely see out the wet windshield, which reflects the coloured pulsations of the streetlights from within the car; in an oscillation, we see the lights reflected on the car windows from the outside, with the faint contours of their bodies behind the blurry wetness of the glass. Both of these abstract intervals punctuate the grounded spatiality and the linear flow of temporality with the potential for reiteration and multiplicity.

Such reiteration and multiplicity produce Augé's excess of time. One of the consequences of this excess, here generated by the interval, is a shift in our sense of the relation between subjective and objective time. As Vivian Sobchack describes it, 'While our sense of subjective time has retained its modernist nonlinear structure, our sense of objective time has been reconstituted from its previous constancy of streaming forward in a linear progression into a nonlinear and discontinuous structure that is, to a great degree, now homologous with the nonlinear and discontinuous structure of subjective time' (2004, p. 156). This homology allows the parameters of the subjective 'inside' and objective 'outside' to become fluid and interchangeable, creating a sense of an excessive and unbounded space.

Augé's second figure – spatial abundance – results not only from this transformation of temporality, but also from changes in scale, from the shifting of objective spatial parameters, which is visibly manifested in the multitude of screens, electronic spaces (such as the Internet), reflecting architectural surfaces, as well as contemporary means of transit and transitory places (airports, hotels, corporate offices, bars), all of them constituting what Augé calls the *non-places* of supermodernity[8] that dislocate the common socially referential framework. These non-places lack the capacity to sustain any organic social life and thus an individual's capacity to constitute and referentially place herself as part of a collective.

Finally we come to Augé's third figure – individualization of references. As Augé puts it, 'Never before have individual histories been so explicitly affected by collective history, but never before, either, have the reference points for collective identification been so unstable'

(1995, p. 37). *Demonlover* reveals the loss of such reference points for collective identity in the corporate world from the very beginning, when Diane makes sure Karen is out of the game, and takes her position. The film then proceeds to show the arrangements of corporate relationships through its focus on shifting individual alliances and hierarchies of power. Clearly, *Demonlover* reveals the characters' individualism to be dictated by the profit-making structure of the large corporations, driven solely by ruthless, individualistic competitiveness. The individual worlds of each character differ greatly from one another, and yet are simultaneously interdependent and dictated by the laws of globally circulating corporate capital. These economic dictates are characterized by digitized communications technologies, which atomize analogue information 'into discrete pixels and bits of information that are then transmitted serially, each bit discontinuous, discontiguous, and absolute – each bit "being-in-itself" even as it is a part of a system' (Sobchack, 2004, p. 153). The characters in *Demonlover* absorb and are restructured by this digitally characterized communications network, which is reflected in the absence of the collective reference points in the corporate world. As the reference points for collective identification have disappeared, so dissolves individuality: Diane's individuality ends up dispersed and multiplied into images simultaneously coexisting in heterogeneous layers of social and psychic space. In one scene Elise even reveals that Diane's identity is forged, although she doesn't reveal who she actually is, because at this point, her discrete identity has no significance. This is because Diane's individual presence has been refracted into a multiplicity of presences, which belong to diverse, although coexistent, social and power relations: she has replaced Karen as Volf's executive assistant while spying for Mangatronics, then she transforms into Elise's subordinate, becomes Hervé's lover and eventually his murderer, then turns into a faceless, drugged woman tortured in the placeless underground of 'The Hellfire Club' and finally turns into nothing more than an image behind the screen (in the computer software). Diane's multiple and reflexive presences are reflective of the electronic iterative process constituted by a series of discrete bits, which in *Demonlover* translates into a series of 'this, and this, and this'. In other words, the functions and the signifying referential network of Diane's bodily and subjective presence are fragmented and iterated and ultimately dematerialized into a solely electronic presence.

Sobchack describes 'electronic presence' as a dispersal[9] across a network, 'its kinetic gestures describing and lighting on the surface of the screen rather than inscribing it with bodily dimension', so that 'all surface, electronic space cannot be inhabited by any body that is not also an electronic body' (2004, p. 159). This logic of a culturally pervasive electronic presence describes the logic of Diane's physical presence, in which the 'outside' is absorbed by the body and then reflected back onto and dispersed in (dislocated on) surrounding space. Diane's subjectivity is therefore like Sobchack's electronic subject, 'at once decentred, dispersed and completely extroverted' (2004, p. 159). This dispersal and display suggest the erasure of what Sobchack describes as 'the modernist (and cinematic) dialectic between inside and outside and its synthesis of discontinuous time and discontiguous space in the coherence of conscious and embodied experience' (2004, p. 159). Electronic presence thus doesn't allow for the coherence of conscious and embodied experience. According to Sobchack, and as problematized by Assayas's film, this lack of coherence is foregrounded in and through a 'self-conscious representational process that is absent in the majority of mainstream uses of electronic technologies' (2004, p. 160). *Demonlover's* nonlinear diegesis highlights the processes of the dematerialization of embodied experience, although, simultaneously, its director attempts to imagine and recreate the phenomenology of this very experience. By exploring and enacting the process of active embodied consciousness and imagination, he creates an account of sensory experience as it is dematerializing and, as Sobchack puts it, the 'fleshly presence of the human body and the dimensions of that body's material world' are being diffused (2004, p. 161).

If electronic presence doesn't allow consciousness and embodiment to cohere and causes their dispersal and diffusion, we need to describe this process whereby materiality becomes more soluble. This 'liquid' or 'gaseous'[10] materiality is characterized by a multitude of micro spaces/intervals, which challenge perception to attune itself to the microdynamics between the subjective 'inside' and objective 'outside' and lead to the development of a 'new sensorium'. Fredric Jameson asserts this new production of the senses privileges sight as the supreme sense (1997). However, as I have already suggested, this 'new sensorium', accentuating the spatial and its fluid dynamics of 'inside'/'outside', emphasizes the haptic. The latter is not primarily visual, but relies on corporeal sensitivity, the acoustic and the affective. On the one hand, this new sensorium 'replicates the specializations and divisions of capitalist life at the same time that it seeks in precisely such fragmentation a desperate Utopian compensation for them' (Jameson, 1997, p. 7), while on the other hand, this new sensorium allows for elements of chance and difference to enter the interval and produce new variations of the dynamics between the visible and the sensible, as well as produce new forms of affect.[11]

Foregrounding the film's spatial aesthetics instead of its narrative logic, *Demonlover*'s cinematographer (Denis Lenoir) elicits these new variations of the visible and the sensible with digitally mastered sped-up dissolves, close-ups of reflective glass surfaces and computer screens and black-screen intervals; against the multilayered sound, this non-representational visual aesthetics creates assemblages of multiple and heterogeneous presences (colour, sound, rhythm and motion) and spaces (screen surfaces), generating affect. Itself an affect, the cinema screen is furthermore reiterated as computer screens, larger than life-sized multiple screens in the Tokyo nightclub, the windows of the underground train, car windows, a glass elevator cage, reflective glass surfaces in the hotels and corporate offices and the black screen inserted between certain scenes of the film. The reflexive and absorbent qualities of the various sizes of these affective screen surfaces reproduce multiple layers of affect, representing new variations of the dynamics between the visible and the sensible.

In the context of digital technology, the interval becomes crucial to these dynamics; it creates a pulsation, generating a series of discrete micro-movements, which are reflected onto the immobile surface of a screen. These reflected micro-movements are expressive, rather than projective or extensive. Their expressive pulsations generate affect. The displayed affect is dispersed and extroverted, yet still expressive. This expressiveness is contained in the interval's pulsation, creating pockets of intensification, keeping affect in its dislocated place. Furthermore, this dialectic between the *containment* and simultaneous *dispersal* of electronically generated affect results in the intensification of the surface (of the screen, façade, skin), provoking an experience of the corporeal as depthless, insubstantial and dispersed 'across a network or a web' (Sobchack, 2004, p. 154), which dissolves the stable ground of embodied experience.

Understanding this particular process of *dematerialized presence* and *dislocated affect* is vital to the contemporary analysis of culture, its artefacts and its hermeneutics.[12] A fluid assemblage of interrelated elements – the presence of a physical body, an electronic device and an interval – transpires through the interstitial containment and simultaneous dispersal of electronically generated affect. Such an instance occurs when Diane, Hervé and their Japanese business partners go to a Tokyo nightclub. The interior of the bar pulsates with loud techno-rave music, a laser lightshow, intervals of darkness, human bodies, all parcelled into different spaces by stages enveloped by large screens filled with various imagery. There are live performers dancing on the stage, merging into the trance-inducing 'electronica' soundscape and the background images flowing on the screen. Their bodies are absorbed into the screen, to the point that the inorganic extensive movements of screens, lights and sound and the organic mass of physical bodies in front of it become indistinguishable micro-pulsations of the electronically configured environment. This merging of the physical bodies into the electronic environment and vice versa triggers the process of dematerialized yet highly sensitized presence, while the intensive micro-pulsating electronic vibrations on the bodily surface generate dislocation of affect. Affect is dislocated from its traditional reference to and centre in the human body and subjectivity onto the aesthetic intensification of space. This scene shows Assayas intentionally exploring the reflexive and absorptive qualities of the body and screen surface so as to spatialize affect. This spatial intensification of affect is enabled by the interval, which punctuates both the merging of physical bodies into electronic environment and the electronic micro-pulsations on the intensive bodies.

In the context of digital culture, the interval (sometimes described as an interstice) is thus the *space of oscillation* between the micro-movements of reflection, projection and absorption, and the expressive surface of the screen. As a space of multiple impulsions, the interval therefore creates not only the previously analysed dynamic of *affective interrelatedness* of the body and spatial environment but also the new spatial aesthetics emergent from the cultural assimilation of digital technology. This affective interrelatedness conceptually bifurcates into a *process of dematerialization* – when affect is dispersed 'outside', bodily awareness is abstracted – and into *affect*, as a specific kind of embodied, sensory experience that stimulates consciousness into corporeal awareness. These are not two separate movements; they palpitate simultaneously and digital technology both generates and emphasizes their operation. Thus, I suggest, although there is definitely a significant tendency towards the dematerialization of the body, there is also a counter-reaction in the simultaneous emergence of an increased awareness of how our senses are engaged, as the latter become more and more critical to our orientation and appropriate responsiveness to our environment.

Assayas thus problematizes the dematerialization of presence by emphasizing the aesthetic intensification of spatiality as it affectively interrelates with the corporeal and sensitizes it for an internal haptic rather than external visual apprehension. This modifies our understanding of how individual and collective interrelate as 'entities' within the 'whole' as a spatio-temporal entirety. The cultural assimilation of digital technology is effacing experiential differentiation between the subjective 'inside' and objective 'outside'. As the 'outside' becomes homologous with the non-linear and discontinuous structure of subjective experience, the boundaries between the 'outside' and 'inside' become more porous. Assayas cinematographically represents this porosity by emphasizing the interval, the space 'in-between'. This means that the experience of the 'whole' is displaced from being an objective 'outside' experienced by a subjective 'inside' to a subjectively and affectively inflected interval.

This 'in-between' disallows a purely cinematic dialectics of the 'inside' and 'outside' to cohere on the (unitary) screen as conscious and embodied experience. Such non-coherence emerges from an aesthetics that highlights sensual experience by dispersing the signifying and unifying power of the purely optic. Instead, that power is given to the interval as a site constitutive of the contemporary digital imagination in a process characterized by spatialization *as* interval, where 'excess' connotes an intensity of expression as affect. The interstitial space of the interval thus generates difference precisely because it forces the visual to a halt and engages the a-signifying, yet significant experience of the sensual and the felt.

## Acknowledgements

I want to thank Professor Vivian Sobchack for helping me learn how to express my ideas and demonstrating a true academic generosity of spirit. I also want to thank Marc Furstenau for his precise and insightful editorial comments, which inspired me and enriched this essay.

## Notes

1. Jason Shawhan (2005) describes these and other such elements as the objects of a 'porn of success', in his review of *Demonlover*.
2. *Demonlover* masterfully represents the varied dynamics of power, affection and desire, where, as Gilles Deleuze notes in his essay 'Désir et plaisir', 'le pouvoir est une affection du désir' (1994, p. 62). That is, 'power is the *affectio* of the encounter between two (or more) bodies, whether collective or individual' (Seigworth, 2005, p. 166).
3. Abbas Akbar defines the difference between displacement and dislocation in his book *Hong Kong: Culture and the Politics of Disappearance*: '[I]nstead of thinking in terms of displacements, a movement somewhere else, it is important to think in terms of dislocation, which is the transformation of place. Such transformations, even after they have taken place, are often indiscernible and hence challenge recognition. That is why cultural survival is also a matter of changing the forms of attention and seeing the importance of even decadent or degenerate cultural objects' (Akbar, 1997, p. 146).

4. There is ample literature available that draws from and critiques Deleuze's application of the Bergsonian concept of affect. I will only mention two authors who engage in such a dialogue in the context of recently published studies on film and visual culture: Brian Massumi in his book *Parables for the Virtual* (2002) and Mark Hansen in his *New Philosophy for New Media* (2004). There are many authors who productively contextualize Deleuze's conceptual apparatus, such as David Rodowick in *Gilles Deleuze's Time Machine* (1997), Ronald Bogue in *Deleuze on Cinema* (2003), Charles J. Stivale in *Gilles Deleuze: Key Concepts* (2005) and Gregory Flaxman in *The Brain Is The Screen* (2000).
5. Gregory J. Seigworth very astutely points out the way Deleuze's study of Spinoza's *Ethics* in his *Expressionism in Philosophy* (Deleuze, 1990) influenced his understanding of affect. Namely, the translation of *Ethics* conflates Spinoza's distinction of *affectio* (or affection as 'the state of a body in as much it affects or is affected by another body'), *affectus* ('a body's continuous, intensive variation (as increase-diminution) in its capacity for acting'), affect as soul and, finally, a 'multitudinous affectivity beyond number (a plane of immanence)' (pp. 160–2). Deleuze (and Guattari) build upon all these notions of affect, which seem to firmly ground it in the body and therefore complicate Mark Hansen's otherwise excellent critique of Deleuze's concept of affect, where he states that 'active affection or affectivity is precisely what differentiates today's sensori-motor body from the one Deleuze hastily dismisses' (2004, pp. 7–8). It may be productive to read Deleuze's use of Bergson in light of his indebtedness to Spinoza's understanding of affect. Deleuze's apparent dismissal of the body (and thus the disembodiment of affect in cinema) is due to his omission of explaining what Vivian Sobchack directly addresses as the *transcendent* (not transcendental) space that 'exceeds the individual body', yet is 'concretely inhabited and *intersubjective*', and 'indirectly taken from and as existential experience' (1992, pp. 25, 295).
6. Deleuze discusses affect in *Cinema 1*, in the chapter on 'affection-image'. See Deleuze, 1986.
7. In *Cinema 2*, Deleuze defines 'movement-image' outside a language system: 'It is a plastic mass, an a-signifying and a-syntaxic material, a material not formed linguistically even though it is not amorphous and is formed semiotically, aesthetically and pragmatically' (Deleuze, 1989, p. 29).
8. In the context of cinema Deleuze uses the term *any-space-whatever* (*éspace quelconque*), which he borrows from Pascal Augé. According to Deleuze, any-space-whatever has two states: it is a space that is 'defined by parts whose linking up and orientation are not determined in advance, and can be done in infinite number of ways' (here we must think of the Internet). In *Demonlover*, this aspect of any-space-whatever is represented by the corporate offices, hotel lobbies and rooms, airports, airplanes, trains, cars and the cellar in a suburban villa of 'The Hellfire Club'. Another state of any-space-whatever figures as 'an amorphous set which has eliminated that which happened and acted in it', such as in the video game-like sequence in which Diane fights with Elaine, kills her and then wakes up in a hotel room only to discover no trace of their bloody encounter. Also acting as any-space-whatever are computer displays of torture scenes, pornographic animé or scenes in the desert of Mexico. Although marked 'as pure locus of the possible' any-space-whatever still reflects 'a preexistent analogy between the

human experience of space and the cinematic any-space-whatever. It is precisely such a preexistent analogical basis that is missing in the case of the digital ASW' (Hansen, 2004, pp. 208–9). The interplay between the cinematic and the digital any-space-whatever in *Demonlover* is key to its operations of de-materialized presence and dislocated affect.
9. Sobchack's concept of 'dispersal' in the context of electronic (digital) technology corresponds to Akbar's concept of 'dislocation' in terms of cultural transformations of place. Just as the cultural pervasiveness of digital aesthetics of affect dislocates the human body onto urban space, the embodied presence can be dislocated onto electronic space (similarly to Diane's subjectivity, ultimately dematerialized into an electronic presence).
10. Deleuze discusses 'liquid' and 'gaseous' perception in *Cinema 1*, in the chapter on the 'Perception-Image.' See Deleuze, 1986.
11. Assayas aims to surpass conventional representation in order to engage the spectator's non-representational thinking, which allows for the birth of 'difference'. According to Deleuze, difference cannot be conceptualized within the dominant 'image of thought' defined in terms of thinking in representations, characterized by four aspects: identity, opposition, analogy and resemblance. Difference, therefore, becomes 'an object of representation always in relation to a conceived identity, a judged analogy, an imagined opposition or a perceived similitude'. Just like the conventional narrative, this 'image of thought' is thus restrictive, 'because it doesn't allow thinking to occur unless there is something with which we can compare' (Pisters, 2003, p. 6). An alternative would be *rhizomatic* thinking, such as in *Demonlover*'s spatially and temporally disjunctive narrative, which doesn't acknowledge hierarchies, beginnings and endings, segmental and oppositional divisions. This kind of thinking implies thinking in *assemblages*, in which heterogeneous aspects come together. It also implies thinking in different terms than those to which we are accustomed, like affect and interval.
12. An example of the latest advance in imaging technologies is a 3D animated model able to reflect a live actor's most sophisticated facial expressions without using motion capture technology. The 3D model thus acts as an avatar possessing, according to a *New York Times* article, 'something more subtle, more ineffable, something that seems to go beneath the skin', imbuing the animated model with the 'soul of the actor'. Indeed, as the *New York Times* writer observes, 'the virtual woman actually seems to have adopted the actress personality, resembling her in ways that go beyond pursed lips or knitted brow' (Waxman, 2006). Exploring the processes of dislocated affect and dematerialized presence thus proves essential not only in terms of the different modes of production of images, but also of the (re)production and multiplication of the world at large.

# 9
# 'Into the décor': Attention and Distraction, Foreground and Background

*Christopher Rodrigues*

The relationship between technologies and film meaning, particularly as they concern the rendering of reality, has been a perennial theme in explanations of how cinema functions, how it exerts its fascination on us. In the new digital world, where an enhanced 'reality' or hyperreality is readily available, it might seem that a qualitatively new ontology of the cinematic image prevails, that in a sense there is an absolute transparency between means and meaning, techné and poesis, that the terms of debate and discussion have been resolved or at least swallowed up in a plenitude of reality. But I want to suggest in this chapter that what Tom Gunning has called the 'excess of mimesis over meaning' (1991, p. 17), the overbearing 'dominance of showing over telling', is ever-present whatever the technological apparatus might consist of, however beguiling the verisimilitude. And this 'dominance of showing' has the potential, in its technological embodiment, to be precisely that – a 'showing off', an instrument for destabilizing and setting in crisis a whole series of narrative and perceptual codes. Eileen Bowser, for example, indicates how the revival of interest in double exposure in 1912 was allied to a greater complexity in narrative form. Double exposure was 'admired by the viewers for its cleverness. Such uses of the device departed from the notion that a double exposure is more "realistic" because less disruptive of the narrative flow than a cut to another scene; on the contrary, the device was now calling attention to itself, breaking the illusion that the screen represents reality' (Bowser, 1990, p. 248). The cinema of attractions can become a cinema of distractions.

I want to pursue this line of thought tangentially by focussing on ways in which certain film-makers, through reflections on different technologies, have explored the tension between background and foreground, between attention and distraction, and in this play have exemplified and reproduced the complex structures of perception themselves. Crucially, each of the chosen film-makers – Jean-Marie Straub/Danièle Huillet, Jean-Luc Godard, Atom Egoyan, Eric Rohmer, Raul Ruiz – have incorporated a distinctive approach to a technology (film, television, home video, digital). The concentration on the more experimental end of film-making is deliberate: it is here that we often find a curiosity about and a willingness to look around the corners of new technologies and techniques.

But the art/experimental cinema bias in this chapter should not preclude us from examining how mainstream film-makers also play on the tension between background and foreground, attention and distraction. To choose an obvious example, Hitchcock, and his deliberately maladroit use of back-projection embodying the duplicity of the narrative, could be seen as akin to what Peter Wollen called the hyperbolic 'misuse of existing technology, its use to transgress the norms implicit in it' (1980, p. 20).

It will be necessary to revisit some earlier theories, ideas about the nature of film and the cinematic experience in particular as they are focussed on ways of formulating the address to the viewer. One set of theories belong basically to notions about the *mise-en-scène* (processes controlled by the film-maker) and the other set of theories about how the spectator is constructed in the screen axis. Somewhat schematically I'm going to arrange these preoccupations into two tropes, one around *background*, the other around *distraction*. These two tropes clearly coalesce and merge: they can be articulated in the proposition that it is in the play between foreground and background that viewers notice things; that they are distracted or, on the contrary, pay attention to phenomena that are relevant or irrelevant to the process of understanding the particular film or sequence of film under consideration. In general, what is irrelevant is most commonly relegated to the 'background', while what is key to the narrative or plot, or to the characters' psychological development and so on, is foregrounded, in other words differentiated from the background.

Perhaps surprisingly – given the amount of recent historical work on researching what audiences carry away with them in terms of sense impressions and memories – little theoretical attention has been paid in film studies to the function of background and the way in which backgrounds can serve a distractive function in the film-viewing experience. It is as if we are convinced that in the hierarchy of information that a viewer is subjected to, there is rarely any dispute as to which is the preferred or dominant reading. But we know from contemporary accounts of the screenings of the early Lumière films that audiences were often more fascinated by the 'irrelevant' – the movement of leaves on a tree – than on the ostensible focus of their attention, the main narrative or event. In addition, ever since the pioneering work of Nöel Burch on early cinema we are aware of the decentred spatial and narrative dimension of the screen frame, how over ten or so years films by Porter, Billy Bitzer (*Tom, Tom The Piper's Son, The Kentucky Feuds*) and others promoted 'a sort of panoramic view – an acentric, "non-directive" image leaving the eye more or less 'free' to roam over the entire frame and to organize the signifiers as it will (at best it can); an image, moreover, in which the presence of the characters never predominates over their environment, but is invariably inscribed within it' (Burch, 1978, p. 96). Lynne Kirby provides another example of the way in which early subgenre of 'Subway' films around 1916 demanded that the spectators themselves made sense of what was going on on the screen:

> In these films the law is shown to be powerless in an urban crowd that moves according to the mechanical rhythm of the trains and responds like nerve endings to the stimulus of constant arrivals and departures. If 'loose' behaviour is to be expected in the subway . . . It cannot be located or fixed; it moves and depends on mobility. . . As in the early rain films, its essence is that it is nonessential; it is an ephemeral representation, like the cinema itself, which draws the spectator into the search for meaning in a tangle of visual disorder.
> (1997, p. 140)

The history of dominant cinema is of course among other things one of ensuring that the viewer is, as Jacques Aumont puts it, 'never completely free when viewing an image, as his or her way of viewing an image is almost always guided by implicit or explicit reading instructions' (1994, p. 120). In spite of an exponential increase in sophisticated readings on the part of audiences, it would be astonishing if this kind of distraction or misdirected attention were not a consistent feature of film viewing. In literature the realm of the background is founded on description, the moment when, crudely put, the narrative is in stasis for a while as the surrounding scene is described (see Marin, 1994, pp. 251–66; Frogier and Poinsot, 1997). And in photography we accept now without question Barthes's distinction between the *studium* and the *punctum*, where the latter is the incidental, 'irrelevant' detail through which the viewers of the photograph can invest their meaning on the image. We are unlikely to be convinced that sequences of film could be seen as *punctums* delivering an idiosyncratic and personalized truth 24 frames a second (to misquote Godard), but then where are the moments when we are free to indulge in perverse and contrary readings? Perhaps it is only in our memories of films, given that these are embodied as stills and not moving images?

If background as information, noise, disturbance, distraction, the anonymous crowd, the architectural or landscape setting, theatrical décor or depth of field has been relatively badly served by film scholars, this is not the case with the second trope, distraction. It has had its critical recognition in Bazin's classical espousal and exposition of deep focus in *Citizen Kane* and other films, and at least as far back as the writings of Walter Benjamin and Siegfried Kracauer. Benjamin in his seminal essay of 1935, 'The Work of Art in the Age of Mechanical Reproduction', made a passing reference to the notion when he compared the distracted modern spectator with the person moving through architecture. But it is principally in Kracauer that we find the notion developed, firstly in a short essay written in 1926, 'Cult of Distraction: on Berlin's Picture Houses', and then taken up in a larger more expository formulation in his book *Theory of Film: The Redemption of Physical Reality*. The early essay was provocative and political. Beneath the apparent playfulness of the introductory remarks 'the interior design of movie theatres serves one sole purpose: to rivet the viewers' attention to the peripheral, so that they will not sink into the abyss' (Kracauer, 2005, p. 325), there is a serious argument that is being articulated: 'Here, in pure externality, the audience encounters itself; its own reality is revealed in the fragmented sequence of splendid sense impressions' (p. 326). The political force of Kracauer's paradoxical way of thinking is then revealed: 'Distraction – which is meaningful only as improvisation, as a reflection of the uncontrolled anarchy of our world' (p. 327). The radical aim is 'a kind of distraction that exposes disintegration instead of masking it' (p. 327). As Thomas Levin comments: 'In the "creative geography" of the specifically cinematic syntagm or sequence, Kracauer recognizes a staging of the relationless jumble that is the signature of modernity' (2005, p. 22). Crucially, Kracauer develops his argument in terms that are surprisingly familiar in a postmodern context. He argues, as Levin puts it, 'that the site of intelligibility which cinema constructs for its spectators is no longer that of the coherent self-identical bourgeois subject. Instead of the immersed and contemplative concentration of this now outmoded paradigm of stable subjectivity and its equally anachronistic, "stabilizing" spectacles, it is "distraction" that now becomes the defining characteristic of cinematic spectatorship. [. . .] Distraction further serves as both a lived critique of the bourgeois fiction of the coherent self-identical subject and as a barometer of mankind's alienation from itself' (p. 26).

Ian Aitken has followed this way of thinking through to its inverse, the opposite of politicized consciousness. He writes, 'the state of being distracted could, like its opposite, absorption, be reactionary in the case of films that organize the multiplicity of effects, the surface fragmentation, into a unified whole and make distraction an end in itself, which is precisely what Hollywood movies do' (1998, p. 141). Aitken emphasizes the 'particular forms of indeterminate mimesis found in film and photography' (p. 141), an indeterminacy that is not far removed from the kind of engaged visuality that Bazin promoted. Kracauer went on to develop some of his ideas adumbrated in his early essays in his now rather unfashionable book, *Theory of Film*, published in 1960. In it he proselytizes for something close to this early 'mimetic indeterminacy'. He sets out his main thesis without equivocation in the 'Introduction' as 'film is essentially an extension of photography and therefore shares with this medium a marked affinity for the visible world around us. Films come into their own when they record and reveal physical reality' (1960, p. ix). Anticipating Lynne Kirby's characterization of the subway genre, (but also recalling Benjamin's famous invocation of the explosion of cinematographic effects in the 'Work of Art' essay), he writes that the individual spectator recalls (in what is now a rather tired trope) the nineteenth-century *flâneur* 'in his susceptibility to the transient real-life phenomena that crowd the screen. [. . .] Along with the fragmentary happenings incidental to them, these phenomena – taxi cabs, buildings, passers-by, inanimate objects, faces – presumably stimulate his senses and provide him with stuff for dreaming [. . .] Through its very concern with cinema-reality, film thus permits especially the lonely spectator to fill his shrinking self – shrinking in an environment where the bare schemata of things threaten to supersede the things themselves – with images of life as such – glittering, allusive, infinite life' (1960, p. 170).

Much more recently and from a sophisticated multidisciplinary perspective, Jonathan Crary has been conducting research on the technologies and archaeologies of visuality in *Techniques of the Observer* and *Suspensions of Perception: Attention, Spectacle, and Modern Culture*. The work is particularly striking in combining insights about the construction of 'attention' as a prerequisite for the acquiring of subjective freedom in the late nineteenth century and as a process for policing the consciousness of the distracted masses. He investigates how 'vision became a kind of discipline or mode of work' and how optical devices 'were techniques for the management of attention, for imposing homogeneity, anti-nomadic procedures that fixed and isolated the spectator' (Crary, 1990, p. 18). The complex thesis of his latest book is structured 'transversally' around the case studies of a few iconic artists of modernity – Manet, Seurat, Cézanne: 'what they have in common is an engagement with a general problem of perceptual synthesis and with the interrelated binding and disintegrative possibilities of attention' (Crary, 1999, p. 9). It is not a book that can be usefully reduced to a few overarching quotations. But where it is relevant to the tentative and speculative notes of this chapter is in suggesting some methods of, firstly, going beyond the Kracauer/Benjamin notion of modern distraction and, secondly, of articulating a cinematic perception that both inhabits a rich and creative 'zone of indetermination' and makes of cinema an autonomous world. I'm going to quote at length from Crary because his analyses provide, it seems to me, a quite brilliant set of insights into how modern visuality and perception are intricately and dialectically part of the spectacle apparatuses. The work of Kracauer and others 'presumed that a distracted perception was central to any account of subjectivity within modernity' (1999, p. 48). His opposing point of view, however, 'is that modern distraction was *not* a disruption of stable or "natural" kinds of sustained, value-laden perception that had existed for centuries but was an *effect*, and in many cases a constituent element of the many attempts to produce attentiveness in human subjects' (p. 49). He uses Deleuze (and subsequently views cinema from the perspective of Cézanne's work) to confront and inhabit 'the instability of perception itself' (p. 288). He relates Manet's intuition to Cézanne's practice – 'the creative discovery that looking at any one thing intently did *not* lead to a fuller and more inclusive grasp of its presence, its rich immediacy. Rather, it lead to its perceptual disintegration and loss [. . .] breakdown was one of the conditions for the invention and discovery of previous unknown relations and organizations of forces' (p. 288). Deleuze's work is important for explaining how cinema is fundamentally distinct from previous historical forms of simulation. It isn't part of some continuous mode of representation; cinema is not about representing a world but about constituting an autonomous world 'made up of breaks and disproportion, deprived of all centres, addressing itself as such to viewers who are in themselves no longer the center of their own perception. [. . .] It is precisely the non-selectivity of the cinema eye that distinguishes it from the texture of human attentiveness. Cinema, as it took shape during the last years of Cézanne's life, is a contradictory form of synthetic unity in which rupture is also part of an unbroken flow of time, in which disjunction and continuity must be thought together' (p. 344).

I now want to ground these theoretical and historical speculations in an exploration of the work of four practitioners whose films embody and express some of these indeterminations and tensions as they are played out in the spaces between distraction and background. (I also want to refer to two other film-makers who have articulated this dilemma in more incidental ways.) In some instances these tensions turn on a self-reflexive aesthetic proposition; at other moments they are phrased in a playful or otherwise political rhetoric. In all instances, however, it is the technological means of production and representation expressly employed in the film that is the important thing. It will not be unnoticed that they could all be described as belonging to the genre or idiom of European Art Cinema.

The first two examples I propose to mention only in passing. Not because they are not worth lingering over – quite the contrary – but their exemplary status in the realm of avant-garde film-making ensures that they are well documented and extensively analysed. In *History Lessons* (1972) by Jean-Marie Straub and Danièle Huillet the movement through the environment, through the real décor of the streets of Rome, becomes the meaning of the film. The film dispenses with commonsense distinctions between foreground and background, only minimally holding on to a framing structure (what would have been the clichéd device of the rear window in clumsily put together back-projection car chases). The background is both metaphorically and literally 'foregrounded'. As Gilberto Perez comments,

> Built into the photographic image are the rectangular frame and perspective of an individual viewing point [. . .] and here our attention is called to that construction, basic to any picture, moving or still made with a camera [. . .] What appears in the picture may move and shift all it wants but the manner of picturing it stays put. [. . .] We are made conscious of the unchanging frame and the gridlike partitioning of our view: it is like watching the set pictorial scheme of a Renaissance painting carried around the city streets and applied to the diverse actualities there encountered.
> 
> (2000, 283–4)

The second film, *Passion* (1982), needs even less of an aide-memoire. Complemented by the short documentary, *Scenario of the Film Passion* (1982), which like its reference (but even more so) is a deliciously mischievous and metaphysical take on spatially and metaphorically going through (the actors colliding with the sets and other actors) 'living paintings' and film sets. Godard, his back turned to us, is superimposed on one of the sequences of his film as he reflects: 'this infinity will end when metaphor will meet up with reality. You know that the film can be made – at the crossroads between reality and metaphor, or between documentary and fiction'. The constructed aspect of the cinematic reality and illusion is explicitly highlighted by comparing it to the (real) factory environment of the film set. In *Scenario* Godard makes quite clear the diagrams of power and image manipulation as they are enforced in television broadcast protocols: 'On television the people who talk, the announcers, never face the screen. The image is always behind them, never in front. On television they never see anything because they turn their backs on the images instead of facing them. The image is behind them: they can't see it. It's the image which sees them, and it's those who manipulate the images who see them. Those who manipulate the image push the announcers up the arse. That's how you get buggered'. Patrick Fuery provides a productive Derridean gloss on *Passion* by discussing its incorporation (the corps – the body – as inversely related to the décor[1]) of the filmic 'supplement': (the way 'in which film constructs a particular type of supplement unique to itself [. . .] the idea that, rather than just representing the supplement (as dangerous or otherwise), film actually incorporates it into its own textual formations and operations' (Fuery, 2000, p. 43). Godard, he goes on to explain, demonstrates in this film 'a type of deconstruction of the impasse that had existed in [the] realist/expressionist – montage/mise-en-scène debate'. He does this by working 'in terms of montage and mise-en-scène operating together, so that neither could be attributed as supplement of the other' (Fuery, 2000, p. 44). As Jacques Aumont puts it, summing up his achievement over the past 10 years (he is referring to *France Tour Detour*), Godard's project is 'a radical training in how to look: about how, little by little, by looking more precisely one can better reveal' (1995, p. 238).

Atom Egoyan's *Calendar* (1993) is among this Canadian-Armenian's lesser-known films. The author of a monograph on his work characterizes it as his most 'most experimental – that is, aleatory – film' (Romney, 2003, p. 97). The film could be seen as a systemic investigation (however playful and at times abstruse) of the ways in which background exists in a dialectical relationship to foreground: the conceit is embodied at one level in quite a literal sense as the background is spatially occupied by Armenian churches (or in the Canadian sequences by the movement to and fro in the apartment – from a tête-à-tête at a dinner table to the telephone sitting on a water cooler adjacent to the unfolding calendar). There are other levels, narrative, symbolic, historical but also personal and autobiographical, which operate in terms of this interleaving of fore- and background: of critical importance is the interpenetration of voices and music, some understood, others translated, some left in their original Armenian. Constantly weaving in and out of the past and the future, the location and the performance, the home video format and the formal set-up shot, the wife and driver-cum-guide coming into and out of frame, interacting with the absent camera operator-cum-husband (the film director), running forwards or backwards into the shot, there is a witty set of permutations on the blurring between documentary and fictional modes. 'Who is he addressing?' asks his wife at one stage. 'Us?' The 'us' presumably refers to her and the driver. But the us could equally well be us, the audience! Or else, 'What's going on in your mind?' The 'you' is the husband but could be just as well the viewer trying to make sense of the linguistic triangle. And so on throughout the film, the conundrum, built on inherited, exiled and disjunctive spaces, is played out as if it were a postmodern minuet. The film is rich in its mediations and *re*mediations (in the sense elaborated by Bolter and Grusin (1999), the refashioning and reconfiguring of representations through different media). At the narrative core is the task of taking pictures for a calendar, but in this process the excess of reality seeps out, just like liquid through a sieve as Perez describes the movement in Straub-Huillet's *History Lessons*. And similarly, (and even more poignantly in the telluric panoramics of *Fortini-Cani*), there is history etched into the very texture and landscape of this film, not least the implicit genocide of the Armenians as viewed from exile in Canada. The child, voiceless, but one of the few in the film – the other is the old man telling us a story we cannot understand – is filmed in full shot without encumbrances of décor or distracting background. The phrase of Straub comes to mind: 'The greatness of film is the humbleness of being condemned to photography' (quoted in Perez, 2000, p. 284).

In *The Lady and the Duke* (Eric Rohmer, 2001) the scenic backdrop is literally that; but a theatrical backdrop brought to life through digitization. The trope works so well because it embodies the distance between the present and the reconstructed past of a moment in the French revolution. It establishes this as among other things a symbolic and mythic event in European culture and history: in seeing the French revolution through the perspective of an Englishwoman it merely replicates a long tradition dating at least from Charles Dickens. It establishes a disjuncture between the apparent authenticity of the verbal accounts from the journal and the facticity of the décor, the actual environment that cannot ever be recreated in its original fullness. 'Rohmer distances things in order to bring them closer to us, he distances the Revolutionary by making it unreal with the use of painted canvases [. . .] Rohmer uses new technologies in order to distance us from contemporary cinema and to bring us back to the period of silent cinema. [There is a confusion] between a cutting edge technology being used in the service of a naïve imagery' (Tesson, 2001, p. 41).

In part the visual divide between protagonists and background seems to be suggesting a mismatch between the lived experience of an individual and the more anonymous and manipulated/mythic status of the revolutionary crowds. The intrigues are recounted and take place in closeted and theatrical interior spaces, while the tapestry or backdrop of history takes place in a more pictorial urban environment and landscape. In this dramatic account of what Marc Fumaroli calls 'a phenomenology of the first modern terror', distant views and viewpoints are 'monstrously blurred, the private moment assaulted by a kind of horror of emptiness' (Fumaroli, 2001, p. 46). (There is a palpable sense of looking forward to the pleasurable visual conceit of the magical painted backdrop opening up into the actual, that reflects the diegetic pleasure that the lady has in escaping from the confines of her house. The past is contained in the décor, the present in the performance.)

When the film was released much attention was paid to the digitization. But Rohmer (with the exception of Truffaut), one of the most Bazinian of all the *nouvelle vague* film-makers, was adamant in interviews that the 'digital is simply a process which allows one to lose nothing in reproduction'. What interested him in the use of blue-screen digital technology was that it 'permitted him to enter into the décor, so that you could have perspective views, that you could go beneath porches and see people at the window'. Above all, Rohmer was insistent on the pictorial aspect of his approach to filming. 'My starting point was a painting. At the start one has the impression that it's a documentary on paintings, and then the paintings come alive. It isn't the painting which enters into reality. On the contrary it's the painting which becomes real'. The kind of truth that he is looking for is not so very differently articulated in the films of Egoyan, Godard and Straub-Huillet. The terms themselves can be transposed and refer just as pertinently to theatre or special effects as in the grand theatricality of Syberberg, and at another but equally inventive level the do-it-yourself (DIY) special effects of Raul Ruiz. 'Pictoriality (*picturalité*) is my first priority. Truth must be embedded in pictorality' (Rohmer, 2001, pp. 50–8).

Ruiz is an appropriate film-maker to end on. For in his work, especially in his middle period (for example, *Les trios couronnes du matelot*, 1983), technological invention and bricolage goes hand in hand with a curiosity about the quiddity of the real, of the pro-filmic event, whether it is occurring in the foreground or background. In endorsing what he calls the 'experimental delinquent'[2] he is celebrating the creative function of distraction and making a virtue of the 'photographic unconscious': 'tiny, inevitable breakaways configure a different type of photographic or cinematographic unconscious, produced no longer by lack of control over the images, but by an excess of control' (Ruiz, 2005, p. 59).

It's exactly the opposite of the excess of mimesis that is boasted about in the recent crop of advertisements for high-definition television sets: they are sold on the premise that reality is stunningly defined and represented so that you can see the very blade of grass on the football pitch. Here we have a flagrant example of the perversion of 'complex seeing' (and consequently of complex knowing).[3] Here we have in its technological and teleological hubris the reduction of reality to its ultimate absurdity.

## Acknowledgements

With thanks to Rod Stoneman

## Notes

1. See also Maurizia Natali, *L'image paysage: iconologie et cinéma*: 'l'image de paysage garde toujours la connotation de décor supplémentaire parce que notre imaginaire est centré narcissiquement sur les corps: notre attente du sens se focalise sur les gestes, les yeux, et sur la bouche qui parle. Dans ce régime symbolique, le plan de paysage produit une faille sensible dans notre identification aux personages. Pour quelques instants notre regard est simplement renvoyé à l'arrière-fond. [. . .] Perpétuer le paysage comme fond signifie attendre la mise en scène du corps et du regard narcissique: pour nous, spectateurs de cinema, un paysage sans personages est toujours un peu une scène vide, un fond filmé en attente' (Natali, 1996, p. 71).
2. Ruiz uses his own fetishistic experience to explain what he means: 'For years I watched so-called Greco-Latin films (toga flicks, with early Christians devoured by lions, emperors in love, and so on). My only interest in those films was to discover the eternal DC6 crossing the sky during Ben Hur's final race, Cleopatra's naval battle, or the Quo Vadis banquets' (Ruiz, 2005, p. 60).
3. For another take on how indeterminacy works in television. See Samuel Weber, *Mass Mediauras: Form, Technics, Media*: 'The reality of television [. . .] no longer follows the traditional logic and criteria of reality. It is no longer a function of identity or of its derived form: opposition. Far and near are no longer mutually exclusive but rather converge and overlap. Such convergence brings a different aspect of reality to the fore – the reality of *ambivalence*' (Weber, 1996, p. 124).

# 10
# Children, Robots, Cinephilia and Technophobia

*Bruce Bennett*

*Terminator 2: Judgment Day* (Cameron, 1991) is a film about the social and affective impact of rapid and unmanageable technological change. The plot interweaves two parallel timelines, moving between present-day Los Angeles and an apocalyptic future 40 years hence in which a 'war against the machines' rages. Glimpsed intermittently throughout the film, this speculative future world is a sunless, blasted charnel house of rubble, twisted metal and corpses, patrolled by gleaming robotic terminators, tanks and 'Hunter-Killer' aircraft. Those humans that survived 'judgment day', the nuclear strike initiated by Skynet, an unprecedentedly powerful computer defence system so sophisticated that it achieves consciousness, are driven underground into tunnels and basements. Led by John Connor, the survivors form a resistance army and are conducting a guerrilla war against the machines. It is reiterated throughout the film that 'the future is not set', and thus the scenes of the imminent war present a cautionary message about the impermanence of our social order and the dangers of integrating technology too fully into our lives, of our dehumanizing, incapacitating prosthetic dependency upon machines.

This hellish future scenario of mechanical rebellion and systematic extermination contrasts with the present-day friendship between the 13-year-old John Connor and the Terminator, one of the colossal robotic killing machines that has travelled from the future in a time machine after being re-programmed by the human resistance movement to protect its future leader. These scenes offer a romantic, optimistic counterpoint in the form of an intimate and supportive friendship between John and the Terminator whom John adopts as substitute father, playmate, bodyguard and manservant. The depth of this relationship is evidenced in John's profound distress in the film's penultimate scene, following a climactic battle in a steelworks, as the robot announces that the time has come for it to be destroyed. The distraught boy, having grown strongly attached to the machine over the course of the film, protests frantically, begging and then ordering the Terminator 'not to go', hugging it tightly as if to prevent it from leaving. However, we have seen John's development from brattish delinquent into a mature figure, conscious of his future role as a military leader, and recognizing the necessity of the machine's sacrifice, he reluctantly releases his hold. The Terminator responds compassionately, 'I know now why you cry, but it is something I can never do', and wipes a tear from John's eye before being lowered into a vat of molten steel to 'die'. The narrative's logic dictates that the Terminator's destruction is necessary to ensure that its components can't be used to develop the Skynet system that eventually precipitates the catastrophic war. Metaphorically, the development of the child/robot relationship in the film constitutes an alternative relationship with technology to the one depicted in the film's apocalyptic future in which the human race is obliterated by the machines that were designed to aid and protect us.

*Terminator 2: Judgment Day*'s production values and aesthetics exemplify contemporary cinematic technology. At the time of its release *Terminator 2: Judgment Day* was one of the most expensive films ever made, and, along with Cameron's other films, demonstrates the technical and logistic possibilities of Hollywood cinema at the end of the twentieth century. For example, the level of 'realism' achieved in the computer-generated imagery (CGI) animation used to render the metamorphosing 'T-1000' Terminator constitutes a historic landmark in special effects. The film is thus a model of a contemporary 'cinema of attractions' in which the spectatorial pleasures of shock, identificatory immersion and audio-visual spectacle are imbricated with a fascination with the film as novel, spectacular technical construction (see Gunning, 2000; Williams, 2000). It is also a film *about* our relationship with cinema technology, since the relationship between John and the Terminator represents the spectator-screen relationship wherein our interaction with screen technology is fulfilling, exciting, disconcerting and intensely moving. This chapter will explore the ways in which the child/robot relationship functions within *Terminator 2: Judgment Day* and a related series of recent science fiction films, as a means of articulating the impact of technology upon our lives and, more complexly, the relationship between the spectator and the cinema screen. I argue that the child/robot couple is a means by which Hollywood cinema represents technology in general and, more specifically, the technological character of cinema itself.

The theme of friendship between children and robots extends back beyond the inception of cinema, and if the category of robot is expanded to include the uncanny figures of clockwork automata, animated dolls, reanimated corpses, living statues, paintings and doppelgängers, the number of accounts is vast. However, while this thematic preoccupation has been explored in various media, it has a particular affective charge in relation to film because of the parallel status of the fantastic mechanical automaton and the captivating apparatus of the cinema as technological constructions.

Perhaps due to its massive commercial success, *Terminator 2: Judgment Day* is frequently invoked by subsequent playfully intertextual child/robot films and TV programmes. However, the less well-known *Star Kid* (Coto, 1997) is an equally archetypal generic model, and between them the two films plot the parameters of the comic, absurd and affecting cinematic relationship between children and robots. Adapted from a series of comics, the title announces its formulaic, generically self-aware approach to its material, and it is littered with allusions and citations from other SF films and TV programmes. *Star Kid* centres on Spencer, a rather solitary boy who happens upon an alien military weapon prototype in a scrapyard near his house. The large, armoured robotic suit was sent to Earth by the Trelkans to avoid its falling into the hands of an invading force, and on climbing inside it, Spencer finds that it is an intelligent, self-aware robot, and sets about exploring its various sensory and motor functions – it has super strength, rocket-powered roller skates and powerful weapons that are discharged inadvertently. The film thus also offers us a literalized representation of the experience of adolescent physical awkwardness, the growing pains, the strangeness and empowerment of an outsized, unfamiliar male body as Spencer lays waste to his house and various parts of his hometown. In the process of mastering the suit, Spencer matures to a point where he no longer needs it, and thus, *Star Kid* explores the theme of transition to adulthood that is central to child/robot films.

The figure of the child has always had a particularly over-determined significance within science fiction cinema, symbolizing difference, otherness, lack of prejudice, political innocence, facility with technology and readiness to communicate. Because the figure of the child connotes process and becoming, children are often represented as universalized figures that have not yet solidified into particularity but rather constitute a loose aggregation of possible future identities. The character, John Connor, is a typical example of this coding of the child as a 'neutral' set of potentialities. In the context of a Hollywood film, the character's white, male, Anglophone, North American identity marks him not as culturally privileged, but, paradoxically, as non-specific, unmarked. This 'superchild' (Slusser, 1999, p. 76) is well placed to assume his predestined future role as messianic representative of humankind or 'in the war against the machines' referred to throughout the film.

What is at stake in child/robot narratives is a struggle/desire for agency, insofar as child and robot are both in the process of acquiring agency through various rites of passage. Children are *becoming-adult*, whereas robots are often engaged in the process of *becoming-human*, a theme made explicit in *Bicentennial Man* (Columbus, 1999), where the central robot character is driven by a carnal desire to become flesh, and even more so in *A.I.: Artificial Intelligence* (Spielberg, 2001), which takes *Pinocchio* as the loose narrative basis for its account of the attempts by the robotic child, David, to become human in a world in which robots are the subaltern class. Fictional robots and children are thus equally under construction, and their common desire for agency or autonomy, their shared experience, accounts for the intimacy of their relationships. Cinematic robots are childlike in their ignorance and curiosity about (adult) human behaviour and, like children, must learn socially acceptable modes of behaviour and values. A comic scene in *Bicentennial Man* has the robot's embarrassed owner awkwardly explaining human reproduction to the curious but increasingly disgusted machine. The children instruct robots in idiomatic language – John Connor educates the Terminator in the finer points of Californian slang – acculturating them and offering them a cultural and conceptual map oriented around a child's perspective; in *Lost in Space* (Hopkins, 1997) young Will Robinson literally uploads his personality directly into the robot when he rebuilds it after it is destroyed in battle. All of these films explore the unstable power relationships between children and robots through these scenes in which robots and boys switch roles as teacher and pupil, and this in turn functions as a metaphor of the relationship between humans and technology, more generally – dynamic, intimate, asymmetrical.

In these films, becoming an adult involves loss – the symbolic death of the child through its fixing as an adult and the physical disintegration or departure of the robot with which these narratives often conclude. The eponymous Iron Giant and the Terminator both selflessly destroy themselves to save their child companions, and Spencer's robotic 'cyber suit' returns to its home planet. The destruction or loss of the robot is both a figure of childhood's end, the robot left behind in the world of children along with other cast-off trappings of childhood, and a sign of the assumption of mortality. The connection between humanity and death is explicit in *Bicentennial Man*, which concludes with the robot's willing death at the moment in which it is legally granted the status of human being.

A compelling way of understanding the child/robot relationship is as the representation of an idealized spectator-screen relationship. What such a reading reveals is a schematic understanding of our relationship with technology that is over-determined by assumptions about progress, capitalism, development, technology and cinema. Although the time-travel drama of *Terminator 2: Judgment Day* ostensibly centres on a child, John Connor serves as the vehicle for Hollywood's commercially and romantically idealized fantasy of the film viewer transported back to childhood – and childish susceptibility to the image – by the apparatus of the cinema. If the boys within these films stand for the film spectator, the screen robot may be understood as a figuration of what theorist Jean-Louis Baudry terms the *'basic cinematographic apparatus'*, that is, 'the ensemble of equipment and operations necessary to the production of a film and its projection' (Baudry, 1992, p. 693). A robot such as the Terminator is the marvellous product of impossible, futuristic or alien technologies and is regarded by other characters with fascination, awe, hostility and disbelief. Its mechanisms are hidden beneath a sleek, anthropomorphous exterior, and so John Connor misrecognizes it as a person who can reciprocate the love he feels for it, rather than a mere 'technical construct' (p. 692).

The on-screen rendering of the robot through special effects, stop-motion or CGI animation, animatronics or robotics, also constitutes a pleasurable, fascinating spectacle of cinematic technologies for viewers. The robot is a spectacular machine that marks the anachronistic irruption of technologies from another space and time and, consequently, serves as the narrative platform for a display of the advanced technical attractions of cinema. Indeed, the Terminator belongs to a family of screen robots that are clearly machinic, the massive, lumbering, highly visible product of old technologies – or, rather, of earlier imaginings of futuristic technology – rather than the discrete, mobile and imperceptible, new and futuristic bioengineering technologies represented by the cyborg in which boundaries between inside and outside, 'orga' and 'mecha', are diffuse and permeable. The final scenes of *Terminator 2: Judgment Day*, in which the massive T-800 Terminator defeats the apparently superior T-1000 model – whose morphing liquid metal body is rendered by CGI animation rather than the older order of special effects technology of prosthetics and animatronic dolls used to realize the T800 – take place in a steel plant, a *mise-en-scène* that strongly reinforces the industrial-mechanical character of the robot and its affinity with the electro-mechanical apparatus of the film camera and projector (and the film factory).

Robots like the Terminator function narratively as screens or mirrors for their child companions, extending the comparison between robot and cinematic apparatus. The mimetic Terminator is an anthropomorphic double, presenting the male child it befriends with an ideal imago (personified in this case by actor and former Mr Universe, Arnold Schwarzenegger, 'the most perfectly developed man in the history of the world'). Children interact with robots in these films through identification, unconsciously and hopefully projecting human characteristics onto them, misrecognizing themselves in the image of the outsized, autonomous and self-sufficient simulating machine like the pre-oedipal infant before a mirror.[1] Significantly, the Terminator is also a 'talking machine' – Baudry's term for the apparatus of sound cinema – that can imitate exactly the voices of others, and in one scene passes himself off as John when on the phone to John's mother, Janelle (although a cutaway reveals that Janelle has been killed and it is the T-1000 on the other end of the line, imitating her voice). Thus, these robots are empty simulating machines, distorting, intensifying mirrors that reflect and amplify the speech, behaviour and mannerisms of the people in front of them.

The recurrent visual motif of a point-of-view shot through the robot's eyes confirms the equation of the robot with the cinematic apparatus. These subjective machine vision shots are an economical means of representing a robot's hyper-mediated perspective and are typically characterized by visual distortion or interference: pixellation, scan lines or monochrome colour, and flashing and scrolling text and diagrams. The shot suggests the interiority of the robot, its subjective 'experience' of the world as it processes and analyses sensory data. In *Terminator 2: Judgment Day*, for example, near the film's beginning when the naked robot appears at a truck stop, the Terminator's non-human identity is affirmed through a point-of-view 'TermoVision' shot showing its surroundings on a red screen overlaid with messages, schematic diagrams, grids and a compass. The film's equation of robot with screen is confirmed by the representation of the precise moment of the Terminator's 'death' as it is submerged in molten steel at the film's end, through a shot of the red screen, filled with warning messages, flickering and then shrinking to a white dot like a television screen being switched off.

Thus, the robot is an apparatus consisting of both camera and screen, a device for recording and projection, mediation or interface between reality and viewer. In a literal rendering of this, the robotic *Bicentennial Man* sports a projector and sound system, housed in its cranium, that can generate large-scale, three-dimensional holographic images with accompanying music, while in *Jimmy Neutron: Boy Genius*, Jimmy's faithful robotic dog Goddard has a similar projector in its mouth, as well as a large circular screen that emerges from its body and relays the view through Goddard's eyes.[2] The cyber suit in *Star Kid* meanwhile provides Spencer with a fully immersive hyper-cinematic experience through a probe inserted into his spinal column. And so we might think of these robots as improbable, fantastic kino-eyes – vision machines or relays that are at once seeing and seen, receptive and projective.

Approached from a slightly different spectatorial perspective, we might also regard cinematic robots as reflective screens. For psychoanalytic film theorist Christian Metz, in his account of the value of psychoanalytic theory for the comprehension of film, there is a close and complex relationship between the cinema screen and the mirror. Metz suggests that in some respects the film screen is like a mirror, presenting the spectator not with a real object but its illusory reflection – 'its shade, its fantasy, its double, its *replica* in a new kind of mirror' (Metz, 1982, p. 45). However, a cinema screen is *clearly* different from a mirror (and from the 'primordial mirror' discussed by Jacques Lacan in the essay on the 'mirror stage') insofar as 'there is one thing and one thing only that is never reflected in it: the spectator's own body. In a certain emplacement, the mirror suddenly becomes clear glass' (ibid.). Although Metz proposes here that the cinema screen is a window (when viewed from some positions) rather than a mirror, he asserts that the film image is nevertheless only comprehensible as a result of the spectator having gone through the mirror stage:

> what *makes possible* the spectator's absence from the screen – or rather the intelligible unfolding of the film despite that absence – is the fact that the spectator has already known the experience of the mirror (of the true mirror), and is thus able to constitute a world of objects without having first to recognise himself in it.
>
> (p. 46)

Spectators can recognize that they are not looking at a mirror but nevertheless make sense of film images through the ongoing process of identification initiated with the infant's (mis-)identification with a mirror image. For Metz, then, the cinema screen has an ambiguous status. It is

> A strange mirror, then, very like that of childhood, and very different. Very like, as Jean-Louis Baudry has emphasised, because during the showing we are, like the child, in a sub-motor and hyper-perceptive

state; because, like the child again, we are prey to the imaginary, the double, and are so paradoxically through a real perception.

(p. 49)

Accounts of cinematic spectatorship by psychoanalytic film theorists such as Jean-Louis Baudry and Christian Metz liken the spectator to a child, both because of the affinities between the film-viewing experience and primordial identification, the physical passivity of the audience in the cinema auditorium, and because of the intensity of the cinema's imaginative and affective engagement of film viewers. Of course, the notion of the childlike viewer is not restricted to psychoanalytic theory. On the release of *Star Wars* (Lucas, 1977), *Time* magazine declared, 'It's aimed at kids – the kid in everybody' (Krämer, 2001), while Francois Truffaut similarly suggests that

> To stay with the audience, Hitchcock set out to win it over by reawakening all the strong emotions of childhood. In his work the viewer can recapture the tensions and thrills of the games of hide-and-seek or blindman's buff and the terror of those nights when, by a trick of the imagination, a forgotten toy on the dresser gradually acquires a mysterious and threatening shape.
>
> (Truffaut, 1985, p. 4)

Whereas for Hollywood film-makers, the regressive experience of film spectatorship may be regarded positively as an opportunity to engage and thrill susceptible audiences, at the same time, Hollywood films are commonly castigated for their infantilizing effects on audiences.[3] Newspaper film reviewers frequently complain about the patronizing register of commercial cinema, while, in a reflection upon the vitiations of capitalism, Theodor Adorno attacks US film-makers for the politically damaging regressive effects of such products of the culture industry:

> It is no coincidence that cynical American film producers are heard to say that their pictures must take into consideration the level of eleven year-olds. In doing so they would very much like to make adults into eleven year-olds.
>
> (Adorno, 1999, p. 36)

Progressive histories of cinema also regularly invoke disparaging notions of childish spectators to mark the difference between viewers of early cinema and the maturity and perceptiveness of contemporary audiences.

As Metz observes, invoking the apocryphal story of the gullible customers at the first commercial cinema screening in Paris

> the credulous spectators at the *'Grand Café'* in 1895, [are] frequently and complacently evoked by the incredulous spectators who have come *later* (and are no longer children), those spectators of 1895 who fled their seats in terror when the train entered La Ciotat station (in Lumiere's famous film), because they were afraid it would run them down.
>
> (Metz, 1982, p. 73)

And so, in centring on the figure of the child-machine couple, *Terminator 2: Judgment Day* functions like a primordial mirror (or perhaps a representation *mise-en-abŷme*) offering a reflection of ourselves as idealized spectators engaged in an affecting exchange with the cinematic apparatus. What James Cameron aims to elicit – and doubtless what we seek in repeated viewing of films – is the experience of watching as if for the first time, to recover the experience of joyful confusion, immediacy and desire that supposedly accompanies the primal viewing. John's relationship with the robot stands as a metaphor for this encounter, his love for the robot a form of cinephilia. Mary Anne Doane suggests that the cinephilia that characterized much film criticism of the 1950s and 1960s has re-emerged recently at the point in history where film is de-materializing, when photographic film base, flatbed editors, film projectors and film theatres are no longer crucial to the manufacture and viewing of films. Such cinephilia is therefore intrinsically nostalgic and 'could not be revived at this conjuncture were the cinema *not* threatened by the accelerating development of new electronic and digital forms of media' (Doane, 2002, p. 228). In other words, the new wave of cinephilia is underpinned by an implicit assertion of the distinct physical and ontological properties of photographic film, its indexical capacity that digital video, supposedly, can only simulate. 'It is the intense and privileged relation to contingency, assured by photographic indexicality in the abstract, which can be loved again, this time as lost' (ibid., p. 229).

Like the cinephile's love for a scratched, fading 35mm 'Technicolor' print, John's love for the Terminator is similarly nostalgic. It is a fatal love for a piece of obsolete hardware that belongs to another period – not least to the original pre-CGI film from 1984 – and that disintegrates steadily during the course of the film until at last, having been burnt, stabbed, shot repeatedly, punched, defenestrated, flayed, thrown from a moving vehicle, smashed in the head with a steel girder, dismembered and impaled, it is terminated.

In a review of *A.I.*, Richard Corliss similarly identifies the parallel between cinephile and technophile:

> Is it so far-fetched to think a human can fall in love with a mecha? Multiplex audiences do just that whenever they surrender to the seductive contrivance of movie emotion. (Each tear you shed has been carefully programmed, folks.)
>
> (Corliss, 2001)

As well as likening the film viewer to a robot lover, then, Corliss also characterizes the spectator as a programmable construction whose capacity for critical processing or resistance is overridden by the affective algorithms of genre cinema. The peculiar scenario suggested here is that of a closed circuit, the spectator-machine moved by watching other machines through the artificial apparatus of the cinema (vision machine). The cinematic encounter involves a temporary collapse of distinctions between spectator and object, orga and mecha, which is experienced as affect. Whereas the Terminator's inability to cry is a mark of its essential inhumanity – 'What is wrong with your eyes?', it asks when it first sees John crying – on the contrary, for many critics, a tearful response to film melodrama is a mark of our uncritical incorporation into the network of industrial mass culture as de-individualized dupes, drones, consumer-subjects.

More generally, the child/robot couple is a means by which Hollywood cinema explores the interaction between humans and technology. Both in academic work on media effects and in popular concerns about the social, physical and emotional impact of new media technologies, children are frequently regarded as particularly sensitive to changes in their technological environment. Casual and scientific observation of children's behaviour and emotional responses provides a litmus test for the social, somatic and psychological effects of the distribution and adoption of new media technology from early cinema to video games, the Internet and cellphones. At the same time, however, this sensitivity means that children are also regarded as being able to adapt to and master these technologies particularly rapidly. The intimate relationship between children and robots is an affective means of exploring the supposedly transformative impact of media technologies upon even the most private, personal areas of our lives.

What distinguishes children's interaction with technology from that of adults is a lack of concern over whether robots are alive or merely appear to be. Anxieties around *animation* do not concern them. Living robots are a given, and there is no irreconcilable contradiction in the notions of 'artificial intelligence' or 'machinic life', or, more specifically, in the idea of an 'emotional machine'[4]. There is an interesting coincidence here with the 'ethnographic and clinical' work of Sherry Turkle, who has observed children playing with electronic toys, such as Tamagotchis, and 'computational objects' (Turkle, 1998, p. 317). Turkle notes the ease with which many children accept the apparent paradox that such machines and programs are neither alive nor simply mechanical, through an unstable and approximate process of rationalization. These children have 'a tendency to see computer systems as "sort of" alive, to fluidly "cycle through" various explanatory concepts, and to willingly transgress boundaries' (p. 328).

So, while there is a distinction to be drawn between ethnographic and fictional representations of children, the assumptions that Turkle observes are shared by children such as John Connor who readily accepts that the Terminator is sort of alive and that it can feel and can die. This assumption is manifested in the children's love for their robots and their conviction that this is reciprocal. All they require of the robotic love-object is that it offer a sufficiently elaborate performance or simulation of affection to allow them to love it in return. They are thus advocates for an affective relationship with robots, an ethical love that is unqualified and uncritical and does not demand proof of reciprocation. As far as cinematic speculations about the future are concerned, the practical and ethical goals of current real-world 'affective computing' research into artificial intelligence and robotics – to produce sensitive, responsive, emotionally intelligent machines – are quite achievable. To her growing horror, the child robot David in *A.I.: Artificial Intelligence* does love his adoptive mother deeply and wants only to be loved in return, and given that David is virtually immortal, his love is a nightmarish gift that can never be repaid in full. His mother eventually finds his constant declarations of love so unbearable – and her biological son is so resentful of David – that she drives him out to the woods and abandons him. Whereas robots like the Terminator traditionally threaten social disorder through physical destruction, this robotic super-child poses a far more subtle and disturbing threat through its inadvertent parody of the perfect child that is at the heart of the American nuclear family.

Vivian Sobchack suggests that a central attraction of the genre is the flexibility and permeability of the literal and symbolic boundaries between the speculative worlds of science fiction and reality, and the possibilities of the spillage of fiction into reality and vice versa (Sobchack,

1990, p. 113). Among the areas of spillage – from cinema to contemporary reality – that characterize science fiction cinema is the relationship between toys and the mass media. Writing about the development and phenomenal uptake of such interactive 'Supertoys'[5] as Furbys, Aibos, Tamagotchis, 'My Real Baby' and Lego Mindstorms, Nigel Thrift observes that children's toys have become 'the touchstone for a digital infrastructure that works' (Thrift, p. 1). Thrift suggests that the first steps towards the 'dream of the information technology industry to produce new kinds of heavily mechanised and highly performative space, "intelligent environments" in which the boundaries of human and inhuman could be redescribed' are being taken with the dissemination of these commodities among children (p. 4). These children are inadvertent participants in consumer trials for 'new ways of doing things' and are involved in the embedding of commodified technology in the private sphere of the home (p. 4). They are not flying freely through a radically new technologized, de-realized environment, but are being wired into a fundamentally familiar exchange system, rehearsing their future roles and social skills in a subtly different world. As Thrift notes, the marketing of 'highly mediatised' toys that allow children to replay scenes from films and radio and TV programmes extends back at least to the 1920s, and so, while this is nothing new – and of course, one of the prophetic seductions of critical writing on technology is the readiness to identify novelty and impending social change – it may increasingly be the case that the fantasy scenarios played out intensely with interactive toys exclude the adults around their children. Playing with toys based on TV and film characters and situations can involve children in an intense imaginary identification/engagement with a thoroughly commodified environment.

Another initially surprising area of spillage is from military-industrial research into toy production as 'many of the information technology innovations of contemporary capitalism and the military complex are being put into toys' (p. 10). Interestingly this point of spillage forms the narrative premise for one of the more knowing child/robot films, *Small Soldiers* (Dante, 1998), which recounts the mayhem committed in a small town by a group of interactive toys that are accidentally fitted with A.I. munitions chips. The mix-up follows the takeover of the toy company Heartland Play Systems by the multinational Globotech Corporation, whose military research division developed the chips. The toys subsequently become self-aware, and the 'Commando Elite' toy marines wage war on a group of alien monster toys, called the Gorgons, who have been befriended by Alan, a toyshop owner's son. In their efforts to destroy the Gorgons, the marines subsequently lay waste to the toy shop and cause chaos as they pursue the aliens across the homely town in which the film is set. In addition to citations of *Terminator 2: Judgment Day*, the film makes numerous allusions to Hollywood war films, horror, and science fiction cinema, but it is not clear whether these appropriations are intended as satirical. *Small Soldiers* is broadly critical of the aggressive capitalism of corporate culture, contrasting Globotech's arrogant and insensitive chief executive officer with Alan's father, a traditional shopkeeper fighting a vain battle against chain stores and the rise of soulless electronic toys. However, predictably, it stops short of criticizing the economic infrastructure of Hollywood film production and, in particular, the well-established practices of cross-marketing and licensing tie-in products to accompany a film's release. Criticizing the film's incoherence, one reviewer remarks that 'it's sometimes hard to tell if the target audience is under ten or over 30, given the plethora of cinephile in-jokes and satiric sideswipes' (Charity, 2005, p. 1221). Of course, for the child/robot film the distinction between a 10-year-old boy and a 30-year-old cinephile is virtually non-existent. To be a cinephile is to be returned to childhood – to boyhood – in various ways, the cinematic apparatus functioning like the time-travel machine that sends the Terminator back from the future.

Child/robot couples are one of the means by which science fiction cinema attempts to understand the mediatization and technologization of our lives. They constitute a case study of the ways in which media technologies are incorporated into our private, psychic lives and reconfigure our physical and sensory environments. However, the tendency for science fiction films to imagine technology in cinematic terms (both in relation to a repertoire of generic representations and in relation to the technical apparatus of film production and distribution) is also one of the reasons why their examination of technical incorporation is constrained by certain limits. Technology is routinely imagined as something to be feared, or something to be loved, rather than as something that is ubiquitous and incidental, and it is always represented as something that is extrinsic and irruptive, and with which we are rarely complicit. The story told about technology – as embodied by robots – is that it is a self-determining cause of change, rather than the effect of a set of other causal factors, such as military-industrial development, commercial technoscience or consumer culture.

The problem with the child/robot relationship in cinema is that in its sensationalism it is incapable of representing – or effaces – the mundane, banal, unsensational and incremental ways in which technology is always already physically, erotically and psychically incorporated. In science fiction cinema, the presence of the robot is always a shocking and anomalous spectacle, an unexpected apparition that, like the Lumière film *L'Arrivée d'un train à La Ciotat* (1895), sends adults running in confusion (and returns them to childhood). Just as the idealized notion of a dreamlike cinematic experience in a darkened auditorium is already being consigned to the past, as the experience of watching films is increasingly characterized by distraction and as viewing platforms become more ubiquitous and mobile (computers, mpeg video players, portable DVD players and laptops), so also the sorts of communications technologies and prosthetic extensions metaphorically represented by the robot have already infiltrated our lives – they are no longer strange or troubling. Of course, science fiction is characterized by excess, exaggeration and temporal displacement; these are the dramatic distancing devices with which science fiction aims to represent the present critically, but they are also the reasons why science fiction cinema misrecognizes the imperceptible and constant process of technologization that has *already* transformed our lives and environment radically. Whereas a technophobic insistence upon such binary oppositions as nature/culture, male/female is deeply nostalgic, the technophilic exploration of a utopian landscape of dissolved borders, collapsed hierarchies and flattened institutions is no less problematic in its failure to recognize the violent persistence of national, racialized, gendered and class boundaries.

We should not be surprised that Hollywood cinema is not engaged in a project of ideological criticism, but what is striking about child/robot films is the limitations of their fantasies of boundary transgression. Far from depicting an imminent future glimpsed from the threshold of the twenty-first century, these anachronistic films offer us an image of the future couched in terms of nineteenth- and mid-twentieth-century concepts of cinema and technology.

## Notes

1. In Hogarth Hughes's first encounter with *The Iron Giant*, for example, the huge robot communicates with the little boy by imitating his movements and speech, with Hogarth playing at getting the robot to copy his gestures in the same way an infant plays with its reflection, touching parts of his body and manipulating objects.
2. The proximity of 'Goddard' to 'Godard' is doubtless merely a happy accident.
3. Orson Welles's famous remark in 1940 that RKO's studios were 'the greatest electric train set a boy ever had' suggests that regression is also a feature of

film-making, a regression, interestingly, that returns the director to a miniature version of cinema's primal content and sensory model, the railway.
4. Or, as Marvin Minsky, A.I. researcher and consultant for Kubrick's *2001: A Space Odyssey* (1969), has it, an 'emotion machine' (Minsky, 2006).
5. A citation of Brian Aldiss's story, 'Supertoys Last All Summer Long', the basis for Spielberg's *A.I.*

# IV
# Movement

'Perception of movement and perception in motion could be said to be just what the cinematographic impulse hinges on', writes Marie-Luise Angerer in her critical overview (Chapter 13) of the increasing centrality in film theory of the concept of affect as intensive movement. The chapters in this section are all concerned in different ways with technologies and techniques of movement, from the representational illusion of movement, through the animating movements of hand and eye, to the constant mobilization of theories of affects as intensive movement.

In a sense, all technology organizes, more or less securely, movement. Three layers of technology as movement can be differentiated in cinema. The first concerns the appearance and perception of movement. How does cinema in moving make movement perceptible? Michelle Langford's chapter (Chapter 11) examines two moments of mobility and technological-infrastructural change in German cinema. Michelle Langford detects a historically located preoccupation with movement through time and space in both *Run Lola Run* (Tykwer, 1999) and *Nosferatu* (Murnau, 1922). Both films can be understood as a reflection upon the way movement is made perceptible in cinema and visual technologies. The looping, repetitive narrative structure and elastic time of *Run Lola Run* invokes related audio-visual media such as computer games, hypertext web pages and TV at the same time that it recalls the looped, animated sequences from pre-cinematic platforms such as the Praxinoscope or Zoopraxiscope. The film, Langford argues, thus foregrounds the technological basis for Lola's movement. Her movement is intimately linked to technologies that give 'birth to her'. In *Nosferatu*, 'technologically mediated movement proliferates' throughout the film. It invokes the earlier entertainment technology of lantern slides, as well as exploits a collapse of distinctions between organic and non-organic forms of cinematic movement. Both films create 'meta-cinematic creatures' that serve as allegories of cinematic technology as movement. A second layer of movement runs through the chapters of this section. Movements of images and movements of spectators, moving and being moved, entwine with greater intimacy in contemporary visual cultures. Angerer discusses how new media theory has theorized both new media interactivity and the turn to affect in theories of the cinema and media as deriving from the movements of spectators. Increasingly, spectator movement is productive of images, just as images move spectators. This point is now fairly well established in theories and studies of new media. But what of the production of movement in cinema? Does the mingling of spectator and movement also occur there? Animation renders this connection between moving images and corporeal movement particularly sharply. Animation bridges between making images move as a spectator (as in interactive media) and making moving images (as in cinema conventionally conceived). Bill Schaffer's chapter (Chapter 12) is concerned with cinema's specific capacity to produce the effect of movement through animation. Historically, the animated cartoon has consistently been marginalized by critics, film theorists and historians, but Schaffer argues that, on the contrary, we might understand animation as properly fundamental to cinema. Debates about the ontological *crisis* induced by digital cinema with the supposed loss of chemical/indexical authenticity have run into a theoretical impasse. By contrast, the concept of cinema *as* animation offers a way out of the unproductive conceptual distinction between analogue and digital cinema. Schaffer discusses the comments of a range of significant animators and (of necessity) theorists from Hans Richter to Chuck Jones, all of whom understand cinematic movement – in its simplest sense – as the organization of intervals or differences. Their reflections upon the technical process of animation also introduce other aspects of movement – a certain mobility or blurring of the distinction between animator and image. The experience of producing images involves animators in an intimate identificatory relationship with the images they are animating wherein, at certain points, the animators are animated by the movements of the images or the characters they are drawing.

The final layer of movement in these chapters is intensive movement or affect. Like several other chapters in this volume, the chapters by Schaffer and Langford deploy Deleuze's work as a conceptual tool for thinking about cinema's struggle with informatics. Marie-Luise Angerer's chapter tracks movements in academic film theory over the last 30 or 40 years that have seen Deleuze's work on intensive movements or affects become prominent. In taking stock of these movements, Angerer's chapter summarizes the shifting debates around film apparatus, visual technologies, and the insistent turn towards the problem/concept of affect. Whereas the notion of the spectator as immobilized by the filmic text was dominant in 'Marxist-psychoanalytic Apparatus Theory' of the 1970s and 1980s, Angerer suggests that this has been superseded by the notion of the mobile, active spectator. This shift takes place alongside the collapse of distinctions between producer and consumer of images that is accelerated by digital video (DV) technology. With the re-conception of the spectator as embodied, theorists explored the capacity for films and related audio-visual media to offer a haptic, immersive or participatory experience. This reconfiguration of the spectator as body/embodied, Angerer observes, is particularly connected to the technological means of recent cinema. That is to say that, for many theorists, the 'framelessness of digital images', and the interchangeability of previously distinct media – the emergence of a 'post-medium condition' – have hastened the realization of full-body spectatorship. This conceptual reframing of the spectator drives a preoccupation with affect and feelings of bodily change. Angerer's conclusions about the 'somatic-affective turn' in theory are ambivalent. A key stake in this reframing is the eventual abandonment of the concept of the subject 'based on language and desire'. She views this with some scepticism. Angerer suggests that the enthusiasm for critical approaches to the affects of embodied spectatorship informed by, say, neurobiology can amount to little more than 'ideological bandwagoning'. From the perspective of this book, the heightened visibility of technology and technical practices of seeing, moving and doing goes hand in hand with a re-theorization of feelings of movement or being moved. Only because bodily movements organize so much of the audio-visual field does affect become important as a way of registering how this movement matters.

# 11
# Lola and the Vampire: Technologies of Time and Movement in German Cinema

*Michelle Langford*

At various moments during Tom Tykwer's *Run Lola Run* (*Lola Rennt*, 1998), as the title character Lola runs relentlessly to save her boyfriend, Manni, by chance she bumps into a variety of incidental characters (Figure 11.1, *Lola Rennt*, 1998). Following each collision, those characters' futures are projected forward into a series of Polaroid snapshots giving us a glimpse into their varied destinies. In an attempt to identify the place Lola inhabits in the history of German cinema, I'd like to imagine what might happen if she were to bump into Count Orlock, the mysterious vampire from F. W. Murnau's *Nosferatu* (1922). Would she see her own destiny? Would she see herself, as I do, as a descendant of the shadowy figures of the fantastic German cinema of the Weimar period? The purpose of this chapter is to tease out a series of 'secret affinities' between Lola and the Vampire to show how, despite their separation by 76 years, they appear to be intimately linked through their respective relationship with cinematic technologies of time, movement and the virtual.[1]

Before exploring the conceptual aspects of this affinity, it will be worthwhile situating each film in its respective context of production, for in both periods technological developments have generated highly ambivalent responses, oscillating between celebration and anxiety. Such competing discourses frequently emerge at historical junctures where technological developments effect rapid social change.[2] The Weimar period was characterized by dramatic shifts in social life brought on by technological advancements in transport, industry and entertainment, as well as the rise of the modern metropolis, which produced an intensification of consumer culture, new forms of entertainment, and witnessed the emergence of the 'New Woman', whose newfound independence, disposable income, sexual freedom and social mobility seemed to pose

*Figure 11.1* Lola Rennt.

a threat to masculinity and the traditional role of the family.³ Among these developments, we see the rise of film as the premier medium for mass entertainment, and with this we see the rapid development of the German film industry. During the Weimar period German cinema thrived, technically, creatively and commercially, with studios investing large sums in the research and development of new film technologies in an attempt to compete with the worldwide hegemony of Hollywood and, in the process, to establish a national film industry that was identifiably German. No other national cinema has seen such a close interdependence between the development of film technologies, and the thematic content and aesthetic realization of the films themselves. Fritz Lang's *Metropolis* (1927) is only the most famous example of this unique interdependence. Indeed, Lang's film could be said to play out these very anxieties about technology while clearly celebrating the technological capacity of the medium. Murnau's *Faust* (1926) is another case in point in that, through highly innovative uses of technology, it took audiences on a virtual tour through time and space at the same time as it raised fears about the wholesale moral corruption of society and the temptations of sex and the commodity. Like Mephisto, film technology made possible the visualization of many of Weimar society's fears and fantasies. On a much smaller scale Murnau's *Nosferatu* also takes part in this process. I need not reiterate the discourses around the fear of invasion and contagion by the 'other', and fears of female sexuality that have circulated in the veritable wealth of critical literature around this film.[4] What has been noted less frequently about this film, however, is the close relationship between technology and the monster himself.[5] Technology serves not only as a vehicle for imaging the monstrous, but the monster may in fact be seen as an allegorical emblem for the monstrousness of cinema technology and its unique capacity to manipulate time and space.

Similarly, reception of *Run Lola Run* tended to revolve around the film's radical manipulation of time and space, its uses of a combination of film-making technologies and its aesthetic and conceptual arrangement derived from interactive video games and MTV. In its punchy deployment of 'hypermedia', according to Ingeborg Majer O'Sickey, the film landed right in the middle of debates around the apparent threat posed by digital imaging technologies to the 'epistemological status of the [film] image' and its claims to authenticity (O'Sickey, 2002, p. 123).[6] While critics of cinema in the 1920s might have accused film of presenting too much 'reality' (at least from a moral perspective), cinema at the turn of the twenty-first century could be accused of presenting too little, of abandoning the photograph's indexical relationship with the real. The increasing digitalization of cinema has given rise to its fare share of critics and celebrants, and it is in the midst of such debates that Lola was born. Additionally, *Run Lola Run* emerged at a time when anxiety about German cinema's waning relationship to the 'national' was being felt in the face of the trend towards the transnationalization of European film industries.[7] Although *Run Lola Run* was an entirely German production, its international success may be attributed to clever transnational marketing and distribution strategies, as well as both technical and aesthetic appeal to a highly globalized youth culture facilitated precisely by its use of a range of old and new cinema technologies[8] and its mixture of high and pop culture sources.[9] While the majority of critics celebrated the film's international success and ability to straddle the divide between art and commercial cinema, one German critic, Olaf Moller, anxiously proclaimed that 'Tykwer represents everything that went wrong with German cinema in the Nineties' (Moller, 2001, p. 11). Calling it 'a Kieslowski-techno rip-off', Moller remarked that it is 'utterly devoid of anything *German*' (ibid.). Underlying such critiques of the film is a certain nostalgia for the highly politicized national imaginary developed during the period of the New German Cinema. Perhaps this anxiety about the film's lack of national specificity highlights a generational shift that has taken place in the German cultural sphere in the era of German unification. German youth culture is far more concerned with globalization and transnational media than by the Second World War, which is becoming a distant memory. This younger generation, too, appears not to fear the epistemological questions raised by digital imaging, and instead celebrates its facilitation of a 'virtual' entry into logically impossible or fantastic worlds. Thus, it is possible to argue that Lola and the Vampire's first secret affinity lies on two adjacent points of a temporal and technological spiral with Lola reinvigorating old debates in a new context.

We might locate their second secret affinity in the fact that both figures are highly fantastic creatures, who place no claims on epistemological authenticity. They are created by and exist solely within the realm of cinema and the other imaginative media to which they have previously belonged: nineteenth-century literature and video games respectively.[10] In addition, they may be considered meta-cinematic creatures drawing attention to and causing us to reflect upon the technologies that bring them to life.

In his book *The Language of New Media*, Lev Manovich has argued that as cinema becomes more digital, it tends to reveal a closer affinity with its roots in proto cinematic technologies of the nineteenth century.[11] He theorizes that the processes involved in the digital creation and manipulation of images derive more from techniques of animation and painting than from photography and narrative. Manovich writes, 'Everything that characterized moving pictures before the twentieth century – the manual construction of images, loop actions, the discrete nature of space and movement – was delegated to cinema's bastard relative, its supplement and shadow – animation' (Manovich, 2001, p. 298). Furthermore, in the age of digital cinema 'live-action' footage is now only one of many possible elements from which a film may be made. It is 'reduced to just another graphic', 'raw material for further compositing' (ibid., pp. 300–1). Indeed, in as far as Lola is represented through a combination of 35mm footage, animation and digital post-production effects, her status as a live-action figure indexed to profilmic reality becomes significantly more difficult to establish. While *Run Lola Run* does not make use of any strikingly 'new' film technology and is therefore not fully a creation of digital cinema, *Lola* (the character and the film) does tend to foreshadow the return to cinema's shadowy origins described by Manovich. The triple 'loop' construction of *Lola*'s narrative does recall loop-based moving image technologies of the nineteenth century – the Zoetrope, Kinetoscope and Mutoscope, for example.[12] At the same time, in *Lola* this loop is subject to a variety of interventions, which renders it more like a spiral, and brings us forward to twentieth-century interactive computer games, which revolve around the mutability of the loop. Indeed, the film is infused with a myriad of spirals, from those in the animated title sequence where Lola is sucked into a spinning vortex, to the use of various spiralling and circular camera movements, the telephone receiver that spirals in the air, the staircase in Lola's apartment block, the 'Spiral Bar', the reference to Hitchcock's *Vertigo* in the painting in the casino and the roulette wheel that forms a vertiginous double spiral. On a more rudimentary level, Tykwer makes the viewer highly aware of the manipulations of the film image and the ways in which this is crucial to generating Lola's movement.

Lola's movements are intimately linked to the technology that gives birth to her. In fact, Lola is even introduced to the film first and foremost as an animated character in the fast-paced title sequence, which betrays her proto-cinematic roots. Furthermore, in the opening sequence of the film proper, following Manni's panicked phone call, Lola appears bewildered and movement takes on a strange quality, having the effect of pausing time. The camera begins to arc around Lola and a series of jump cuts create an effect that lies somewhere between stop-motion animation and time-lapse photography. A set of faces and names then flash on screen, as though in a video game, representing possible solutions to her financial dilemma. Lola settles on the image of her father, which is framed and edited in such a way that suggests Lola and her father are looking at one another. He even shakes his head, suggesting that he disapproves of her selection, and then turns his head to watch her leave. Cinematic devices have the effect of connecting these two characters across space, despite the logical impossibility of this. It is only once she has made her selection that 'play' really starts, and she becomes fully 'animated'. Tykwer further highlights the cinematically mediated character of her movement through his frequent use of slow-motion photography combined with the fast-paced techno music on the soundtrack. Moreover, any claims to indexical authenticity her image may have had are further relinquished when she quite literally becomes animation, as the camera momentarily leaves Lola's physical body behind and follows her animated avatar into the television set. This explicit emphasis on the mutability of Lola's image and cinema's ability to reconstitute movement from still images tends to situate Lola wholly within the realm of the fantastic, where she is unconstrained by the laws of logical, organic movement. We might say, as Gilles Deleuze said of the creatures of German Expressionist cinema that she exceeds 'the wisdom and limits of the organism' (Deleuze, 1986, p. 51). Writing of Expressionist cinema of the Weimar period, Gilles Deleuze identified 'the non-organic life of things' as the 'first principle of Expressionism' (ibid., pp. 50–1). This is

> ... valid for the whole of nature, that is, for the unconscious spirit, lost in darkness, light which has become opaque, *lumen opacatum*. From this point of view natural substances and artificial creations, candelabras and trees, turbine and sun are no longer any different.
> (ibid.)

Prefiguring Manovich's theorization of live-action's loss of its privileged status in digital cinema, Deleuze argues that in Expressionist cinema the distinction between the organic and the inorganic is rendered irrelevant primarily through its emphasis on the fantastic. This brings me to my discussion of the vampire Count Orlock and his relationship to movement in *Nosferatu*.

The first 20 minutes of *Nosferatu* are organized according to the logic of narrative storytelling, employing various techniques of cinematic narration, including continuity editing, point-of-view shots, close-ups and an attempt at the psychological development of the main characters, who are portrayed through a verisimilar style of performance that was common to silent films of the time.[13] Until this point, movement in the film is treated naturalistically and the image maintains an unproblematic relationship to pro-filmic reality. Once Jonathan Harker reaches the outskirts of Count Orlock's estate, however, identified in the film as the 'land of phantoms', the film's logic of movement takes on a strange quality. From the moment the phantom carriage collects Jonathan at the border of the estate all movement associated with the vampire becomes a function of film technology. Murnau employs negative film and a stop-motion effect to propel the carriage along. This technique helps to suggest that the natural world has been subverted by the logic of the non-organic life of things. Once Harker has arrived at the castle this technologically mediated movement proliferates: doors open of their own accord, and Murnau employs the stop-motion effect yet again as the vampire packs himself into his coffin for the journey to Bremen. Much later in the film Murnau employs a series of dissolves to represent the vampire's ability to penetrate solid surfaces. His amorphous and shape-shifting qualities are provided directly by the possibilities for optical illusions presented by the film medium. In fact Orlock's movement and all movements associated with him are presented in an overtly inorganic way. Additionally, Max Schreck does not subscribe to verisimilar codes of screen performance. His physical motions do not appear to be derived from an integrated sensory motor system, but are granted primarily by film technology (stop motion, dissolves, lighting devices). Perceptive viewers may become aware that it is frequently not the vampire who moves, but it is the cinematic apparatus that *moves him*, animates him, fills him with non-organic life.

While as with *Lola* these effects are not the result of particularly 'new' developments in film technology, Murnau (like Tykwer) does seem to revel in these rather primitive film attractions familiar from early trick films in order to give his vampire the semblance of life. However, the rather obvious use of these primitive techniques enables us to see the vampire more broadly as a uniquely cinematic figure. It is perhaps no coincidence that one particular proto-cinematic device for the projection of moving images was the nineteenth-century *Phantasmagoria*, which also, by way of primitive animation techniques, brought to life various phantoms, gesturing towards the fantastic worlds the cinema would eventually make visible. In terms of making visible this relationship between cinematic technology and artificial movement, while the majority of films in the 1920s had deeply buried their connection to these origins, Murnau's *Nosferatu* seems to acknowledge its debt to this heritage. *Lola*, too, appears to look back, at the same time as it looks forward, linking this forgotten moment of cinema's past to its future in digital imaging technologies.

If both films testify to the cinema's unique capacity to manipulate time and space, then to analyse their respective approaches to movement only reveals half the picture. Both the vampire and Lola also have complex relationships with time. Not only do clocks feature prominently in *Run Lola Run*, my repeated viewings of *Nosferatu* have left me haunted by the image of a clock.

Twice in *Nosferatu* a clock appears, twice we encounter its image as it silently strikes six and twice its movement is doubled by its shadow deeply chiselled onto the wall behind. Twice this clock beats out the impending doom that is to befall Jonathan Harker. The first time, its strokes startle him as he cuts a slice of bread at Orlock's table, slipping and cutting his finger, drawing the precious blood that so attracts the vampire. The second time it announces the approach of the vampire as he is about to feed on Jonathan for the second time. The clock, like the vampire, is infused with non-organic life. Both clock and vampire are composed of time, shadow, and are driven by mechanical rather than organic movement. Indeed one thing that fascinates me about this clock is its movement. Rather than simply being presented as an instrument for measuring time, marking the time just before dawn when the vampire must feed, this clock is fascinating for what it does *not* do. Murnau does not use parallel editing to generate suspense and the hope that Jonathan might be able to escape the vampire just in time to avoid becoming his victim for a second time. Instead, we see the clock beat out six o'clock twice – the second instance an identical repetition of the first. Furthermore, the clock is somewhat fragmented from its surroundings, occupying a privileged position in its own one-shot, but never visible in an establishing shot that would fix its position in space. Although it is evidently not an extra-diegetic image, because Jonathan is clearly startled by its 'sound', it is not integrated 'organically' into the film. Rather, it has that startling, disconnected quality of an insert or close-up that functions to interrupt the 'natural' flow of cinematic images (Figure 11.2, F. W. Murnau's *Nosferatu*, 1922).

I would argue, therefore, that through its repetition, the clock does not represent the *movement* of time at all but rather the *suspension* of time. It is possible to say that *virtually* no time has passed between the

*Figure 11.2*  F. W. Murnau's *Nosferatu*.

two chimes of six. In other words, this clock suggests a time that does not *flow* or *pass*, but one that *collects* in this land of phantoms, and this causes movement to do strange things. Similarly, the vampire is a creature unaffected by the flow of time. One of the vampire's traditional traits is the ability to exist for hundreds of years without ageing, without suffering the deteriorating effects of time. I would also like to suggest that he embodies a kind of temporal suspension where time and the experience of ages *collect* within him, yet do not flow through him, just as no blood (the organic life-giver) flows through his veins. He certainly exceeds the wisdom and limits of the organism. He therefore represents time as eternal rather than fleeting. This makes him a contradiction, because on the one hand, he is the quintessential figure of modern, artificial cinematic movement, yet he does not embody that linear, progressive, homogeneous time characterized by modernity. In him, time and movement have become disengaged.

Lola similarly exhibits a very complex relationship with time, and she too manages at various moments to exceed the limits of the organism. Just as I am drawn to the image of the clock in *Nosferatu*, Tykwer draws the viewer into the strange temporal logic of the film from the very first image of the title sequence. A giant pendulum swings from side to side across the screen. The pendulum takes the form of a face, a particularly fierce, gruesome face. On the soundtrack we hear a fast 'tick, tick, tick, tick', like that of a battery-powered wristwatch. This sound seems to have little correlation to the slow swooping motion of the pendulum. Suddenly, the pendulum stops and the camera begins to pan upwards towards the face of the clock. The ticking continues on the soundtrack, but now we see that the hands of the clock are racing, hours passing in a matter of seconds. Just as the pendulum's movement is out of sync with the ticking on the soundtrack, so too the hands are disjointed from the rhythm of the pendulum. The clock is elaborately carved in a quasi-gothic style, with another more gruesome face perched above the clock face. As the camera pans further upwards, the mouth slowly opens and swallows the camera and us with it: we have now entered the strange temporal logic of *Run Lola Run*.[14]

Certainly, time and clocks function very differently in *Run Lola Run* than in *Nosferatu*, and in *Lola*, another clock comes to dominate the image: a modern railway-style clock on the wall above the Bolle supermarket where Manni waits. It is true that, informed by the logic of the video game and conventions of narrative suspense, this clock does function as a countdown device, giving Lola a limited amount of time (20 minutes) to complete her mission. Where this departs from a traditional countdown device is provided by the structure of the film that allows Lola to repeat this time three times. In a way, therefore, this clock *is* like the clock in *Nosferatu* in that it repeats a short segment of time without progressing past that quasi-magical hour of 12 o'clock where the game stops, or as in a fairytale the carriage turns into a pumpkin. Like *Nosferatu*, this too is not time as flow or progress, but time as repetition, accumulation or loop. This is evidenced in the way that Lola clearly learns from each turn of the game, each loop of the spiral, just as video game players learn how to beat the game with every turn. In doing so they effectively (su)spend time. This is apparent initially when Lola calls 'stop' at the end of the first round, as though she is hitting the reset button on an imaginary gaming console, but also from the way she seems to remember how to unlock the safety catch on the gun, avoid the group of nuns and use her piercing scream to manipulate the roulette wheel. For Lola time is knowledge. The repeatability of time afforded by the cinema allows her to exceed the limits of the organism. In this sense she is like the vampire as time does not simply pass through her, but collects within her, making her also a figure of temporal suspension. As with the clock in *Nosferatu*, *Lola*'s clock is also privileged with a close-up of sorts towards the end of the first and second episodes when the very top portion of the clock occupies the bottom quarter of the screen in a tripartite split-screen construction in which Manni and Lola appear to face one another.

It is in this close-up that we see the clock reach 12 o'clock, but as it does so, time is momentarily suspended as the second hand pauses for a few seconds before moving on, as if to extract this moment from the flow of time. Both Lola and the vampire therefore share this secret affinity with time, where time is not measured by the logic of 'normal', organic movement, but rather by the non-organic lives generated by the cinema itself.

There is one further secret affinity shared by Lola and the vampire, and that is their relationship to a technologically generated virtuality. I would like to suggest that it is in this secret affinity that the 'monstrousness' of cinematic technology is highlighted. By this I mean the uncanny ability for cinema to record and reproduce organic life photographically at the same time as it harbours the capacity to animate the non-organic, at times even collapsing the distinction between the two.

One further aspect of *Nosferatu* (the film and the vampire) is suggested by the image of the clock: light, or rather, light's absence in shadow. Deleuze believes that Expressionist cinema is dominated by a struggle between light and shadow.[15] This, I believe, is evidenced by a characteristic shared by both vampire and clock. What fascinates me most about the clock in *Nosferatu* is its deeply chiselled shadow that doubles the movement of the skeleton's arm as it strikes six o'clock. It is this skeletal shadow, more so than its 'face', that, for me, anthropomorphizes the clock – renders it part human and secures its home among the non-organic life of things. Human, yet not human, the clock is like the vampire 'nosferatu', the 'un-dead'.

But Orlock has an even more complex relationship to light. He is literally 'light become opaque': shadow, or the negative projection of light on the cinema screen. Recalling Manovich, who referred to animation as 'cinema's bastard relative, its supplement and shadow', it is light, as much as (or perhaps more than) blood, that Orlock craves. In fact it is light that brings him, virtually, into the land of the living, but ironically, this light that he craves so much will ultimately obliterate him. We are reminded of this yearning for light in *Shadow of the Vampire* (E. Elias Merhinge, 2000). This film 'interprets' Orlock/Schreck's longing for light in a fascinating way in a scene in which Max Schreck in full costume as Orlock wanders around the empty studio at night. He happens upon a projector containing the day's rushes, switches it on and passes his hand through the throw of light. Seeing this does him no harm, he proceeds to bask fully in the projector's artificial light.[16] I read this scene to be exemplary of the desire for light invested in Murnau's vampire, and he invests this desire for light in the character of Nina, Harker's wife.

Frequently in discussions of this film, the vampire's desire is understood as libidinal or sexual; however, I would like to read Nina's function in the film slightly differently. It is not the *woman* he desires, but the virtual light she represents. It is Nina's brightness, figured by the whiteness of her nightgown that draws the vampire to her room, like a moth to a flame, and his fixation for light and her ability to imitate it enables her to keep him with her until 'the cock has crowed'. She provides the white screen upon which he literally and palpably projects himself as shadow, projects his unfettered desire for light. But Nina's brightness is virtual, like the vampire who is virtually 'light become opaque'. She is meant to sate him long enough for the first rays of daylight that will ultimately obliterate him to appear. Here again, we can say that the vampire is like the cinema, for light too will obliterate any image from the silver screen. The vampire as 'light become opaque' can therefore only exist in the flickering light cast upon a darkened screen. He *is* light, yet light is that which will ultimately obliterate him. The vampire therefore exists in a state of pure virtuality and reveals to us the virtual wonders made possible by the unique interdependence between technology and cinema in the Weimar period.

Like *Nosferatu*, *Run Lola Run* aesthetically, conceptually and technically privileges the virtual over the actual. Through its use of hypermedia the film generates a virtual, fantastic or supernatural world, unconstrained by the laws of logic and physics, just as Murnau had with his 'land of phantoms' over 70 years before. Like Orlock, this world revolves (spirals) around Lola and her desires. O'Sickey has argued that what Lola really wants is to get into sexual synchronicity with Manni, but I believe Lola wants a whole lot more: she wants everything (O'Sickey, 2002, p. 130). Goaded by the security guard in the second episode who says to her, 'you can't have everything', Lola seems to gain further momentum and desire to have it all. She craves, time, money, knowledge, a meaningful relationship with her parents and with Manni; she craves to know the future, and perhaps even change the past. This is further expressed in the lyrics of the songs that accompany her on her run, which are full of contradictory wishes and wants. For example as she runs, Lola expresses her desires through the words of the extra-diegetic music. Here we learn that she wishes to be both hunter and animal, to have 'unlimited breath' and a 'heartbeat that never comes to rest', a 'stranger', a 'starship', a 'princess', a 'ruler', a 'writer', a 'prayer', a 'forest of trees'. With no clear distinction between human and non-human, material or ephemeral, Lola expresses her desire to be all and everything, regardless of the logical 'impossibility' of becoming any of them. As Deleuze writes of German Expressionism, we may discover 'a supra-organic spirit which dominates the whole inorganic life of things: then we lose our fear, knowing that our spiritual "destination" is truly invincible' (Deleuze, 1986, p. 53). By the third episode, Lola has indeed lost all fear, and gains the knowledge that in this veritable land of phantoms (the hybrid cinema/gaming environment), she can indeed have it all. Her wishes will be realized. These wishes not only express her desire to exceed the limits of the human organism, which she is *like* yet ultimately not like, they also privilege the cinema, both analogue and digital, as that which harbours the possibility of realizing these wishes. Like the cinema, Lola too seems to embody this potential. Although she appears human, she does possess some of the shape-shifting qualities and supernatural powers that Orlock possessed more than 70 years before – the difference, however, being that rather than taking life, Lola has been granted the power of restoring life, just as the cinema 'restores' life to, or 'animates' a series of still images. Interestingly, this ability to restore life is not recognized until the third episode, when she has lost all fear, represented by the dog in the stairwell, and accumulated enough knowledge to anticipate the ambulance carrying the security guard, whose life she saves.

O'Sickey has argued that Lola's supernatural qualities are inherently tied to the technological means that produce her. She writes, 'the audience recognizes the 'supernatural' aspects of her character as built cumulatively in a combination of live action and digitally produced effect' (O'Sickey, 2002, p. 126). I would add, just as the vampire's supernatural characteristics are produced primarily by film technology, so too are Lola's supernatural aspects produced by and through the technological possibilities of the now increasingly hybrid film medium. I'd like to imagine that if Lola were to bump into Orlock on the street, she would indeed see snapshots of herself, and in doing so, she may see both German cinema's past and future and take pleasure in the secret affinities shared by herself and the vampire as both fantastic creations of German cinema. Lola effectively re-vivifies the triumph of the non-organic in German cinema and re-invents the Expressionist impulse towards the technological fabrication of illusory worlds. This is nowhere more evident than in her cry, her scream that can break glass and stop a roulette wheel – this is the cry attained by Expressionism: 'Margueritte's cry, Lulu's cry, which marks the horror of the non-organic life as much as the opening-up of a spiritual universe which may be illusory' (Deleuze, 1986, p. 54).

## Notes

1. Lola's lineage could be traced via alternate paths through German cinema, for example, via her relationship to her cinematic namesakes: the 'Lola' of Josef von Sternberg's *The Blue Angel* (1930), the title character of Fassbinder's *Lola* (1981) and perhaps even Pabst's 'Lulu' of *Pandora's Box* (1928). To do so would situate her in terms of discourses on the 'New Woman' and sexuality, which is not my intention here. My title, however, is intended to evoke Thomas Elsaesser's work on Weimar cinema. See Elsaesser, 2000, and Elsaesser, 1988/1989.
2. Recently these ideas have been discussed in relation to the 'world music' industry and its relationship to technology, culture and globalization. See S. Feld, 2001.
3. The social aspects of Weimar culture have been discussed at length within studies of Weimar cinema. See for example Elsaesser, 2000, and see also Petro, 1987. Siegfried Kracauer, writing in Germany during the 1920s, also keenly observed the impacts on German society and culture of technological and urban development. See, for example, Kracauer, 1994.
4. See Williams, 1996, Elsaesser, 2000, pp. 235–39, and Elsaesser, 1988/1989.
5. See S. Abbott, 2004, for an account of the 'symbiotic relationship' between the vampire and cinema.

6. O'Sickey defines hypermedia as the mixing of 'sound, text, graphics, video and 35mm film' (O'Sickey, 2002, p. 123).
7. See Halle, 2002.
8. Ibid., 39–44.
9. See Haase, 2003.
10. Specifically Bram Stoker's novel *Dracula* upon which *Nosferatu* was based, the repetitive structure of *Run Lola Run*, which is derived from video games.
11. See Manovich, 2001, especially pp. 293–308.
12. Manovich also mentions the Phonoscope and Tachyscope and points out that Edison's Kinetoscope also arranged its moving images into loops. Ibid., pp. 297–98.
13. Roberta Pearson prefers the term 'verisimilar' to 'naturalistic' in her discussion of performance codes in the films of D. W. Griffith, Pearson, 1992. I use it to mark the fact that acting in this film is still highly theatrical, although far from the histrionics of earlier periods.
14. In the director's commentary of the DVD edition of the film, Tykwer remarks that he included this clock as a reminder to himself to make a horror film one day. *Run Lola Run* collector's edition DVD, (USA: Columbia Tristar Home Video & Australia: Sony Pictures, 1999).
15. Deleuze writes, 'Light and shadow no longer constitute an alternative movement in extension and enter into an intense struggle which has several stages'. *Cinema 1*, 49.
16. An episode of the *Buffy* spin-off series *Angel* includes a similar example. The episode opens with the title character basking in sunlight on a Californian beach, but the camera pulls back to reveal the fact that this is not an actual beach at all, but a film set!

# 12
## Inbetweening: Animation, Deleuze, Film Theory

*Bill Schaffer*

Why Deleuze and animation? Why this bizarre conjunction of Daffy Duck and a dead French philosopher? The purely pragmatic reason I offer for proposing this liaison is that certain commonly overlooked aspects of Deleuze's work seem uniquely able to respond to the *fact of animation*. In particular, I have come to view Deleuze's attempt to define the threshold of filmic specificity – that hypothetical point at which technological developments open up the possibility of a new and relatively autonomous artform – as one that allows us to approach both cinematography and animation as distinct yet simultaneously possible modes of a single medium. It is precisely this element of Deleuze's work, however, that has been neglected or dismissed on the grounds that it rehearses a form of old-fashioned essentialism guilty of over-generalising on the basis of selective technical facts.[1] I argue, to the contrary, that the concepts of the *any-instant-whatever* and the *intermediate image* offer valid points of departure for new forms of research and theorisation.

Most 'theorisation' that has departed from Deleuze's work on cinema seems to be concerned with reproducing, extending, sometimes 'deconstructing' his distinctions between the movement-image and the time-image and their different realisations. Few have paused to develop the implications of Deleuze's opening claim that at the most general level – prior to the subsequent distinction between the movement-image and time-image – *all* cinema may be defined by the use of the technical principle of 'any-instant-whatever' as a means for the production of moving images. The important thing to note here from the perspective of animation theory is that this formulation of the threshold of filmic specificity does not concern the content of individual frames or the implications of the photographic registration of light – as does the 'ontological' model developed by Bazin and his many followers – but instead addresses the way in which frames are *related*. It is, in short, fundamentally concerned with happens *between* frames, rather than with the content of frames, and is therefore equally able to allow for *both* animation and cinematography as equally valid, distinct modes of film.

Instead of deducing the phases of movement from pre-established 'transcendental poses', an approach Deleuze argues had previously dominated Western conceptions of movement, the logic of the any-instant-whatever depends on the automatic sampling of movements through time at a rate that is standardised and independent of content. Each moment of the movement under analysis is initially given equal weight and registered purely as 'any instant', rather than being selected as offering a significantly revealing or decisive 'pose' according to preconceived criteria. Deleuze thus tells us,

> The cinema is the system which reproduces movement as a function of any-instant-whatever that is, as a function of equidistant instants, selected so as to create an impression of continuity.
>
> (Deleuze, 1986, p. 5)

An initial confirmation that this conception of film is *not* determined by photographic ontology may be found in Deleuze's inclusion of animation in the very same paragraph where the any-instant-whatever is initially defined:

> ... if it [animation] belongs fully to the cinema, this is because the drawing no longer constitutes a pose or a completed figure, but the description of a figure which is always in the process of being formed or dissolving through the movement of lines and points taken at any-instant-whatevers of their course. The cartoon film ... does not give us a figure described in a unique moment, but the continuity of the movement which describes the figure.
>
> (Deleuze, 1986, p. 5)

Here a distinction between moments of movement-analysis and movement-synthesis becomes crucial: cinematography and animation both employ the same principle for the synthesis of movement (the moment of projection), but approach the analysis of movement (the process of recording) in radically different ways. Deleuze himself distinguishes expressly between the any-instant-whatever as principle of analysis and as principle of synthesis only when differentiating the aesthetic possibilities of film from the scientific analysis of movement. Cinema thus becomes possible when the physical result of photographic analysis of movement according to the principle of the any-instant-whatever, a strip of regularly sampled and separated images preserved in their consecutive order, is unexpectedly seized upon as a machine of synthesis for the purposes of art and entertainment (Deleuze, 1986, p. 4). Film alone, then, emerges as an industrial art for which the any-instant-whatever is a *necessary* condition of possibility. From the perspective of creative practice, the any-instant-whatever becomes the operative principle of a machine that can disconnect any image from its original context and reconnect it with any other image. Film art thus takes a principle intended for the recovery of 'whatever happens' independently of human perception, and turns it into a method for synthesising unprecedented and aberrant movements that exist only as effects of linkage.

Seen in this way, the any-instant-whatever does not impose a restrictive norm upon the possibilities of film art; to the contrary, it announces the threshold of an unprecedented and potentially infinite field of invention. Moreover, beyond the explicit formulations offered by Deleuze, the distinction between the use of this principle for analysis and synthesis carries immense implications for a theory of film that seeks to account for the fact of animation. There seems to be no need at any level, however, for temporal 'equidistance' in the *production* (or recording) of frames in the case of animation, even if these frames must be produced in *anticipation* of the equidistances imposed by the film strip. In the case of drawn animation, for example, each cel is produced not as an instantaneous perspectival unity, but as a layering of graphical processes unevenly distributed in time and space. Instead of a *transfer* that refers to the movement of already existing bodies, as with the Deleuzian account of cinema, there is in animation a *double movement of imposition and generation*. From the point of view of individual compositions, considered in isolation, recording onto a film strip involves the imposition of an indifferent measure; from the point of view of the emergent moving image, this same process involves a pure act of generation, a veritable 'giving of life'.

This is precisely what Deleuze manages to formalise in his brief reflections on the cartoon form: the animated figure *as such* is defined less by the enclosing outlines characteristic of traditional drawings than by 'the continuity of a movement', which cuts across and through any fixed pose. The specific dynamics of figuration allowed by this tension between figure and movement in animation become ('become' is appropriate here because the verb refers to something that was manifest in the very first cartoon. It cannot be 'has become' because there was no prior period in which this did not apply. If you are unable to accept this perfectly valid usage, the only alternative is 'animation has been'. That is correct, but also bland) a recurrent, reflexive theme from the time of the 'first cartoon', Emile Cohl's *Fantasmagoria* (1908). From beginning to end, as the viewer witnesses the animator's ability to bring whole cellular worlds out of dots, turn them inside out and fold them just as inexplicably back into inky nothingness, this seminal piece explores a specifically *animatic* conflict between the *freedom of lines* and the *integrity of bodies*. The hapless clown figure in *Fantasmagoria* simply never gets a chance to play out his destiny in relation to a stabilised environment, nor even to consolidate the definition of his own form. Within seconds of finding himself thrown into existence, he is forced to see his very own form doubled inside the head of another character, turned inside out, reduced to a vanishing point, inflated like a balloon to the point of explosion and unravelled into the void of surrounding space. From moment to moment, frame to frame, this literally prototypical cartoon character is threatened at the level of his most intimate definition by the very same lines that initially define him and allow him to emerge as a figure against a ground.

The freedom of the line at stake here is not just the familiar exercise of spontaneity as an artist draws; it also implies a higher-level freedom, bought precisely at the cost of subordinating manual activity to the mechanically regular demands of the any-instant-whatever – the freedom to metamorphose and evolve figures unpredictably in time. This transformative, mobile capacity of the animated line at once allows animated figures to emerge, as Broadfoot and Butler stress, by defining their borders and marking them off from the surrounding surface, and, *at the same time,* leaves them permanently vulnerable to the possibility of being undone from within, turned inside out or deprived of all dimension at any instant (Broadfoot and Butler, 1991, p. 270). In a cartoon world, indeed, nothing stops the very same line that forms the edge of a body from suddenly becoming an active, animated agent in its own right. Nothing prevents space itself from inverting all its dimensions so that environments become bodies and bodies become environments; borders become contents and contents become borders. In the context of animation, the any-instant-whatever, intended by scientific pioneers such as Marey and Muybridge as a principle for the objective time/control analysis of bodies, inverts itself to become a method not only for the synthesis of movements, but for the generation (and repeated destruction) of bodies that may be disarticulated and transformed at will. The 'first cartoon' in film history thus amounts to a reflexive demonstration of the purely *intermediate* status of bodies that emerge as a function of the any-instant-whatever.

## Invisible hand: Intermediacy and the cartoon condition

*Intermediacy* may be understood as the state of living in-between. It defines the cartoon condition and opens a whole range of possibilities of figuration and characterisation that are specific to the world of animation. Perhaps the most compelling description of animated intermediacy comes not from Deleuze himself, but from the entirely independent reflections of art animator Norman McLaren. McLaren, an artist responsible for moving films that often literally dispensed with cameras altogether, was never just a practitioner, but inseparably a theorist of animated art. In the most frequently cited attempt to define the specificity of drawn animation, he wrote,

> Animation is not the art of drawings-that-move, but rather the art of movements-that-are-drawn. What happens between each frame is more important than what happens on each frame.
> (McLaren, quoted in Solomon, 1987, p. 11)

Animated figures, it seems, are irremediably intermediate for McLaren: they exist only in moving, only in passing, only in-between, but they nonetheless exist effectively on their own plane of becoming, which must be distinguished from the level at which fixed drawings are created or encountered. Recognition that the any-instant-whatever implies a general threshold of transformation and intermediacy therefore becomes a matter of creative necessity. In a less well-known formulation McLaren generalised his definition of animation in order to allow for forms of animation that do not depend on drawings:

> If I were asked for a definition of animation it is where you can stop between any frame of film and the next frame of film and make a controlled adjustment . . . it is manipulating the difference . . .
> (McLaren, quoted in Solomon, 1987, p. 11)

McLaren's formulation here could not be more felicitous in the way it brings together a seemingly banal observation concerning the technical threshold of animation – 'you can stop any frame' – with a startlingly concise evocation of the unique possibilities implied by the animator's relationship to the any-instant-whatever – 'it is manipulating the difference'. What distinguishes animation from cinematography here is not the 'stuff' of each frame, but *the way the animator puts himself in between frames*. Animation remains this uniquely *generative* art of direct interaction with every interval of the any-instant-whatever, even when the animator chooses to leave many frames strategically blank:

> ... *Blinkity Blink* intentionally set out to investigate the possibilities of intermittent animation and spasmodic imagery. This meant that the film was not made in the usual way, one frame of the picture following inexorably after the next, each second of time crying out for its pound of visual flesh—its full quota of 24 frames; instead, on the blankness and blackness of the outstretched strip of celluloid on my table top I would engrave a frame here and a frame there, leaving many frames untouched and blank—sprinkling, as it were, the images on the empty band of time; but sprinkling carefully—in relation to each other, to the spaces between, to the music, and to the idea that emerged as I drew.
>
> (McLaren, 1976, p. 127)

One sees here the animator's typical experience of the any-instant-whatever as a matrix of emergence that effectively transforms the act of drawing and all other forms of manual manipulation. Released into intermediacy and variation, each 'sprinkling' must be carefully executed 'in relation to the other', and it is this immanent relationship that *will have* conditioned 'the idea that emerged as I drew'. The animation process *always* involves an encounter with 'the empty band of time' automatically generated by the any-instant-whatever as soon as it is deprived of a cinematographic object. Throughout McLaren's career, animation is continually rediscovered as a kind of 'meta-art' whose primary object is the creative process itself, unfolding in time, as the paradoxical discovery of something that emerges and exists only in this very process of discovery. One must now say that each frame *will have been* an any-instant-whatever in the movement of a body generated by the process itself. A specifically *animatic* temporality thus informs the possibilities of cartoon composition and characterisation, yet this can only be articulated in terms of the more general specificity of the intermediate image enabled by the any-instant-whatever.

The manual time of composition thus enters into a complex and specific relationship with the automated time of film that has no obvious parallel in the arts of drawing *or* cinematography, even when it precisely involves bringing the two into intimate relation. The animating hand becomes invisible not just, as with the camera in cinematography, because it is an object in space, occupying a point of view that can never directly appear in its own field, but because the very *time* of its generative, creative activity has *necessarily* been elided in the continuous flow of a moving image. The time of the hand is uniquely implied and potentially alluded to with every instant of animated film, yet at the same time, this time of intimacy and creation is automatically erased. In a further twist, however, the artist's manual interactions may be 'remembered' by the very same intervallic process that obliterates every trace of manual intervention:

> ... if you looked at a single frame of film you'd say that doesn't mean anything there, there's no images there, but once the thing goes into motion, the things that are there, no matter what kind of shape they may be, can behave in a human or animal way, which echoes something quite human in a person.
> (McLaren, quoted in Solomon, 1987, p. 11)

As McLaren's remarks here on the vanishing threshold between abstraction and figuration emphasise, the self-effacing process of animation can leave its trace within the image as *implied motivation of movement*. It becomes possible here to re-raise the question of *indexicality* in the context of animation. The formative activity of the animation process necessarily and uniquely renders itself invisible as an effect of the necessary temporal asymmetry between analysis and synthesis. The world-creating hand of the animator has, in other words, 'disappeared between frames', yet at the same time, it continues to charge the temporal structure of the image. The creative process of animation itself is thus at once recorded and erased by the effect of the any-instant-whatever in a way that has no parallel in traditional graphic arts or cinematography – it is recorded *in* being erased; erased *in* being recorded. The indexicality of animation is not one figured in traces of light – as is the indexicality traditionally privileged in film studies – but through the logic of the any-instant-whatever.

The cartoon film may be based on drawing; but the animator's practice becomes unlike any other form of drawing as soon as he ceases to relate to the drawing taken in isolation and projects himself into the automatic in-between of the any-instant-whatever. Chuck Jones says more or less the same thing:

> One of the odd misunderstandings about animation even by those who work in the field is that an individual drawing has the same

importance as an illustration. Animation is a chorus of drawings working in tandem, each contributing a part to the whole of a time/space idea. If a single drawing, as a drawing, dominates the action, it is probably bad animation, even though it may be a good drawing.
(Cawley, 1990, p. 39)

It is in precisely this sense, as we have already seen Deleuze claim, that in the cartoon film 'the drawing no longer constitutes a pose or a completed figure, but the description of a figure which is always in the process of being formed or dissolving'. Fated to intermediacy, the animated figure finds itself always 'opened' up to the next interval by the same force that would 'close' it in relation to the preceding interval: the force of a movement to which its own life is immanent. The *animated figure*, always already caught up in the any-instant-whatever as in its own life, can never be definitively 'figured' on any single frame of the film strip, and this 'fate' of cartoon figures has more than merely technical consequences, repeatedly entering into the emotional lives of characters. At the level of content, this *cartoon condition* is repeatedly revealed as a source of hilarious tragedy in the lives of cartoon characters. This existential predicament is perhaps most memorably illustrated in Chuck Jones' famous *Duck Amuck* (1953), in which Daffy is not only forced to see himself transformed into a bulbous, flower-headed, polka-dotted alien, then squashed and stretched by the drooping mass of the film frame itself, but even has to endure the experience of seeing his visible form erased altogether.

The animator, however, also finds himself fated to a kind of intermediate practice in which the exercise of total control and immersion in a process that exceeds conscious control come together. The documentary film *Norman McLaren: Creative Process* (Huyce & McWilliams, 1990) makes visible this irreducibly intermediate condition of the working animator as it is experienced from the independent, self-consciously experimental end of the animatic continuum. As we watch McLaren inking directly onto the film strip, the anticipated accompanying musical soundtrack is previewed for the viewer. This music effectively reminds us of the rhythmic, continuously varying image that the animator aims to produce, but it is also made to stutter and grind to a halt as McLaren moves from to frame, rendering tangible for the viewer the strangely interrupted continuity that animators must internalise. Alongside the film strip on which McLaren works, we observe the 24 numbered registration points necessary for each second of film. In search of spontaneity, McLaren moves quickly from one frame to the next, as if trying to reiterate the momentum and integrity of a single unfolding gesture across 24 frames, but each new second's worth of film requires that this momentum be suspended and interrupted at a higher level as the entire setup is realigned. McLaren is at one level like a god surveying the extent of his creation as it emerges, but only within a narrow temporal span:

> I wasn't aware of the general line of what was going to happen 10, 20 seconds from now. I was always aware of how things were developing, this was going to happen in the next five seconds, but a minute from now in the film, what was going to happen, I just didn't know.
> 
> (McLaren, quoted in Solomon, 1987, p. 11)

The conditions of creativity in the context of animation always more or less forcefully generate this kind of rhythm between manual spontaneity and the indifferent measure of the any-instant-whatever. This rhythm, which articulates the paradox of a controlled loss of control, an intended escape from intention, apparently takes the isolated animator beyond himself, just as it takes the isolated graphic figure beyond itself. McLaren's own words thus suggest that the peculiar forms of creativity associated with the animation process can only be understood in relation to, rather than in spite of, the mechanical regularities imposed by the film strip. The creative process in animation implies an irreducible paradox whereby creative spontaneity is at once compromised *and* facilitated by mechanical regularity.

## A strange shape: Becoming cartoon

Four very different evocations of creative process, as quoted below, in the context of animation begin to resonate irresistibly here. The first of these comes to us from the animator Bob Clampett; the second from stop-motion animator Lou Bunin; the third from a spoken interview with Norman McLaren; the fourth from Peter Canning's paraphrasing of Deleuze's philosophy of time:

> If I'm doing Porky Pig I don't stand off removed from Porky directing him; I get inside of Porky and I think Porky. I talk like Porky. I have a s-s-s-s-speech problem. I walk like Porky, and I feel like Porky ... I'm helpful, trusting, concerned, kindly and sometimes a trifle

pu-pu-pu-put out. S-s-s-s-shucks, I am Porky... Bugs' personality is quite the opposite of Porky's. And much more fun to do. When I do Bugs Bunny I get inside of him, and I not only think like, feel like, and walk and talk like Bugs [whispers] but confidentially, Doc, [yells] *I am the wabbit!*

(Lenburg, 1983, p. 57)

If you interpret somebody else's acting ideas, the result can't possibly be important. If you have no inner reaction that you can express by becoming the puppet, then you have no way to transmit vital elements to a performance. You have to be the character in order to make it believable.

Suddenly as a performer, if you have the good sense to follow the performance of the puppet while you are that character, you sense what is right, what is funny or dramatic. You can't anticipate that on your exposure sheets . . . Then you get that creative feeling that is so familiar to every good animator I know; you become the performer in a strange shape, and become the audience at the same time. You are amazed at what is happening, the thing that you yourself are doing. I don't know of another art form that gives such a dual experience to the artist.

(Culhane, 1986, p. 381)

When doing *Hen Hop* for instance, I felt that I was . . . that [hen] . . . doing the dance . . . I sort of got imbued with the spirit of henliness, I think. So, in a way when you're animating a creature, if the creature is moving, you are that animal, you feel the motion.

(McLaren, quoted in Solomon, 1987, p. 11)

[T]he strings of the marionette or the body of the actor are not connected to the will of the puppeteer or actor or author, but to the second order automaton of the human body-brain rhizome . . . From virtual to actual and back, in the ever-renewing feedback loop of self-motivation. [. . .] The difference 'of' immediacy 'with' itself 'in' time forms the smallest internal circuit between the self and itself . . . as in the mirror or mime.

(Canning, 1994, p. 79)

The artist *becomes* the emerging character. To evoke the idea of 'becoming' in this context is not, of course, to make the absurd claim that the animator's physical body somehow metamorphoses to resemble the cartoon character's body. Nor is it a mere matter of metaphor. In a quite specific sense, the animator or puppeteer discovers the character acting in himself, in the virtual, from moment to moment. There is a temporal loop between two bodies, one actual, the other virtual, which must be qualified as neither separable nor identical in their relationship to each other. The moments of acting out oneself and witnessing the bodying forth of another become entwined and begin to chase each other in an open loop of creativity. The self-affective element implied in all acting (indeed, for Bergson, in all creativity) is taken to a specific limit and instantiated in a uniquely animatic feedback circuit between 'human inwardness' and 'mechanical externality' that is at once played out, experienced, recorded *and* erased *as* time.

The animator, as Clampett's words have it, finds himself re-animated in turn by the characters he animates and feels himself becoming a cartoon. According to McLaren's testimony, the artist allows himself to become 'imbued with henliness' when animating a hen. The character must thus come to life within the body of the animator if it is to have any chance of coming alive for the viewer. Rather than remaining above and separate to the material he transforms – the animating artist puts himself into a circuit from which new forms of movement and motivation emerge. The animator's or puppeteer's experience of his own creativity is thus shaped by an irreducible paradox of control in time that hardly could be stated more boldly than by Bunin: he follows the character, even though the character exists and moves only as an effect of the animator's own controlling movement. The animator becomes the performer, the character and the audience, simultaneously following himself and pre-empting himself as other-in-himself, self-displaced from self, moment to moment. The animator *himself* thus becomes an image of variation and intermediacy. Character and performer thus become indiscernible and meet in the emergence of 'a strange shape'.

According to Canning, explicator of Deleuze, the multiple strings of the moving puppet are never simply controlled from a single point embodying the 'will' of the puppeteer. Powers of influence are ramified in every direction across all the scales of a network of control that cannot be monitored from any point simply external to itself without killing the entire process. The puppeteer or animator may initiate this dance of strings and displaced bodies, but once set in motion, it reverberates unpredictably, takes on a life of its own, one in which the artist's entire body becomes but one of many dancing limbs. Resonances of influence are conducted back through the pencil into the vibrating network formed by the strings of the artist's nervous system. We approach, here, the heart of the paradox of animatic intention already encountered in McLaren. It is as though the emerging character draws out an inner reaction that at the same time functions as an intentionality directed towards drawing the character itself out of the void of each cel.

The irreducible difference of animation, both as a mode of film and as a form of manual art, thus seems to be intimately related to a singular experience of time implied by the use of the any-instant-whatever for the synthesis of virtual bodies. It has been testified to repeatedly by practitioners working across the continuum that stretches from commercial character animation to avant-garde experimentation:

> Animation is not a simple form to pin down; it has surprisingly little to do with other graphic arts, because it adds that elusive element—time.
> (Chuck Jones, backcover dedication, Klein, 1993)

> We were in a new medium altogether. It was not only the orchestration of form but also of time-relationship that we were facing in film. The single image disappeared in a flow of images, which made sense only if it happened to articulate a new element—time.
> (Hans Richter, quoted in Russett and Starr, 1976, p. 53)

Reflecting on their experience of animation, Chuck Jones, the American master of commercial cartoonery, and Hans Richter, the European avant-gardist, say almost exactly the same thing, even down to the way they leave the word 'time' dangling from a dash at the end of their sentences – like a cartoon character who has just gone charging over an abyss. The self-affective, intrinsically temporal nature of creative process is, of course, not confined to animation. In Deleuzian terms, it is at the basis of all art. Nonetheless, the paradoxes of self-affectivity are taken to a new level by the practice of animation, to the point where self-division becomes a kind of graphic obsession within a popular art form.

In conclusion, I wish to suggest that the richest promise of Deleuze's work for the future study of film lies not in treating his already established categories as templates for faithful reproduction, but in the use of the most neglected and derided aspect of his work – the attempt to define the threshold of filmic specificity – as one possible *launching pad* for the testing of new approaches to film that no longer arbitrarily privilege cinematography over animation. Such a shift seems especially appropriate at a time when digital technologies are bringing the world of cartoons and movies into unprecedented, unexpected forms of relationship.

## Note

1. For the dismissal of Deleuze's work by a committed detractor on the grounds that the entire project of defining the specificity of cinema is bankrupt, see David Bordwell, *On the History of Film Style* (1997, p. 116). Bordwell clearly conflates Deleuze's analysis of the implications of the automatic synthesis of movement automatic with the far more familiar theme of the automated/chemical registration of light developed in the work of Bazin. Bordwell thereby reduces Deleuze's arguments to a mere reiteration of the very film-theoretical prejudices that I suggest his work allows us to escape.

# 13
# Affective Troubles and Cinema

*Marie-Luise Angerer*

Thinking about the links between cinema and affect is not necessarily original. After all, cinema has always operated with affective charges, physical reactions and imaginary escapes. But the current discussion on affect and film/media is different. Rather than the question of how film addresses the imaginary dimension within the viewer, the primary focus is now on the brain activity that triggers the affective response. In this theory, a focus on affect replaces the focus on representations and desire in structuralist/psychoanalytical film theory. A first criticism was formulated by Gilles Deleuze in his books *Cinema 1* and *Cinema 2*, which are currently receiving new and increased attention. But Deleuze's notions of affect are now being combined with findings from neurology. Mark B. N. Hansen's *New Philosophy for New Media* is a good example. Film, media, art on the one hand, brain and affect on the other are now being linked via Spinoza (Damasio, 2003) and Bergson (Hansen, 2004). This frames the image/spectator pair in a new way, with the unconscious dimension replaced by affect.

## From the pleasure of looking to the emotion machine

From 1970 through the mid-1980s, film theory was dominated by Marxist-psychoanalytical Apparatus Theory, which viewed cinema as an extremely influential ideological state apparatus (in the Althusserian sense) that caught the viewer – like a small child – in the mirror phase of screen, camera and gaze. Everything that takes place between the viewer and the screen was analysed in terms of these three elements and their imaginary productions. Apparatus Theory is interested not so much in the impact of film, but in why it can exert such a libidinous attraction. And the answer it gives is, because sexuality and desire are always already inscribed in the field of the visual (or vanish into it) as driving forces of the human subject.[1] Since then, Apparatus Theory has been replaced by cognitive film theory, which now dominates the discussion on emotion and affect in cinema, taking as its basis psychology and its repertoire of empirical theories of emotion. The techniques used in film are linked with the viewer's cognitive make-up, which is supposed to explain cinema's emotional impact. Accordingly, the question asked by David Bordwell and Kristin Thompson, the chief proponents of cognitive film psychology, could be summed up in simplified terms (Bordwell and Thompson, 1994) as, 'How do the staged emotions shown on screen manage to produce the emotions felt by the viewer?' One factor contributing to the rise of cognitive film theory is the tendency of recent years in cognitive science to attempt to pin down emotions and affects using digital calculation and imaging techniques. In her essay in the collection *Mediale Emotionen,* Sigrid Weigel analyses the notion of emotion that these new recording and localization techniques claim to capture. For it is clear, as the author emphasizes, that it is not emotions that are being measured here but brain activity that is interpreted as feelings. In Weigel's view, 'the current conception of feelings (or emotions) [. . .] represents the return of a notion of pathos from the age of *sensibilité*' (Weigel, 2005, p. 244). This is a reference to the eighteenth century, when emotion was conceived of as a medium that had to communicate between a 'sensibilité morale' and a 'sensibilité physique' to bridge the gap between body and intellect.

In the same book, Andreas Keil and Jens Eder summarize the relationship between audio-visual media and emotional networks to show how broad today's understanding of 'affective phenomena' has become. It covers intensive, short-lived emotions as in a romantic happy end, diffuse, subliminal moods like at the start of a horror film and reflex-like affective reactions like those triggered by the explosions in a spectacular action scene, but also empathy, liking and desire, aesthetic pleasure and political-ideological sympathy (see Keil/Eder, 2005, p. 224). The authors begin by explaining that the early '90s saw a shift within film theory, with 'psychoanalytical affect theories' like those developed by Laura Mulvey and Louis Baudry being sidelined as undifferentiated and unempirical (p. 238). It should be emphasized here, however, that affect was not an explicit theme of the psychoanalytical-structuralist film theories of the '70s and '80s, as Apparatus Theory dealt with here; instead, the focus was on unconscious identification and the ideological production of the subject.

Today, however, in the process of a comprehensive emotionalization of media and cultural theories, psychoanalysis (and with it the associated film theory of the '70s and '80s) is accused of having neglected affect. In *Moral Spectatorship* (Cartwright, 2008), Lisa Cartwright summarizes the debate on representation versus affect in psychoanalysis and film theory as the basis for her claim against psychoanalysis, and especially against feminist film theory of this period, that its blindness to affect was based on political premises. In other words, the stronger party at the time was psychoanalysis with its focus on language, Freudian slips and symptoms. According to Cartwright, affect was not acceptable to advocates of feminism for political reasons, as it was always located too close to the body, especially the female body. But today, as she writes, affect must be taken into account in a reorientation towards theoretical premises of the object relations theory of Donald Winnicott and Melanie Klein, as well as the psychological affect theory of Silvan Tomkins. Both Cartwright's work on media and affect and Eve Kosofsky Sedgwick's publications on Silvan Tomkins' affect theory are at pains to privilege a subject framed in terms of affect over the sexually coded subject of psychoanalytical film theory.[2]

## The return of the repressed of cinema

But the shift within film theory predates these recent developments. Gilles Deleuze's books *L'image mouvement* and *L'image-temps* (1983 and 1985 in French, available in English from 1986 and 1989 as *The Movement-Image* and *The Time-Image*) opened up another language of cinema, and with it another theoretical approach to the nature of film. Deleuze talks about the body of the viewer, about affect, about framing and about informatics. As Deleuze states in the second volume, 'The life or the afterlife of the cinema depends on its internal struggles with informatics' (Deleuze, 1989, p. 270).

In the wake of Deleuze's *Cinema 1* and *Cinema 2*, publications began to appear that spoke out more or less openly against psychoanalytical film theory, criticizing it as overly rigid and not capable of doing justice to the moving nature of film. In his *Cinematic Body* from 1993, for example, Steven Shaviro writes that the body becomes lost in cinematic space, thus moving beyond the reach of time, the generator of meaning. He speaks of a 'somatic gaze' and about speed and motion as the primal gestures of cinema (Morsch, 1999, pp. 21–44). Feminist film theory, too, has now focused on Deleuze, criticizing terms like gender and identification and foregrounding the body and its becoming-other through affection.[3] Deleuze's cinema books have also been a major influence in the debate on the digital image, which was seen from the outset as having a special relationship with the affective and the physical.

In the film and media theory of the '90s, then, the body of the spectator becomes not only more important, but also more mobile, integrating itself into the filmic spectacle. For a short period, older approaches such as Vivian Sobchack's phenomenological film analysis competed with the gradual spread of digital images (in the form of computer games, digital photography, TV and cinema images) in a kind of desperate struggle for the body of the spectator/viewer. In the '80s, Sobchack heroically defended cinema against the new digital images: the experiential body, she explained, is awakened to life by the movie screen – since the film is experienced not as a thing but as an image that presents an objective world, the viewer can partake of this embodied experience. In her view, whereas film gives access to experience, photography mummifies and electronic media build a meta-world where everything revolves around representation per se, producing a system of simulation without reference – referentiality becomes intertextuality, entailing a process of disembodiment (cf. Sobchack, 1994).

Unlike the affective pull of images that is postulated today, however, this physical involvement in film is not direct, being understood instead in symbolic-phantasmatic terms. When discussed in the context of digital images today, on the other hand, the body is viewed primarily in terms of its pure – and affective –materiality.

In her 2000 book *The Skin of the Film*, Laura Marks spoke of a haptic visuality[4] that allows the film to be 'seen' through the skin. In her more recent book *Touch: Sensuous Theory and Multisensory Media* (2002), video, multimedia and even TV are used to experience haptic realities. Marks describes the trend of making digitally perfect images 'dirty' again as 'analog nostalgia':

> Paradoxically, the age of so-called virtual media has hastened the desire for indexicality. In popular culture, now that so many spectacular images are known to be computer simulations, television viewers are tuning in to 'reality' programming, and Internet surfers are fixing on live webcam transmissions in a hunt for unmediated reality. Among digital videomakers, one of the manifestations of the desire for indexicality is what I call analog nostalgia, a retrospective fondness for the 'problems' of decay and generational loss that analog video posed. In the high-fidelity medium of digital video, where each generation can be as imperviously perfect as the one before, artists are importing images of electronic dropout and decay, 'TV snow,' and the random colors of unrecorded tape, in a sort of longing for analog physicality. Interestingly, analog nostalgia seems especially prevalent

among works by students who started learning video production when it was fully digital.

(Marks, 2002, p. 152)

## Affective framing

In terms of perception, traditional cinema kept its viewers immobile and cast a spell over them by means of the camera, editing, montage, sound and so on. As numerous analyses suggest, digital images appeal to viewers in their entire physicality. A much-cited hallmark of the new image worlds is immersion, which overrides self-control, activating the body.

This active body is explained with reference to the specific quality of the digital image, that is, its lack of frame. In the current debate on the status of the digital image, attention focuses on two issues: firstly, that of a post-medium condition, in which digitization has deprived each individual medium of its specific difference. Be it cinema, television or photography – they are all subject to the same conditions of production and postproduction. The cinematic image is thus no longer enclosed within a frame, mirror or window. Instead, it is integrated into a network of images that requires an entirely different form of viewing. 'Our perception has very much become an affective processing that is constant spatial and temporal fluctuation' (Laine, 2006). And secondly, this abolition of difference between media corresponds to a deframing of images as such: not only do the various media flow into one another, but the images themselves have also lost their stability,[5] which is why there has recently been such renewed interest in affective body, as we will see below.

This framelessness of digital images is a constant theme discussed by, for example, Lev Manovich and Mark Hansen, who come to different conclusions. Lev Manovich argues that only the invisible basis of image production has changed and that what we see is still images: 'Since its beginnings fifty years ago, computerization of photography (and cinematography) has by now completely changed the internal structure of a photographic image; yet its "skin", i.e. the way the image looks, still largely remains the same. It is therefore possible that at some point in the future the "skin" of an image would also become completely different, but this did not happen yet. So we can say at present our visual culture is characterized by a new computer "base" and old photographic "superstructure." [. . .] What remains to be seen is how the "superstructure" of a photographic image—what it represents and how—will change to accommodate this "base"' (Manovich, 2004).

In his *New Philosophy for New Media* (2004), Mark B. N. Hansen refers to Manovich's analysis, but states that his expectations are disappointed by it. Manovich, he says, adopts an ultimately humanist position, only according images relevance in terms of their relationship with the viewer (consumer), and only perceiving and interpreting them as filmic images. As a result, Hansen claims, Manovich completely fails to identify the specific quality of digital images because he clings to the primacy of the cinematographic. Unlike classical cinema, the pre-cinema era already offered technical options linking perception and tactility: the stereoscope, the panorama, the mutoscope – in all of these cases, the viewers are required to use their hands, to move, to adopt a position in order to see the pictures in question, obliged to manoeuvre themselves physically into the corresponding receptive position. As Hansen goes on to explain, this is comparable with today's virtual realities like computer games and simulation environments, which therefore call for a new philosophy that puts the body in touch with its sensuality as an active agent. In Hansen's view, the philosophy of Henri Bergson is appropriate, since it understands the various visual registers always and exclusively in connection with the affective body. In *New Philosophy*, as well as relating Bergson's theory of the affective body to digital media, Hansen also subjects Deleuze's theory of cinema to a comprehensive critique: unlike Bergson, he points out, Deleuze separates affect from the body and attributes it to the technical procedure. As Hansen underlines, this reduces affect to a technical effect. According to Henri Bergson, however, perception without affect is not possible, as suggested by his writing 'that our body is not a mathematical point in space, that its virtual actions are complicated by, and impregnated with, real actions, or, in other words, that there is no perception without affection. Affection is, then, that part or aspect of the inside of our body which we mix with the image of external bodies; it is what we must first of all subtract from perception to get the image in its purity' (Bergson, 1994, p. 58). For Hansen, this means that where the reception of digital images is concerned, the central role played by the viewer's body is not only new but also exclusive: 'In a very material sense the body is the 'coprocessor' of digital information' (Hansen, 2004, p. xxvi), with the production of framing taking place 'in and through our own bodies' (p. 76).

It is striking, however, how little attention is paid to the auditive dimension, even in Hansen's work, although it seems quite obvious that affect and hearing are profoundly linked. One of the few studies of this is Sean Cubitt's *Digital Aesthetics* (1998) in which the author emphasizes the role played by sound technologies. According to

Cubitt, the domination of contemporary cinema by sound is at odds with the medium's two-sided claim to reality. The perfecting of sound technology and the organization of audio data in the space create an antagonist to the image. This antagonist is the sound and its auditive space. In Cubitt's view, digital sound technology acquires the status of a three-dimensional art form that intervenes in the old alliance of film apparatus and its production of signs of reality. The audio space of the cinema forms the interface between the media virtuality of the events on the screen and the reality of the listener's body, which is completely captured by what it is hearing. What Cubitt describes here can be heard and experienced particularly well in the works of Janet Cardiff and George Bures Miller. In *The Paradise Institute* (2001),[6] in *The Berlin Files* (2003) and in the *Audio and Video Walks* (since 1991), the soundtrack and the images are separate, each producing its own rhythm. This leads to disorientation, or to a more intensive perception of one's own physical position in space, as Cardiff has repeatedly underlined. Jörg Heiser has described what Cardiff and Miller do in their works as follows: '[they] translate the classical philosophical and religious body-and-soul-dualism debate into a contemporary art chiasmus [. . .] of physical presence and absence on the one hand and media-psychological making-present and making-distant on the other' (Heiser, 2005, p. 30). Rather than the kind of simulation featured in so many media art projects, he continues, what is rendered newly accessible here is the original experience of the cinema.

## Affective relays

The mental work required of the film viewer is characterized by two aspects in particular – and both are specifically linked with the human subject: 'seeing oneself see' and a special relation to duration, that is, to time, which always becomes subjective time. 'Seeing oneself see' is how Jacques Lacan describes the fundamental rift in the cogito, which is then 'healed' by the image, the mirror, the screen. With digital imaging operations, this mechanism now takes place under amplified conditions. At the same time, these images intensify the experience of time passing, which, via memory, allows the self to emerge. As Deleuze has explained on this subject, memory is the 'true name of self-reference or self-affection. According to Kant, time is the form in which the self affects itself, just as space is the form in which the self is affected by something else: consequently, time is 'auto-affection' and forms the essential structure of subjectivity. But time as subject, or rather as the constitution of subject, is called memory' (Deleuze, 1988, p. 23).

No other medium than film is better able to deploy and present these two aspects, 'seeing oneself see' and 'affection through time' – they take us to the core of cinema, to its very heartbeat. Perception of movement and perception in motion could be said to be what the cinematographic impulse hinges on.

And this axis – seeing and movement – is also at the centre of negotiations in cybernetics. As both act and subject matter, writes Stefan Rieger, seeing movement is a prototypical arena for negotiating 'that which—in whatever semantic nuance of the unconscious—eschews both control and monitoring, allowing it to become one of the showpieces of cybernetics in the broadest sense' (Rieger, 2003, p. 100). This means that human perception can only be understood and reproduced in technical terms to a certain degree, part of it remaining in the unconscious, an unconscious that is credited, at least by the physicists of the nineteenth century (and by today's neurobiologists), with extreme efficiency. Human perception always involves an element of the fantastic, which can be neither measured nor otherwise pinned down. This fantasy or capacity for virtuality, this ability to imagine things that have yet to come into being and to transpose oneself from an actual state of being into another potential state of being, is speculatively and of course anthropomorphizingly attributed and transferred to digital image production.

Affect now seems to be opening up as an inter-zone between unconscious virtuality and digital virtuality – a definition particularly linked with Deleuze's cinema books, in which the author presented his adaptation of Bergson to the cinema. For Bergson, rather than being separated from the visual, the auditive is included within the image, in which movement and interval are also inscribed. Following Bergson, Deleuze now defines affect in terms of this interval, but without the interval being filled by it. Instead, he sees affect as indicating a movement, but one that is not yet action:

> Affection is what occupies the interval, what occupies it without filling it in or filling it up. It surges in the centre of indetermination, that is to say in the subject, between a perception which is troubling in certain respects and a hesitant action. [. . .] There is therefore a relationship between affection and movement in general [. . .] But, it is precisely in affection that the movement ceases to be that of translation in order to become movement of expression.
> 
> (Deleuze, 1986, pp. 65–66)

For Deleuze, however, affect is still associated with the spectator/image relation as an affective link, creating a space he refers to as the 'any-space-whatever' (Deleuze, 1986, p. 122) – an empty, separate space that is neither geometric nor geographic nor social, not actually a space in any strict sense of the term. These 'any-space-whatevers' are marked by optical or acoustic situations; and these 'opsigns and sonsigns' refer, as Deleuze writes, to a 'crisis of the action-image' (p. 120).

Mark Hansen picks up on this 'any-space-whatever', identifying it now in digital art praxis, but this time outside of any cinematographic framing. This difference between Deleuze and Hansen is important insofar as the autonomy of affect in Deleuze is one that goes beyond the subject, and then recaptures it from outside, from the screen. Hansen, on the other hand, links it with a neurobiological approach that has in general terms ceased to be interested in the question of the subject (its language, its desire).

Hansen thus follows a current trend of playing affect off against language, against representation, against concepts of the subject as a whole. However far removed Silvan Tomkins' theory of affect may be from Henri Bergson's concept of affect, the distance is reduced to nothing in the moment of their exclusive central focus on affect. Here, then, media and cultural theories with their current orientation toward Tomkins and his new focus on shame (see Kosofsky Sedgwick, 1995 and Cartwright, 1995) meet with Hansen's exclusive emphasis on the 'affective body' (in the Bergsonian sense), which is less visual than sensual: 'The affective body does not so much see as feel the space of the film; it feels it, moreover, as an energized, haptic spatiality within itself' (Hansen, 2004, p. 232).

With his Bergsonist affective body-centrism, then, Hansen opens up a potential link to current research in neurobiology. When the response to images is seen primarily in terms of secretions, with a particular focus on the activities of the brain (as the seat of affective cognition), then the distance from Antonio Damasio's 'I feel therefore I am' (Damasio, 1999) and the affect theory of Silvan Tomkins is merely a question of degree.

In her introduction to Silvan Tomkins, Eve Kosofsky Sedgwick underlines that for someone with a background in cultural or media studies, it is doubtless hard at first to accept the biological approach. But once this hurdle has been cleared, she writes, then one recognizes the high degree of freedom in Tomkins' theory of affect. It states that the computer is more free than the calculator, since the latter can only perform specific calculations, whereas the computer, as a universal machine, can process everything – image, sound, language:

> Affect, unlike the drives, has a degree of competency and complexity that affords it the relative ability to motivate the human to greater degrees of freedom. For freedom is measured quantitatively, in degrees of cognitive competency and complexity. Tomkins even proposes a principle for freedom, suggesting Freud's pleasure principle as the model. He calls it the information complexity, or "degrees-of-freedom principle"'.
>
> (Kosofsky Sedgwick/Frank, 1995, p. 35)

This example makes very clear what the introduction of a central and primary focus on affect will mean for thinking about the subject in the long term – as a subject based on language and desire, it will gradually disappear.

## Emotional navel-gazing

The affect-related developments described here are not a sign of a general revival of sensual pleasures; they should be interpreted instead in terms of a conquest of the affective dimension of the body. This may sound banal, but against the backdrop of the widespread frenzy of feelings that appears to have gripped even the theorists of emotion and affect, we should not lose sight of it entirely.

In his essay *Zu spät, zu früh?* (Elsaesser, 2005), Thomas Elsaesser addresses this, speaking of the emotion of the protagonists in the film theory business. Elsaesser, too, finds that they do not more than celebrate cinema as an event, radically distancing themselves from psychoanalysis, especially in its Lacanian form. In his view, however, this discontent with theories of viewing is in itself an emotion that is shared by various fractions, even where they operate with completely different sets of concepts. He attributes central importance within this discussion to the concept of 'experience', which, as he says, does not enable access to immediacy and presence. Interestingly enough, however, he goes on to note, particular emphasis is placed not only on the experience of time, but also, in the same context, trauma. Just as Walter Benjamin saw 'shock effects' as characteristic of his time, for Elsaesser, we are now clearly living in a situation characterized by 'Erlebnis ohne Erfahrung' (experience that leaves no trace, p. 415). In his opinion, this is to be blamed in part on the media with their superabundance of images and their sonic onslaughts: they produce a 'somatic context for perception that is so saturated with media experiences that its modes of reception, reaction, and action require various forms of detachment and unpicking of the sensomotory apparatus [. . .] in order to function' (p. 438). Elsaesser understands this somatic-affective turn, then, not as a new, intensive relationship between spectator and movie screen, but as a sign of a wound, as the expression of a *new malady of the soul* (Kristeva, 1995) – 'affective troubles'.

### Closing credits: Affective ideology?

In my opinion, the affective turn that can be identified in film and media studies is not a new turn in the development of the humanities; instead it signals a movement at a deeper level. My impression is that the uncritical reception and repetition of neurobiological concepts in film and media theory should be interpreted more as ideological bandwagoning. Brian Massumi stated in an interview that 'it is really important to understand affect 'after a society of ideology'. Ideology is still around but it is not as embracing as it was, and in fact it does operate. But to really understand it you have to understand its materialization, which goes through affect' (Massumi, 2003). This would also make sense of Slavoj Žižek's definition of ideology, according to which it works today because we believe that we know. We know, but in spite of this belief, or perhaps precisely because of it, we follow the mainstream. Ideology is therefore to be situated entirely on the side of doing and is completely excluded from knowing.

### Notes

1. The main proponents of Apparatus Theory include Jean-Louis Baudry, Christian Metz, Jean-Louis Comolli and Laura Mulvey. For a survey of these positions, see Angerer, 1999, pp. 56–99.
2. In Anglo-American media and cultural studies, there is an unmistakable trend towards affective theories, with the American psychologist Silvan Tomkins beginning to play a prominent role. See in particular Kosofsky Sedgwick; Adam, 1995; and Cartwright (forthcoming).
3. See for example Rosi Braidotti (2002, 2006) and Elizabeth Grosz (1994).
4. 'Haptic cinema appeals to a viewer who perceives with all the senses. It involves thinking with your skin, or giving as much significance to the physical presence of an other as to the mental operations of symbolization. This is not a call to willful regression but to recognizing the intelligence of the perceiving body. Haptic cinema, by appearing to us as an object with which we

interact rather than an illusion into which we enter, calls on this sort of embodied intelligence. In the dynamic movement between optical and haptic ways of seeing, it is possible to compare different ways of knowing and interacting with others' (Marks, 2000, p. 18).
5. 'The digitalization explodes the frame, extending the image without limit not only in every spatial dimension but into a time freed from its presentation as variant series of (virtual) images. In this sense, the digital image poses an aesthetic challenge to the cinema, one that calls for a new "will to art" and one whose call is answered by the neo-Bergsonist embodied aesthetic of new media art' (Hansen, 2004, p. 245).
6. Canadian Pavilion, 49th Venice Biennale, 2001.

# 14
# Afterword – Digital Cinema and the Apparatus: Archaeologies, Epistemologies, Ontologies

*Thomas Elsaesser*

## Can film history go digital?

The spectre stalking film history is that of its own obsolescence. It is widely assumed that the digital convergence between image, audio and print media – and thus the practice of multimedia – must inevitably modify and eventually overturn our traditional notions of film history. Even if we concede that this assumption rests on several unstated premises, both about this convergence and about film history, it is evident that the electronic media do not fit neatly into a linear or chronologically conceived film history, focussed on film as text, autonomous work or artefact. However, it is not at all obvious that digitization is the reason why the new media present such a challenge, historically as well as theoretically, to cinema studies. Perhaps it merely forces into the open inherent flaws and contradictions, shortcomings and misconceptions in our current picture? Does the digital image constitute a radical break in the practice of imaging, or is it merely a logical-technological continuation of a long and complex history of mechanical vision, which traditional film theory has never fully tried to encompass? Is film history vulnerable because it has operated with notions of origins and teleology that even on their own terms are untenable in the light of what we know, for instance, about early cinema? This chapter takes the latter question as its working hypothesis, and in order to do so, I want to start with identifying a number of what I take to be typical attitudes among film scholars when it comes to responding to the new media or multimedia.

## We have to draw a line in the silicon sand

To some of my generation, the electronic media (TV and digital media) do not belong to the history of cinema at all. On this side of the divide are above all those for whom the photographic image is sacred, and for whom celluloid is the baseline of a 150-year visual heritage that must not be plundered, devalued, faked or forged. Jean Douchet, a respected critic in the tradition of André Bazin, thinks the loss of the indexical link with the real in the digital image presents a major threat to mankind's pictorial patrimony, as well as to a cinéphile universe, of which he feels himself to be the guardian:

> The shift towards virtual reality is a shift from one type of thinking to another, a shift in purpose, which modifies, disturbs, perhaps even perverts man's relation to what is real. All good films, we used to say in the 1960s, when the cover of *Cahiers du cinéma* was still yellow, are documentaries, . . . and filmmakers deserved to be called 'great' precisely because of their near obsessive focus on capturing reality and respecting it, respectfully embarking on the way of knowledge. [Today, on the other hand], cinema has given up the purpose and the thinking behind individual shots, in favour of images – rootless, textureless images – designed to violently impress by constantly inflating their spectacular qualities.[1]

At the limit, multimedia for Douchet is a revival of the old futurist and fascist obsession with speed and kinetics, the most superficial kind of activism, kinetic avant-gardism and sensationalism, making digital effects a childish toy, a grimace disfiguring the face of the seventh art.

On the other side of the silicone divide stand those for whom, with the promise of 'virtual reality', Bazin's prediction of an age-old dream is finally fulfilling itself, that of man creating his own immortal double. According to this argument, all previous audio-visual media, and especially the cinema, are but poor cousins and incomplete sketches of such an aspiration. Now, in the digital domain, thanks to virtual reality, we can really 'break through' the screen: 'no more actors, no more story, no more sets, which is to say that in the perfect aesthetic illusion of reality, there is no more cinema.' (Bazin, 1971, p. 60).[2]

## It's business as usual

For those holding the view that it is business as usual, the argument might go as follows: The film industry, for nearly a hundred years, has been delivering the same basic product, the full-length feature film, as the core of the cinematic spectacle and the institution cinema. Technological innovations there have been all along, but they have always been absorbed and accommodated, possibly reconfiguring the economics of production, but they have left intact the context of reception and the manner of programming. Digitization does not appear to have changed this state of affairs. On the contrary, the contemporary industry standard – the star- and spectacle-driven blockbuster – dominates the audio-visual landscape more visibly than ever, attracting vast global audiences, incorporating digital effects in live action and perfecting computer-generated graphics for fully animated narrative films. As one of the blockbuster's most successful practitioners ever, George Lucas, has opined, 'Digital is like saying: are you going to use a Panavision or an Arriflex [camera]? Are you going to write with a pen or on your little laptop? I mean, it doesn't change a thing' (Quoted in Kelly and Parisi, 1997, p. 164).

Even though Lucas, as owner of the most innovative and lucrative special effects factory (Industrial Light & Magic), may have changed his mind since, there is, among film scholars, a sizeable and respected group who would concur with such a downgrading of the importance of the digital revolution for feature film-making. They maintain that the formal system that has underpinned Hollywood and other mainstream commercial cinema practices for the past 80 years, based as it is on the three- or five-act model of Western drama, which is itself more than 2500 years old, namely 'classical narrative', is alive and well in the digital age. Against all comers and all odds, David Bordwell and Kristin Thompson, for instance, never tire to point out how the classical model has adapted itself to different media and technologies, adjusting to the introduction of sound as well as to other technical innovations, be it colour, widescreen, animation or electronic imaging techniques, by what they call the principle of 'functional equivalence'.[3]

Another section of the film-studies community, notably those familiar with Early Cinema, might go further, but also change direction, by refusing to make 'classical narrative' the gold standard. When you know the trick and animation work of Georges Méliès, Segundo de Chomon, Emile Cohl, or the experiments of Oskar Messter with three-dimensional (3-D) projection and synchronized sound (all before 1910!), there is little that can be called fundamentally new about the effects achieved by digital images, or the spectacle attractions generated by contemporary multimedia. One could even argue that our present state of the art of visual magic and virtual imaging is a throwback to the beginnings of the cinema and before. To spectators at the turn of the twentieth century, the Lumières, too, were magicians. In their 50-second films, the spectacle of curling smoke, moving clouds or leaves shaking in the breeze was more enchanting and did more to amaze them than Méliès' conjuring tricks, many of which were already familiar from magic theatre, circus and vaudeville. This would be the stance of Tom Gunning, and his 'cinema of attractions' (Gunning, 1989; 1990). Finally, scholars of especially the Russian avant-garde of the 1920s would argue that you can fold film history around the 1950s and see how the two ends overlap, that is, the '20s with the '80s. This is Lev Manovich's position, who argues that Vertov's *Man with a Movie Camera* very much converges with the work now done by digital artists experimenting with new kinds of graphics: his film-within-film is not unlike certain computer generated images (CGI)-techniques, his split screen and superimpositions are similar to video overlay and morphing and his form of montage is close to today's compositing (Manovich, 2001, pp. xiv–xxiv). The futurist and constructivist ideas of how both art and everyday reality would be transformed with the help of new technologies of sight and sound, of bodily prosthetics and precision engineering, seem to be coming true in the computer age. Also, the priority of good design for objects of everyday use, first pioneered by international modernism, has become the default value of practically every computer software application, as well as of hardware, interfaces or new technological gadgets.

## As usual, it's business

A slightly longer view, not necessarily confined to our field, would hold that both the technologically determinist and the formalist-modernist case are misconceived: what gives the digital image its uncertain status is that the search for a 'killer application' has not yet produced a decisive winner. Digital storage and delivery may have exponentially increased the production and circulation of images both in quantity and accessibility, but digitization has yet to transform the way people use these images. Except for computer games, admittedly a very lucrative market, where digital imaging has opened up innovative and challenging possibilities above all for 3-D graphics, the vast majority of digital images produced today still serve traditional aims: besides live-action feature films, they have taken over the home. Domestic use of the camcorder and digital cameras are the instantly recognizable and thus profitable products in the mass market, but they serve very traditional ends. By contrast, when in the 1980s the video recorder and the remote control were introduced, they not only powered a new consumer industry and changed people's entertainment habits, they also transformed the television industry (programming, advertising needed to take note of zapping), along with the film industry (opening the secondary market for video rentals and purchase). In the 1990s, the economic-technological basis for a vast industrial and infrastructural expansion did not turn out to be the digital image, but the mobile phone. With its universal popularity, its wildfire penetration of everyday life, its mythology of mobility, ubiquity and interactive instantaneousness, it is probably the more likely candidate for also redefining the use and function of images in our culture. The DVD, despite its economic impact, its extras and bonuses, is nonetheless only a digital clone of the gramophone disc (cross-breeding it with the videotape), while it actually encourages a form of cinephilia and collector's mania that everyone thought was passé in the 1970s. In the meantime, the iPod, a music-based device seems more likely to transform our way of interacting digitally with the environment than game-boys, data-gloves or VR helmets, as well as with the cultural image databanks, which are films, television programmes and museums – assuming that very soon, our iPod will be permanently online, allowing us to download not just music and audio information, but also images of any kind, both still and moving. The technology of telephony and wireless Internet access is moulding the sociocultural dimension of a new killer application, one that might well make the DVD as obsolete as the videotape and the CD already are.

Lowering the unit price and increasing availability of previously scarce commodities is the chief parameter that wins a new 'hardware' the sort of users who encourage the development of demand-driven mass-market products. According to this 'as usual, it's business' perspective, only consumer acceptance can impose a medium, not a technology, however superior it may be: witness the victory of the (technically) inferior VHS standard over the BETA system, or Apple's astonishing comeback from personal computer limbo, thanks to the iPod.

But if we take the longer view, we may have to be even more sceptical regarding the digital image. A few years back, even before the high-tech bubble burst, *The Economist* ran a sobering survey about the IT revolution. While it was true that the computer and modern telephony had brought a massive fall in the cost of communication and thus had increased the flow of information through the economy, it was not yet proven whether the 'new economy' will be remembered as a revolution, in the same way as the invention of the steam engine had been a revolution, which – via the railways – created the modern city and mass-market consumer society. Or that of electricity, which – via the assembly line, artificial lighting, the extension of the working day, the invention of leisure and entertainment – brought about not only new and more efficient ways of making things, but led to the creation of new things altogether. The cinema, as we know, is very much a consequence of both these revolutions, that of urbanization and electrification. According to *The Economist*, besides the cost of information, it is the cost of energy that is the real variable in a major, epochal social transformation, which is why it suggests that the development of new fuel cells may well be a bigger breakthrough on a global scale than either the computer or the mobile phone: a prediction that seems hard to believe from our present vantage point, not to mention for those of us interested in film and digital media. But as we also know, genetic engineering and nanotechnology are just waiting in the wings as the true transforming technologies of the twenty-first century (*Economist*, 1999).

## The digital: Technological standard or epistemological rupture?

Where, in these different stances towards the digital, does one locate oneself as a film historian? What about the optico-chemical image's unique value as a record with its evidentiary as well as its enunciative status of authenticity? Take film archivists, the guardians of this heritage. Admittedly they are finally agreed that celluloid (or its polymer successor) is still a more durable and reliable material support of audio-visual data than digital storage media. Yet when it comes to restoration and preservation, they now rely on digital intermediaries, only then to reintroduce the analogue artefacts, like grain or soft focus, the natural 'special effects' typical of celluloid. Others, such as Lev Manovich, look at the photographic mode from the vantage point of the post-photographic age and see the photographic image as merely a historically special instance of the graphic mode, much older than the cinema and the photograph, and destined to outlive it (1999, p. 309ff). But Manovich was not the first to argue that the photographic mode (so heavily fetishized in our culture) is merely one of the graphic mode's possible articulations. At the height of the semiological turn and well before digitization, it was Umberto Eco who deconstructed the so-called indexical level of the photographic image into a dozen or so iconic and symbolic codes (1972, pp. 195–292, esp. 214–30). The Czech media historian Vilem Flusser also pointed out, some 30 years ago, that in any photograph, the distribution of the grain already prefigures both the dots of the video image and the numerical grid of the digital image (2000).[4] Other scholars and film-makers have likewise drawn analogies between the mechanized loom of Jacquard in the eighteenth century, the Hollerith cards that made the fortune of IBM in the late nineteenth century and the television image of the de Forester cathode ray tube in the early twentieth century.[5]

All this to say that, with regard to the indexical nature of the photographic image and its place in our cultural episteme, one may be well advised to regard digitization less as a technical standard (important though this is, of course) and more like a zero degree that allows one to reflect upon one's present understanding of both film history and cinema theory. And as a zero degree, it is, necessarily, an imaginary or impossible place from which one speaks. From this impossible place, digitization can serve as a heuristic device, helping me as historian to displace myself in relation to a number of habitual ways of thinking. For instance, it allows me to suspend judgment on the usual range of options. I need not decide whether digitization is, technically speaking, a moment of progress, but aesthetically speaking a step backward; whether it is, economically speaking, a risky business-bubble, and politically speaking the tool of a new totalitarianism of ubiquitous surveillance and relentless data mining. But neither do I need to mourn the death of cinema.

## The cinema: An invention that has no origins

Instead, we can look at digital multimedia through the lens of early cinema and judge early cinema from a media-archaeological perspective, rather than a chronological or a genealogical one. One can even go a step further, and displace the cinematic apparatus (as we know it from the theories of Christian Metz, Jean Louis Baudry or Stephen Heath)[6] by adding to it its four S/M practices or perversions, depending on one's point of view. These are, to list them briefly, the *scientific and medical* cinematic apparatus (on which there are some excellent books, notably by Lisa Cartwright (1995)); the *surveillance and military* apparatus (theorized by, among others, Paul Virilio (1989) and Friedrich Kittler (1999)); the *sensory-motor-schema* apparatus (of Gilles Deleuze's (1986; 1989) philosophy); and the *sensoring and monitoring* apparatus (celebrated by Kevin Kelly (1999)), which speaks of feedback loops, pull technologies, searchability and augmented reality. In other words, by going back to early and pre-cinema, and by duly noting the non-entertainment uses of the cinematic apparatus, I am advancing the proposition that the cinema has many histories, only some of which belong to the movies, in order to – if not to answer – then at least to approach the question whether digital media constitute a new apparatus, whether they are parasitic on the pre-existing ones or whether in the case of digital media it is altogether inappropriate to speak of a cinematic apparatus?

A brief word about such a media-archaeological perspective: Among film historians it is now generally accepted that the cinema has too many origins, none of which adds up to a chronology, but also makes for doubtful genealogies. For instance, if one goes back to the genealogies of the cinema printed in the textbooks of only 20 years ago, one can observe the kind of self-evidence that today seems startling for its blind spots. There, the history of photography, the history of projection and the 'discovery' of persistence of vision are listed as the triple pillars that sustain the temple of the Seventh Art. Or, to change the metaphor, they appear as the three major tributaries that finally – miraculously but also inevitably – join up around 1895 to become the mighty river we know as the cinema. But as we also know, archaeology is the opposite of genealogy: the latter tries to trace back a continuous line of descent from the present to the past; the former knows that only the presumption of discontinuity and the *pars-pro-toto* of the fragment can hope to give a present access to a past.

A media archaeologist would therefore notice above all what is missing or has been suppressed and left out in our genealogical chart. Sound, for instance, since we now know the silent cinema was rarely if ever silent, in which case, why is the history of phonograph not listed as another tributary? Or what about the telephone as an indispensable element of what we would now understand by the cinema in the multimedia environment? Radio waves? Einstein's wave and particle theories of light? Electromagnetic fields? The history of aviation? Do we not need Babbage's difference engine ranged parallel to his friend Henry Fox-Talbot's Calotypes, combined with Ada Lovelace's first attempts at programming? (Batchen, 1997).

Or take the so-called 'delay of cinema'. If we were to time-travel, and place ourselves at the end of the nineteenth century, we could see the cinematograph in 1895 as both a sleepy latecomer and a perilously premature birth – a latecomer, because the technology of moving images had been known for almost 50 years, and also that the Lumières' invention was in some respects no more than a mechanized slide-show, whose special effects for a brief time were inferior to any twin or triple-turret magic lantern, worked by a singer-lecturer assisting the skilled lanternist-operator, which could supply sound and image, verbal commentary and colour, abstractly moving designs and representations from life. But the cinema was also premature or (some would say) an irrelevant detour altogether, because the late nineteenth century might have been poised on the brink of a quite different imaging technology, which the popularity of the cinema in some ways 'delayed'. There is even a sense in which the cinema was not only a bastard, but an unwanted child altogether. According to television scholars, both Edison's peep show and Lumière's public projection was not what the nineteenth century had been waiting for. What it was imagining for its techno-topic future was domestic television, and preferably two-way television. The Victorians not only dreamt of television. They were as hungry for mobility, instantaneity, for simultaneity and interactivity as we are today, and they also had a good idea of what it would mean to be connected to an Internet: after all, they had developed the telegraph-system! (Standage, 1999).

Few of us now recall that many of the so-called pioneers – among them Pierre Jules César Janssen, Ottomar Anschütz, Edweard Muybridge and even the Lumière Brothers – were either not at all or not primarily interested in the entertainment uses and storytelling possibilities of the cinematograph, thinking of it in the first instance as a scientific instrument. Were they blind to the economic potential of entertainment and its social role in the late nineteenth century, or had they something in mind that only the emergence of an entirely different set of needs and uses nearly a hundred years later could bring to light? It seems the 'losers' of yesterday may turn out to have predicted the winners of today. Whenever historians have begun to think in these terms, their findings are producing at times dramatic shifts in our conception of early cinema, but also of the cinema in general. So much so that, today, near-forgotten figures such as Étienne-Jules Marey or his assistant Georges Demenÿ look more interesting than the Lumière Brothers (as in the books of Mannoni (1995), Marta Braun (1992) and Mary Ann Doane (2003)), and to those historians interested in German cinema, Oskar Messter seems as emblematic for an archaeology of multimedia as Thomas Alva Edison used to be for the history of the cinema and the origins of the film industry.[7] Never very well known outside Germany, Messter's Alabastra 3-D projections of 1900, his synchronized sound pictures from 1902, his medical films from 1904 or his airborne surveillance cameras from 1914 nonetheless strike one as more fantastic than Jules Verne's novels, but just as prescient and a lot more practical. Messter's indefatigable search for applications of the moving image parallel to its entertainment uses testify to such a pragmatic understanding of the different potentials of the cinematic apparatus that he stands at the intersection of several histories, many of which we are only now beginning to recognize as being histories – precisely those configurations and applications of the basic apparatus I just listed as its S/M practices.

We have come to know a good deal more about the complex War and Cinema – or 'surveillance and the military' – than even two decades ago (Virilio, 1989; Kittler, 1999). But it is the practical impact of satellite technology, space exploration and airborne or terrestrial surveillance that have sensitized us to a continuous, if submerged, alternative history of cinema, which is gradually being recovered in the form of an 'archaeology' of the present (Levin et al., 2002). Yet it is worth recalling that much else that we are now beginning to consider as belonging to early cinema was not initially intended or indeed suited to performance in a movie theatre: scientific films, medical films, training films, for instance. The pioneer of nervous diseases, Jean-Martin Charcot at the Salpêtrière Hospital in Paris had very sophisticated photographic equipment, and his successors used the moving image alongside still photography, to document the symptoms of his patients (Didi-Huberman, 2003). Many prominent surgeons also belonged among early users of the cinematograph. On the other hand, even such classics of early cinema programming as the tourist view, the actualities and many other types of films or genres initially relied on techniques of vision and on a habitus of observation that had to be 'adjusted', in order to fit into the movie theatre. Think of the landscape view, or the painted panorama: prior to the cinema, they relied on the mobile observer, optimizing his varying point of view. Think of the stereoscope (so important in Jonathan Crary's (1990) techniques of the observer), or the so-called 'Claude glass' and the *camera lucida*, both recently revived by David Hockney as precursors of the digital camera (Hockney, 2001). Think of the phantasmagorias or fog pictures: they and a multitude of other devices were in everyday or specialized use, and besides serving public spectacles they were also handled in private or, like the Mutoscope, by a solitary spectator. Yet the cinema borrowed from all these genres and practices, adapting them and significantly transforming their cultural meaning. In the process, both the mode of presentation and the audiences had to be 'disciplined' – 'disciplined through pleasure' one might call it – in order to become suitable for collective, public reception (Elsaesser, 2006).

What this suggests is that the different ways in which the moving image in its multi-medial electronic form is today 'breaking the frame' and exceeding, if not altogether exiting, the movie theatre (giant display screens in airport lounges or railway stations, monitors in all walks of life, from gallery spaces to museum video art, from installation pieces to football stadiums, from tiny mobile screens to IMAX theatres), we may be 'returning' to early cinema practice, remembering Lumière's giant screen for the 1900 Paris World Exhibition, Pathé's Baby projector for living room use, or W.K. Dickson's experiments with 68mm film stock to capture the grandeur of Niagara Falls.

On the other hand, as I suggested with my iPod example, we may be on the threshold of another powerful surge of 'disciplining' and normatively prioritizing one particular standard of the multimedia image over others. What can be said is that the instability of the current configuration is by no means unique in the history of the moving image. In fact we seem to have been there before, even if less dramatically – when, for instance, the drive-in cinema was competing with the television screen, converting the automobile into a living room, or trying to combine the erotic intimacy of home with a giant outdoor screen, not to mention the better-remembered 3-D and Vistavision experiments.

Let us finally recall how unstable, around 1895, were the definitions and minimal conditions that eventually led to exactly dating the 'birth' of cinema: why does chrono-photography not qualify as cinema? Why was Émile Raynaud's continuously moving strip of paper with painted images projected on to a screen not good enough as the birth of cinema? Why should only images taken with a camera and fixed on celluloid qualify? If photographic images, why not Edison's peep-hole kinetoscope, instead of the Lumières cinematograph (derivative from Edison's machine and reverse engineered in London, by Robert Paul) for projecting images on a screen? Did it make a difference whether these moving images were first shown to a scientific community or before a paying public? As we know, it was decided that only the paying audience 'really' counted, with the result that in the end it took four or five different (some would say, arbitrarily selected) qualifiers or limiting conditions, in order to make 28 December 1985 the date, and the Lumière Brothers the authors of the 'invention' of the cinema! (Rossell, 1998). In this sense, the history of the cinema responds not so much to the Bazinian enquiry 'what is cinema?', but has to start from the question, 'when is cinema?' And it is clear that for the first ten years of its life, the cinema did not, strictly speaking, 'exist' at all. As Bazin could not help wondering, after reading Georges Sadoul's history of the cinema, 'looking at all the technical possibilities [of moving images] that have appeared in the past, one can only conclude that the cinema still needs to be invented' (Bazin, 1967, p. 22).

## Film in the expanded field

I hope I have been able to suggest that in film history, even before one gets to digitization, the case for a wider agenda, as well as a different range of issues, is a compelling one. That it has not been an insight exclusively owed to the new media is proven by a century of avant-garde cinema, and what has been variously described and celebrated by historians such as Gene Youngblood as expanded cinema (1970). It was practiced by, among many others, Peter Weibel and Valie Export in Vienna and by Standish Lawder, Andrew McCall and Ken Jacobs in New York (Michalka, 2001).

But even here, we must beware, as an anecdote once told to me by Vivian Sobchack might illustrate. One day, when she was still teaching at Santa Cruz, she was driving on a San Francisco freeway behind a van with the words 'Pullman's Underground Film' written on the back. Being a film scholar with wide-ranging interests, she became curious, since in all her years of teaching the American avant-garde, she had never come across a film-maker or a collective by that name. As she accelerated and levelled with the van, in order to see whether she recognized anyone inside, she read, neatly stencilled across the driver's door: 'Pullman's Underground Film: The Bay Area's Specialists in Electronic Sewer Inspection'.[8]

Perhaps only in the city or the region that is home to the Pacific Film Archive could the industrial users of the cinematic apparatus salute the artistic film community with such a handsome tribute. But as the case of the so-called pioneers (as well as many examples discussed in the previous chapters) show, the non-entertainment and non-art uses of the cinematic apparatus at the turn of the nineteenth to the twentieth century did not disappear with the arrival of narrative cinema or the feature film around 1907; they merely went underground. But this underground was in many instances contiguous with the above ground, and in several cases it was the very condition of possibility for the developments of the entertainment uses, making the cinema as we know it no more than the visible tip of the proverbial iceberg – certainly when one recalls once more how many of the technical innovations in the fields of photography, the cinema and the new media were financed and first tested for warfare and military objectives. To name just a few of the best known: the powerful searchlights of World War I, the 16mm portable camera, radar, the Ampex (audio- and video-) recording tape, the television camera, the computer, the Internet.

As so often in the history of inventions, some of the most influential or momentous ones were the by-products of other discoveries, or turned out quite differently from what their makers intended with them: technological 'progress' rarely takes the form of a Eureka-experience and nothing seems more the result of *bricolage* than the cinema. Consider the film projector – to this day film technology's equivalent of the platypus. Apart from being a mechanized magic lantern, it still shows quite clearly that what allowed this magic lantern to be mechanized were the treadle sewing machine, the perforated Morse telegraph tape and the Gatling machine gun. All three have disappeared in their respective areas of applications, but are miraculously preserved in the retrofitted adaptation still to be found in every projection room (though probably not for much longer).

Let me try and sum up what these brief forays into media archaeology might tell us about the electronic multimedia as part of the history of cinema. By positing the digital not only as a technology of signal conversion and data transmission, but as a moment of cultural rupture, I first wanted to disarticulate the cinematic apparatus in its historical dimension, and to re-articulate it across its many entertainment and non-entertainment practices. These practices in their diversity, but also our 'digital' perspective on them, suggest that the cinema may well have ceased to be important because of this particular cinematic apparatus of camera, projector, screen and auditorium, and instead, it has become digital culture's internal reference point. If we follow Friedrich Kittler, and take seriously the multimedia, multi-modal dimensions of our sound, image and text machines, we need to speak of discourse networks rather than an apparatus, with its suggestion of fixity, ocular alignment and rigid geometries of space (Kittler, 1990). If we follow Gilles Deleuze, we should forget about narrative, subjectivity and interpellation (that is, the psychic dispositiv) and instead start from the raw physiological given of movement, flow, folds, energies, intensities as they animate matter, memory and brain (Deleuze 1986; 1989). For Lev Manovich, the cinema constitutes the digital media's symbolic form, the way Erwin Panofsky talked about perspective as the Enlightenment's symbolic form, the way Michel Foucault described the *Order of Things* during the classical age by pointing to Velasquez' ingenious perversion of perspective in his *Las Meninas* painting or the way Martin Heidegger spoke about the Age of the World-Picture: 'the basic dynamic of modernity is the conquest of the world as image. The word image here means: the enframing of man's imagined production of the world' (Heidegger, 1977).

The camera is in our head, even before it is in our hand, or its images on the screen. For Kittler, this is an epistemic problem: how do we know what we know in the discourse network of our age? It is a question of our modes of seeing no longer being our ways of knowing, our form of agency become mere performativity and our bodies the material residues, the 'wetware' of information processing. For Deleuze, on the other hand, the cinema stands for the promise of a new ontology: a mode of immanence without (the need for) transcendence.

Nonetheless, what is the ground that can ground the groundlessness that is the moving image, both might ask, Heidegger-fashion? Film theory over the last 50 years has answered them with a long list of metaphors: reality as God had intended to reveal it (Bazin), a natural language without a language system (Metz), the very logic of our subjectivity (Baudry, Heath via Lacan-Althusser), the tragic destiny of gendered identity (Mulvey), the nature of human consciousness (Michelson), the unsymbolizable real (Žižek), the figural (Lyotard), the body, the senses, touch and skin, the death drive, affect, attraction, time, the brain, the perceptual modelling of our hard-wired cognitivist schemata and so on. The digital as rupture thus leaves us with a paradox: just as it installs the cinema as episteme or ontology, it does away with cinema as a unique technology of imaging. Its vantage point or vanishing point, so to speak, is a cinematic apparatus no longer grounded in the eye, in vision or visuality. The digital inaugurates a cinema for the blind, or of the blind ('*ein Blindenkino*'), as Franz Kafka is supposed to have imagined it. And if we take my last S/M practice – of sensors and monitors – and think of the electronic traces and digital footprints we leave behind every time we go online or move through the circuits of computerized transaction, transport and exchange that make up our lives, then the corresponding 'cinematic' apparatus is indeed at the very threshold of the visible, or altogether beyond it. The visible would be, as it already is for the computer, a mere interface for our convenience, a sort of prosthetics of our data-doubles, since the digital machine needs neither time, motion, image, light or object. A spectre is indeed haunting film history – that of the disappearance of the cinema as a *machine of the visible* (Comolli, 1980). And here the digital may indeed come to our rescue: by not itself belonging to the order of the visible, the digital can close the gap between the visible and the invisible of the world, and thus be the 'ground' on which the cinema can indeed be reinvented, as it has been so many times. In this respect at least, it is neither business as usual, nor is it, as usual, business. At most, it is our business, and we have to make it so – to see the cinema anew, as archaeology, theoretical object, practice, epistemology, ontology, but above all as a philosophical *perpetuum mobile*, as an intellectual automaton and a source of self-renewing energy.

## Notes

1. Jean Douchet, lecture given in Paris on 20 March 1995 at a symposium called 'Le Cinéma: vers son deuxième siècle'.
2. The link between the aesthetics of neorealism and immersive virtual reality is also made implicitly in the opening section ('The Logic of Transparent

Immediacy') of Jay David Bolter and Richard Grusin, *Remediation* (1999), pp. 21–31.
3. See a recent edition of Bordwell's and Thompson's *Film Art*, with the bullet-time effect from *The Matrix* on the cover, and Kristin Thompson, *Storytelling in the New Hollywood. Understanding Classical Narrative Technique* (1998).
4. Some of Flusser's key essays have been published posthumously as *Ins Universum der technischen Bilder* (Flusser, 2000).
5. Harun Farocki's *Wie man sieht/As you see* (Germany 1986, 16mm, col., 72 min) explores this 'archaeology' that links Jacquard, Hollerith, the television image and the computer.
6. See the essays by these authors in Rosen (1986).
7. On Messter's diverse activities, see Martin Loiperdinger (1994).
8. Vivian Sobchack, personal communication, June 1998.

# Bibliography

Abbott, S. 2004, 'Spectral Vampires: *Nosferatu* in the Light of New Technology', in Steffen Hautke ed. *Horror Film: Creating and Marketing Fear* Jackson: University of Mississippi Press, pp. 3–20.

Abel, R. 1999, *The Red Rooster Scare: Making Cinema American 1900–1910* Berkeley: University of California Press.

Adorno, T. 1999, 'Culture Industry Reconsidered', in Marris, Paul, and Thornham, Sue, eds. *Media Studies: A Reader* Edinburgh: Edinburgh University Press, pp. 31–7.

Aitken, I. 1998, 'Distraction and Redemption: Kracauer, Surrealism and Phenomenology', *Screen*, 39.2, 124–40.

Akbar, A. 1997, *Hong Kong: Culture and the Politics of Disappearance* Minneapolis, London: University of Minnesota Press.

*American*, 1913, Chicago, 'Heroism Averts "Movie" Panic, Girl Plays Piano When Smoke Terrifies Audience'. 24 March, 1913, 3rd edn, 2.

Angerer, M.-L. 1999, *Body Options* Vienna: Turia & Kant.

Arnheim, R. 1971, *Film As Art* Berkeley: University of California Press [1933].

Artaud, A. 1972, *Collected Works*, Vol. 3, Calder and Boyars.

Augé, M. 1995, *Non-Places: Introduction to an Anthropology of Supermodernity*, John Howe, trans. London and NY: Verso.

Aumont, J. 1995, *L'Oeil interminable* Paris: Séguier.

——, 1994, *The Image* London: BFI.

Barry, N. 2003, 'Telling Stories on Screens: A History of Web Cinema', in Shaw, J., and Weibel, P., eds. *Future Cinema: The Cinematic Imaginary After Film* Cambridge, MA and London: MIT Press, pp. 544–51.

Batchen, G. 1997, *Burning with Desire: The Conception of Photography* Cambridge, MA: MIT Press.

Baudry, J.-L. 1986, 'The Apparatus: Metapsychological Approaches to the Impression of Reality in the Cinem', in P. Rosen, ed. *Narrative, Apparatus, Ideology* NY: Columbia University Press, pp. 199–318.

——, 1986, 'Ideological Effects of the Basic Cinematic Apparatus', in P. Rosen, ed. *Narrative, Apparatus, Ideology* NY: Columbia University Press, pp. 286–98.

——, 1992, 'The Apparatus: Metapsychological Approaches to the Impression of Reality in Cinema' in Mast, G., Cohen, M., and Braudy, L., eds. *Film Theory and Criticism: Introductory Readings, Fourth Edition* Oxford: Oxford University Press, pp. 690–707.

Bazin, A. 1967, *What is Cinema?*, Vol. 1, Gray, H., trans. Berkeley: University of California Press.

——, 1971, *What is Cinema?*, Vol. 2, Gray, H., trans. Berkeley: University of California Press.

Belton, J. 2002, 'Digital Cinema: A False Revolution', *October*, 100, 98–114.

Benjamin, W. 1973, *Illuminations*, London: Fontana.

——, 1999, *The Arcades Project*, Eiland, H. and McLaughlin, K., trans. Cambridge, MA and London: The Belknap Press of Harvard University Press.

## Bibliography

Benjamin, W. 2005, 'The Work of Art in the Age of Mechanical Reproduction', 1935, in Utterson, A., ed. *Technology and Culture, The Film Reader* London and NY: Routledge, pp. 105–26.
Bergson, H. 1911, *Creative Evolution* London: Macmillan.
——, 1994, *Matter and Memory* Paul, N. M., and Palmer, W. S., trans. NY: Zone Books.
*Billboard*. 1910, 'Coolness of Crowd Averts Panic in Minneapolis.' 13 August, 4.
Bogard, W. 'Distraction and Digital Culture' Available at http://www.ctheory.net/articles.aspx?id=131 (Accessed 18 January 2007).
Bogue, R. 2003, *Deleuze on Cinema* London: Routledge.
Bolter, J. D., and Grusin, R. 1999, *Remediation: Understanding New Media* Cambridge, MA: MIT Press.
Booth, M. 1965, *English Melodrama* London: Herbert Jenkins.
Bordwell, D. 1997, *On the History of Film Style* Cambridge, MA and London: Harvard University Press.
——, Thompson, K., 1994, *Film History: An Introduction* NY: McGraw-Hill.
Bossin, H. 1951, 'Canada and the Film: The Story of the Canadian Motion Picture Industry', in H. Bossin, ed. *Yearbook of the Canadian Motion Picture Industry* Toronto: Canadian Film Weekly, pp. 21–41.
——, 1963, 'In Those Days X-Rays were More Popular.' *Star* Toronto. 8 June, 19.
Bottomore, S. 1999, 'The Panicking Audience?: Early Cinema and the "Train Effect"', *Historical Journal of Film, Radio and Television*, 19.2, 177–216.
Bourdieu, P. 1990, *In Other Words: Essays Towards a Reflexive Sociology* Cambridge: Polity Press.
Bowley, D., Honour, J., and Speyer, B., 1997, 'Ultra High-Speed Electronic Imaging', *Industrial Physicist* December, 28–31.
Bowser, E. 1990, *The Transformation of Cinema 1907–1915* NY: Macmillan.
*Box Office*, 1938, 'Local Industry Heads Oppose 16mm – United Artists sell indies again', June 1938.
Braidotti, R. 2002, *Metamorphosis. Towards a Materialist Theory of Becoming* Cambridge, Oxford UK: Polity Press.
——, 2006, *Transpositions. On Nomadic Ethics* Cambridge UK: Polity Press.
Brandt, N. 2003, *Chicago Death Trap: The Iroquois Theatre Fire of 1903* Carbondale: Southern Illinois University Press.
Braun, M. 1992, *Picturing Time. The Work of Etienne-Jules Marey 1830–1904* Chicago: University of Chicago Press.
Broadfoot, K., and Butler, R. 1991, 'The Illusion of Illusion', in A. Cholodenko, ed. *The Illusion of Life: Essays on Animation* Sydney: Power Publications in association with the Australian Film Commission.
Brown, T. 2007, 'The DVD of Attractions', *Convergence*, 13.2, 169–83.
Buck-Morss, S. 1989, *The Dialectics of Seeing: Walter Benjamin and the Arcades Project* Cambridge, MA and London: MIT Press.
Bunton, R., and Petersen, A. 2005, *Genetic Governance: Health, Risk and Ethics in the Biotech Era* London and NY: Routledge.
Burch, N. 1978, 'Porter, or ambivalence', *Screen*, 19.4, 91–105.
Burrow, M., Farnell, G., and Jardine, M., eds. 2004/2005, *Reading Benjamin's Arcades, New Formations*, 54, Special Issue.
*Business Wire*, 2001, 'Media 100 Technology Drives Success Behind the Scenes of BMWfilms.com With Media 100 I and Cleaner 5' Available at http://www.

findarticles.com/p/articles/mi_m0EIN/is_2001_July_23/ai_76691092 (Accessed 21 August 2004).
Butler, J. 2004, *Precarious Life: The Powers of Mourning and Violence* London: Verso.
*Canadian Independent,* 1938, 'Ontario Enactments on 16mm', 1 July 1938.
Canguilhem, G. 1989, *The Normal and the Pathological* New York: Zone Books.
Canning, P. 1994, 'The Crack of Time and the Ideal Game', in C. Boundas and D. Olkowski, eds. *Gilles Deleuze and the Theatre of Philosophy* NY: Routledge.
Cardinal, R. 1986, 'Pausing over Peripheral Detail', *Framework* 30.31, 112–30.
Cartwright, L. 2008, *Moral Spectatorship: Technologies of Agency, Voice, and Image in Postwar Institutions of the Child* Durham, North Carolina: Duke University Press.
——, 1995, *Screening the Body: Tracing Medicine's Visual Culture* Minneapolis and London: University of Minnesota Press.
Casetti, F. 1999, *Theories of Cinema, 1945–1995,* Chiostri, F., Bartolini-Salimbeni, E. G., and Kelso, T., trans. Austin: University of Texas Press.
Cawley, J., and Korkis, J. 1990, *How To Create Animation* Las Vegas: Pioneer.
Charity, T. 2005, '*Small Soldiers*', in Pym, J., ed. *Time Out Film Guide, Fourteenth Edition, 2005* London: Time Out Guides, 1221.
Chun, W., and Keenan, T. 2006, *New Media Old Media* London: Routledge.
Clément, C. 1990, 'Charlatans and Hysterics', in M. Budd, ed. *The Cabinet of Dr. Caligari: Texts, Contexts, Histories* New Brunswick: Rutgers University Press.
Comolli, J.-L. 1980, 'Machines of the Visible', in T. de Lauretis and S. Heath, eds. *The Cinematic Apparatus* NY: St Martin's Press, pp. 121–42.
——, 1986, 'Technique and Ideology: Camera, Perspective, Depth of Field', in P. Rosen, ed. *Narrative, Apparatus, Ideology* NY: Columbia University Press, pp. 421–43.
Cook, D. 1996, *A History of Narrative Film,* 3rd edn NY, Norton.
Corliss, R. 2001, '"A. I."—Spielberg's Strange Love', *Time,* 17/6/01, Available at http://www.time.com/time/nation/printout/0,8816,130942,00.html.
Craik, W. A. 1961, 'The Fight Will Not Be Shown Tonight.' *Telegram,* Toronto. 2 June 1961, 6.
Crary, J. 1990, *Techniques of the Observer: On Vision and Modernity in the Nineteenth Century* Cambridge, MA: MIT Press.
——, 1999, *Suspensions of Perception: Attention, Spectacle, and Modern Culture* Cambridge, MA and London: MIT Press.
Cubitt, S. 1998, *Digital Aesthetics* London and NY: Sage Publications.
——, 2004, *The Cinema Effect* Cambridge, MA: MIT Press.
Culhane, S. 1986, *Talking Animals and Other People* NY: St Martins.
Daly, J. 1997, 'Hollywood 2.0' How technology is transforming film-making', *Wired,* 5.11 1997. Available at www.wired.com/wired/5.11/hollywood.html.
Damasio, A. 1999, *The Feeling of What Happens. Body and Emotion in the Making of Consciousness* NY, San Diego and London: Harcourt.
——, 2003, *Looking for Spinoza* San Diego and London: Harcourt.
Darley, A. 2000, *Visual Digital Culture* London: Routledge.
Deleuze, G. 1986, *The Movement-Image, Cinema 1* trans. Tomlinson, H. and Habberjam, B., Minneapolis: University of Minnesota Press.
——, 1988, *Foucault* London: Athlone Press.
Deleuze, G. 1989, *The Time-Image, Cinema 2* Tomlinson, H., and Galeta, R., trans. Minneapolis: University of Minnesota Press.

——, 1990, *Expressionism in Philosophy: Spinoza,* Joughin, M., trans. NY: Zone Books.
——, 1994, 'Désir et plaisir', *Le Magazine littéraire,* 325, 59–65.
——, 1994, *Difference and Repetition* NY: Columbia University Press.
——, 2000, 'An Interview with Gilles Deleuze', in Flaxman, G., ed. *The Brain is the Screen: Deleuze and the Philosophy of Cinema* Minneapolis: University of Minnesota Press.
Derrida, J. 1978, *Writing and Difference* London: Routledge.
Didi-Huberman, G. 2003, *Invention of Hysteria: Charcot and the Photographic Iconography of the Salpetrière* Cambridge: MIT Press.
Dixon, W. W. 1998, *The Transparency of Spectacle: Meditations on the Moving Image* Albany: SUNY press.
Doane, M. A. 2002, *The Emergence of Cinematic Time. Modernity, Contingency, the Archive* Cambridge: Harvard University Press.
Eco, U. 1972, 'Zu einer Semiotik des visuellen Codes', in *Einführung in die Semiotik* München: Wilhelm Fink, pp. 195–292.
——, 1994, Eco, U. *Apocalypse Postponed,* R. Lumley, ed. Bloomington: Indiana UP.
*The Economist,* 1999, 'A Survey of Innovation in Industry', Special Supplement, 20 February 1999, 5–8.
Edgerton, D. 2006, *The Shock of the Old: Technology and Global History Since 1900* London: Profile.
Eisner, L. 1973, *The Haunted Screen* Berkeley: University of California Press.
Elias, N. 2000, *The Civilizing Process* Malden, MA: Blackwell.
Elkins, J. 1999a, *The Domain of Images* Ithaca NY: Cornell University Press.
——, 1999b, 'Logic and Images in Art History', response to Galison's *Image and Logic,* in *Perspectives on Science,* 7.2, 151–80.
——, 2004, 'Harold Edgerton's Rapatronic Photographs of Atomic Tests', *History of Photography,* 28.1, 74–81.
——, 2005, 'What Do We Want Photography to Be?' [a reply to Michael Fried's 'Barthes's *Punctum,* also in *Critical Inquiry*]' *Critical Inquiry,* 31.4, 938–56.
——, 2006, 'Einige Gedanken über der Unbestimmtheit der Darstellung', in Gerhard Gramm and Eva Schürmann, eds. *Das unendliche Kunstwerk: Von der Bestimmtheit des Unbestimmten in der ästhetischen Erfahrung* Berlin: Philo.
——, 2007a, *Photography Theory,* vol. 2 of *The Art Seminar* NY: Routledge.
——, 2007b, *Visual Practices Across the University* Paderhorn: Wilhelm Fink Verlag.
Ellis, J. C., and Wright Wexman, V. 2001, *A History of Film,* 5th edn Boston: Allyn and Bacon.
Elsaesser, T. 1988/1989, 'Secret Affinities' *Sight and Sound,* 58:1, 33–39.
——, 1990, 'Social Mobility and the Fantastic: German Silent Cinema', in Budd, M. ed., *The Cabinet of Dr Caligari: Texts, Contexts, Histories,* New Burnswick: Rutgers University Press 171–89.
——, 2000, 'Lulu and the Meter Man: Louise Brooks, G. W. Pabst and *Pandora's Box*' in *Weimar Cinema and After: Germany's Historical Imaginary* London: Routledge.
——, 2005, *'Zu spät, zu früh? Körper, Zeit und Aktionsraum in der Kinoerfahrung',* in M. Brütsch et al., eds. *Kinogefühle. Emotionalität und Gefühl* Marburg: Schüren, pp. 415–39.
——, 2006, 'Discipline Through Diegesis: The Rube Film Between "Attraction" and "Integration"', in Wanda Strauven, ed. *The Cinema of Attractions Reloaded* Amsterdam: Amsterdam University Press, pp. 205–24.

Everett, A. 2003, 'Digitextuality and Click Theory: Theses on Convergence Media in the Digital Age', in Everett, A., and Caldwell, J., eds. *New Media: Theories and Practices of Digitextuality* NY and London: Routledge, pp. 3–28.
Ezra, E. 2000, *Georges Méliès: The Birth of an Auteur* Manchester: Manchester University Press.
Fallon Worldwide, 2005, 'Hire I', Available at http://www.fallon.com.
Feenberg, A. 2002, *Transforming Technology* NY: Oxford University Press.
Feld, S. 2001, 'A Sweet Lullaby for World Music', in Appadurai, ed. *Globalization* Durham: Duke University Press, pp. 189–216.
Figgis, M. 2007, 'Into the Abstract', *Sight and Sound*, 17.3, 18–19.
Flaxman, G., ed., 2000, *The Brain Is The Screen: Deleuze and the Philosophy of Cinema* Minneapolis and London: University of Minnesota Press.
Flew, T. 2002, *New Media: An Introduction* South Melbourne: Oxford University Press.
Flusser, V. 2000, *Ins Universum der technischen Bilder* München: European Photography.
Foucault, M. 1972, *The Archaeology of Knowledge* London: Tavistock Press.
——, 1977, *Discipline & Punish: The Birth of the Prison* London: Viking Books.
——, 1990, *The History of Sexuality: An Introduction,* Vol. 1. New York: Vintage Books (first published 1978).
Franklin, S. 2000, 'Life Itself. Global Nature and the Genetic Imaginary', in Franklin, S., Lury, C., and Stacey, J., eds. *Global Nature, Global Culture* London: Sage.
Franklin, U. 1999, *The Real World of Technology,* Revised edn, Toronto: Anansi.
Frayling, C. 2003, *Mad, Bad and Dangerous? The Scientist and the Cinema* London: Reaktion Books.
Freud, S. 1964, 'The "Uncanny"', *The Complete Psychological Works of Sigmund Freud.* Standard ed. Vol. 17. London: The Hogarth Press, pp. 217–56.
Friedberg, A. 2000, 'The End of Cinema: Multimedia and Technological Change', in C. Gledhill and L. Williams, eds. *Reinventing Film Studies* London: Arnold, pp. 438–52.
Frisby, D. 1986, *Fragments of Modernity* Cambridge, MA: MIT Press.
Frogier, L., and J.-M. Poinsot, eds., 1997, *La description* Actes du colloque Rennes: Archives de la critique d'art, Université de Rennes.
Fuery, P. 2000, *New Developments in Film Theory* NY: St Martin's Press.
Fumaroli, M. 2001, 'Cinéma et Terreur', *Cahiers du Cinéma*, 559, 40–9.
Galison, Peter, 1997, *Image and Logic: A Material Culture of Microphysics* Chicago: University of Chicago Press.
Gane, N. 2005, 'Radical Post-humanism: Friedrich Kittler and the Primacy of Technology', *Theory, Culture & Society*, 22.3, 25–41.
Gibson, W. 1996, *Idoru* NY: Putnam.
*Globe* Toronto, 1908, 'Hundred and Sixty Bodies Taken from Theatre Ruins.' 15 January, 1.
Graham, G. G. 1989, *Canadian Film Technology, 1896–1986* Cranbury, NJ: Associated University Presses.
Grant, B. K. 1999, 'Sensuous Elaboration: Reason and the Visible in the Science Fiction Film', in Kuhn, A., ed. *Alien Zone II: The Spaces of Science Fiction Cinema* London: Verso.
Gray, W. C. 1973, *Movies for the People: The Story of the National Film Board of Canada's Unique Distribution System* Montreal: National Film Board.

Grieveson, L. 1999, 'Why the Audience Mattered in Chicago in 1907', in M. Stokes and R. Maltby, eds. *American Movie Audiences From the Turn of the Century to the Early Sound Era* London: British Film Institute.
Grosz, E. 1994, *Volatile Bodies. Toward a Corporeal Feminism* Indiana Univ. Press.
Gunning, T. 1989, 'An Aesthetic of Astonishment. Early Film and the Incredulous Spectator', *Art & Text*, 34, 31–45.
——, 1990, 'The Cinema of Attractions: Early Film, Its Spectator and the Avant-Garde', in T. Elsaesser and A. Barker, eds. *Early Cinema: Space, Frame, Narrative* London: BFI, pp. 56–62.
——, 1991, *D. W. Griffith and the Origins of American Narrative Film: The Early Years at Biograph* Urbana & Chicago: University of Illinois Press.
——, 2000, 'The Cinema of Attraction: Early Film, Its Spectator, and the Avant-Garde', in Stam, R., and Miller, T., eds. *Film and Theory: An Anthology* Oxford: Blackwell, pp. 229–35.
Gutteridge, R. W. 2000, *Magic Moments: First 20 Years of Moving Pictures in Toronto 1894–1914* Whitby, ON: Gutteridge-Pratley.
Haase, C. 2003, 'Running for Your Life: *Lola rennt* and the Flight of Popular German Film', in Halle, R., and McCarthy, M., eds. *Light Movies: New Directions in German Film Studies* Detroit: Wayne State UP.
Halle R. 2002, 'German Film, Aufgehoben: Ensembles of Transnational Cinema', *New German Critique*, 87 Autumn, 7–46.
Hansen, M., 2002 'Cinema beyond Cybernetics, or How to Frame the Digital Image', *Configurations*, 10:1: 51–90.
——, 2004, *New Philosophy for New Media* Cambridge, MA and London, England: MIT Press.
——, 2004, 'Realtime synthesis and the differance of the body: technocultural studies in the wake of deconstruction', *Culture Machine*.
——, 2004, 'The Time of Affect, or Bearing Witness to Life', *Critical Inquiry*, 30, 584–626.
Hansen, Mark B. N. 2004, *New Philosophy for New Media* Cambridge, MA, London: MIT Press.
Haran, J., Kitzinger, J., McNeil, M., and O'Riordan, K. 2007, *Human Cloning and the Media: From Science Fiction to Science Practice* London: Routledge.
Harries, D. 2002, 'Watching the Internet', in D. Harries, ed. *The New Media Book* London: BFI, pp. 171–82.
Harris, R. 1996, *Unplanned Suburbs: Toronto's American Tragedy, 1900 to 1950* Baltimore: Johns Hopkins University Press.
Hayles, N. K. 1999, *How We Became Posthuman: Virtual Bodies in Cybernetics, Literature, and Informatics* Chicago: The University of Chicago Press.
Haynes, R. 2003, 'From Alchemy to Artificial Intelligence: Stereotypes of the. Scientist in Western Literature', *Public Understanding of Science*, July 2003, 12.3, 243–253.
——, 1994, *From Faust to Strangelove: Representations of the Scientist in Western Literature* Baltimore: John Hopkins University Press.
Heath, S. 1980, 'The Cinematic Apparatus: Technology as Historical and Cultural Form', in T. de Lauretis and S. Heath, eds. *The Cinematic Apparatus* NY: St Martin's Press, pp. 1–13.
Heidegger, M. 1977, 'The Age of the World Picture', in *The Question Concerning Technology and Other Essays*, Lovitt, W., trans. NY: Harper and Row, pp. 115–54.

Heiser, J. 2005, 'The Making Of Imagination', in *The Secret Hotel*, exhibition catalogue, Kunsthaus, Bregenz.
Hendershot, H., ed., 2006, 'In Focus: The Death of 16mm?', Special Issue, *Cinema Journal*, 45.3, 109–40.
Hespos, T. 2002, 'BMW Films: The Ultimate Marketing Scheme' Available at http://www.imediaconnection.com/content/546.asp, (Accessed 21 August 2004).
Highfield, R., and Wilmut, I. 2006, *After Dolly: The Uses and Misuses of Human Cloning* London: Little Brown.
Hills, M. 2004, 'The Genetic Engineering of Monstrosity: Appropriation of genetics in 1990s species level bio-horror', Conference paper at MECCSA, 2004, University of Sussex.
Hockney, D. 2001, *Secret Knowledge* London: Phaidon.
Hutchins, E. 1995, *Cognition in the Wild* Cambridge, MA: MIT Press.
Huyssen, A. 1986, *After the Great Divide: Modernism, Mass Culture, Postmodernism* Bloomington: Indiana University Press.
Isin, E. F. 1992, *Cities Without Citizens: The Modernity of the City as a Corporation* Montreal: Black Rose.
Jacobs, L. 1967 [1939], *The Rise of the American Film: A Critical History* NY: Teachers College Press of Columbia University Press.
Jameson, F. 1997, *Postmodernism, or, The Cultural Logic of Late Capitalism* Durham: Duke University Press.
Jancovich, M., Faire, L., and Stubbings, S. 2003, *The Place of the Audience: Cultural Geographies of Film Consumption* London: British Film Institute Press.
Kay, H. 1938, '16mm Marches On!', *Canadian Independent*, 1 November 1938.
Kay, L. 2000, *Who Wrote the Book of Life? A History of the Genetic Code* Stanford: Stanford University Press.
Keil, A., and Jens, E. 2005, 'Audiovisuelle Medien und neuronale Netzwerke', in O. Grau and A. Keil, eds. *Mediale Emotionen. Zur Lenkung von Gefühlen durch Bild und Sound* Frankfurt am Main: Fischer Tb, pp. 224–41.
Kelly, K., and P. Parisi, 1997, 'Beyond *Star Wars*—What's Next for George Lucas?', *Wired*, 5.2, 164.
——, 1999, *New Rules for the New Economy* NY: Penguin.
Kember, Sarah, 2003, *Cyberfeminism and Artificial Life*, London and NY: Routledge.
Kirby, L. 1997, *Parallel Tracks: The Railroad and Silent Cinema* Exeter: University of Exeter Press.
Kittler, F. 1990, *Discourse Networks 1800/1900* Stanford CA: Stanford University Press.
——, 1997, *Essays: Literature, Media, Information Systems* Amsterdam: G+B Arts.
——, 1999, *Grammophon, Film, Typewriter*, Geoff Winthrop-Young and Michael Wutz, trans. Stanford: Stanford University Press.
——, 1999, *Gramophone, Film, Typewriter*, Stanford CA: Stanford University Press.
——, 1999, 'The History of Communication Media', *Ctheory*: Available at http://www.ctheory.net/articles.aspx?id=45 (Accessed January 7).
——, 2001, 'Computer Graphics: A Semi-Technical Introduction', *Grey Room*, 2: 30–45.
Klein, N. M. 1993, *Seven Minutes: The Life and Death of the American Animated Cartoon* London: Verso.
Kosofsky Sedgwick, E., and Adam, F., eds., 1995, *Shame and its Sisters. A Silvan Tomkins Reader* Durham, London: Duke University Press.

Kracauer, S. 1960, *Theory of Film: The Redemption of Physical Reality* Oxford & NY: Oxford University Press.

——, 1994, 'Girls and Crisis' in Jay, M., Kaes, A., and Dimendberg, E., eds. *The Weimar Republic Sourcebook* Berkeley: University of California Press.

——, 2004, *From Caligari to Hitler: A Psychological History of German Cinema* Princeton, NJ: Princeton University Press.

——, 2005, *The Mass Ornament*, Levin, T. Y., ed. and trans. Cambridge, MA: Harvard University Press.

Krämer, P. 2001, '"It's aimed at kids—the kid in everybody": George Lucas, *Star Wars* and Children's Entertainment', *Scope: An Online Journal of Film Studies*. Available at http://www.nottingham.ac.uk/film/journal/articles/its-aimed-at-kids.htm.

Kristeva, J. 1995, *New Maladies of the Soul*, Columbia University Press.

Laine, T. 2006, 'Eija-Liisa Ahtila's affective images in The House', paper delivered at the conference *Thinking through Affect*, Maastricht Sept 8–9 2006.

Landecker, H. 2006. 'Microcinematography and the History of Science and Film', *ISIS*, 97, 121–32.

Lastra, J. 2000, *Perception, Representation, Modernity: Sound Technology and the American Cinema* NY: Columbia University Press.

Latour, B. 1987, *Science in Action: How to Follow Scientists and Engineers through Society* Milton Keynes: OU Press.

——, 2005, *Reassembling the Social: An Introduction to Actor-Network Theory* NY: Oxford University Press.

LeBon, G. 2002 [1895], *The Crowd: A Study of the Popular Mind* Mineola, NY: Dover.

Leigh, D. 2002, 'Wheels within Wheels' [WWW] Available at http://film.guardian.co.uk/features/featurepages/0,4120,752100,00.html (Accessed 7 June 2005).

Lemke, T. 2002. 'Genetic Testing, Eugenics, and Risk', *Critical Public Health*, 12.3, 283–90.

Lenburg, J. 1983, *The Great Cartoon Directors* North Carolina: McFarland.

Leslie, E. 2000, 'Dreamsleep: Walter Benjamin's *Arcades Project*', *Things*, 13, 49–67.

*Letterbooks of the Chief Constable of the City of Toronto*. 1908, City of Toronto Archives Box 106157-1, 1908, 447–48, 678.

Levin, T. Y. 2005, 'Introduction', in S. Kracauer, *The Mass Ornament* Cambridge, MA: Harvard University Press.

——, Frohne, U., and Weibel, P., eds., 2002, *CTRL [SPACE]: Rhetorics of Surveillance from Bentham to Big Brother* Cambridge: MIT Press.

Lewis, R. 1938, 'Ray Presents', *Canadian Moving Picture Digest*, 24 September 1938.

——, 1938, 'Ray Presents', *Canadian Moving Picture Digest*, 29 October 1938.

——, 1938, 'Ray Presents', *Canadian Moving Picture Digest*, 12 November 1938.

Loiperdinger, M., ed., 1994, *Oskar Messter—Ein Filmpionier der Kaiserzeit* Frankfurt am Main und Basel: Stroemfeld/Roter Stern.

Lunenfeld, P. 2002, 'The New Intertextual Commodity', in Harries, D. ed. *The New Media Book* London, BFI, 69–81.

Macpherson, C. B. 1962, *The Political Theory of Possessive Individualism, Hobbes to Locke* NY: Oxford University Press.

*Mail and Empire* Toronto, 1907, 'Five Cent Theatre Harmless Here.' 4 May 1907, 6.

Mannoni, L. 1995, *Le grand art de la lumière et de l'ombre. Archéologie du cinéma* Paris: Nathan.

Manovich, L. 1997, 'Reality Effects in Computer Animation', *A Reader* in J. Pilling, ed. *Animation Studies* Sydney: John Libbey.
——, 2001, *The Language of New Media* Cambridge, MA: MIT Press.
——, 2004, 'Image_future' Available at www.manovich.net (Accessed 9 October 2004).
Marin, L. 1994, *De la representation* Paris: Gallimard/Le Seuil.
Marks, L. U. 2000, *The Skin of the Film: Intercultural Cinema, Embodiment, and the Senses* Duke University Press.
——, 2002, *Touch: Sensuous Theory and Multisensory Media* University of Minnesota Press.
Marshall, P. D. 2004, *New Media Cultures* London: Arnold.
Marvin, C. 1998, *When Old Technologies Were New* NY: Oxford.
Massumi, B. 2002, *Parables for the Virtual: Movement, Affect, Sensation* Durham and London: Duke University Press.
——, 2003, 'Navigating Moments' interview with Mary Zanazi, in *21C Magazine*.
McLaren, N. 1976, 'Technical Notes, 1955' reprinted in R. Russett and C. Starr, *Experimental Animation: An Illustrated Anthology* NY: Van Nostrand Reinhold Company.
McNay, L. 2000, *Gender and Agency: Reconfiguring the Subject in Feminist and Social Theory* Cambridge: Polity Press.
McSwain, J. B. 2002, 'Fire Hazard and Protection of Property: Municipal Regulation of the Storage and Supply of Fuel Oil in Mobile, Alabama, 1894–1910.' *Journal of Urban History*, 28.5, 599–628.
Mebold, A., and Tepperman, C. 2003, 'Resurrecting the Lost History of 28mm Film in North America', *Film History*, 15.2, 137–51.
Merleau-Ponty, M. 1964, 'The Film and the New Psychology', *Sense and Non-sense* Northwestern University Press.
——, 2002, *The Phenomenology of Perception* Routledge Classic Series London: Routledge.
Metz, Christian, 1974, *Language and Cinema*, Donna Jean Umiker-Sebeok, trans. The Hague: Mouton.
——, 1982, *The Imaginary Signifier: Psychoanalysis and the Cinema*, Britton, C., Williams, A., Brewster, B., and Guzzetti, A., trans. Bloomington: Indiana University Press.
Michalka, M., ed., 2001, *X-Screen: Film Installations and Actions of the 1960s and 1970s* Cologne: Walther König.
Miller, T. 2001, 'Cinema Studies Doesn't Matter, or, I Know What You Did Last Semester', in M. Tinkom and A. Villarejo, eds. *Keyframes: Popular Cinema and Cultural Studies* London: Routledge, pp. 303–11.
Minsky, M. 2006, *The Emotion Machine: Commonsense Thinking, Artificial Intelligence and the Future of the Human Mind*, NY and London: Simon and Schuster.
Moller, O. 2001, 'Film critic Olaf Moller reflects of the current state of German Cinema in the wake of *Run Lola Run*,' *Film Comment*, 37.3, May 2001, 11.
Morris, P. 1978, *Embattled Shadows: A History of Canadian Cinema 1895–1939* Montreal: McGill-Queen's University Press.
Morsch, T. 1999, 'Die Macht der Bilder: Spektakularität und die Somatisierung des Blicks im Actionkino', in *Film + Kritik*, 4, 21–44.

Münsterberg, H. 1970 [1916], *The Photoplay* NY: Arno Press.
Murray, J. 1997, *Hamlet on the Holodeck: The Future of Narrative in Cyberspace* Cambridge, MA: MIT Press.
Natali, M. 1996, *L'image paysage. iconologie et cinéma* Saint-Denis: Presses Universitaires de Vincennes.
Nelkin, D. 2004, *The DNA Mystique: The Gene as Cultural Icon* Michigan: University of Michigan Press.
*News* Toronto, 1907, 'Thaw Pictures Are Forbidden.' 12 April 1907, 1.
*News* Toronto, 1908, 'Theatre Panic Cost 150 Lives.' 14 January 1908, 1.
Novak, W. J. 1996, *The People's Wefare: Law and Regulation in Nineteenth Century America* Chapel Hill: University of North Carolina Press.
O'Riordan, K. 2008, 'Human Cloning in Film: Horror, Ambivalence, Hope' *Science as Culture* 17 (2), June, 145–162.
O'Sickey, I. M. 2002, 'Whatever Lola Wants, Lola Gets Or Does She?: Time and Desire in Tom Tykwer's *Run Lola Run*', *Quarterly Review of Film and Video*, 19, 123.
Ontario. *Statutes*, 1908, 'An Act to amend the Act to Regulate the Means of Egress from Public Buildings.' 8 Edward VII. Chapter 60. 14 April 1908, 452.
Park, R. E. 1972 [1904], 'The Crowd', in *The Crowd and the Public and Other Essays* Chicago: University of Chicago Press.
Pashler, H. E. 1998, *The Psychology of Attention* Cambridge, MA: MIT Press.
Pearson, R. E. 1992, *Eloquent Gestures: The Transformation of Performance Style in the Griffith Biograph Films* Berkeley: University of California Press.
Pearson, R. E., and Uricchio, W. 1999, 'The Formative and Impressionable Stage: Discursive Constructions of the Nickelodeon's Child Audience', in M. Stokes and R. Maltby, eds. *American Movie Audiences From the Turn of the Century to the Early Sound Era* London: British Film Institute.
Pendakur, M. 1990, *Canadian Dreams and American Control: The Political Economy of the Canadian Film Industry* Detroit: Wayne State University Press.
Peranson, M. 2003, 'Reattaching the Broken Thread: Olivier Assayas on Filmmaking and Film Theory', *CinemaScope*, 14, 30–9.
Perez, G. 2000, *The Material Ghost: Films and their Medium* Baltimore & London: The John Hopkins University Press.
Petro, P. 1987, 'Modernity and Mass Culture in Weimar: Contours of a discourse on sexuality in the early theories of perception and representation', *New German Critique*, 40.
Pisters, P. 2003, *The Matrix of Visual Culture: Working With Deleuze in Film Theory* Stanford: Stanford University Press.
Primedia, 2001, 'Effecting BMW Shorts' Available at http://www.findarticles.com/p/articles/mi_m0HEN/is_2001_July_1/ai_76848790 (Accessed 21 August 2004).
Prince, S. 1996, 'True Lies: Perceptual Realism, Digital Images, and Film Theory', *Film Quarterly*, 49.3, 27–37.
Quilley, S., and Loyal, S. 2004, *The Sociology of Norbert Elias* NY: Cambridge University Press.
Rabinow, P., 1999, *French DNA: Trouble in Purgatory* Chicago: Chicago University Press.
Rank, O. 1971, *The Double: A Psychoanalytic Study* Chapel Hill: University of North Carolina Press.
Reid, S. 2002, 'On car chases, and BMW Films' Available at http://www.tagliners.org/archive/001117.html (Accessed 21 August 2004).

Rieger, S. 2003, *Anthropologische Kybernetik*, Frankfurt am Main: Suhrkamp.
Rodowick, D. N. 1997, *Gilles Deleuze's Time Machine* Durham and London: Duke University Press.
Rohmer, E. 2001, 'Je voulais que la réalité devienne tableau', *Cahiers du Cinéma*, 559, 50–8.
Romney, J. 2003, *Atom Egoyan* London: BFI.
Rose, N., 2001, 'The Politics of Life Itself', *Theory, Culture and Society*, 186, 1–30.
Rosen, C. M. 1986, *The Limits of Power: Great Fires and the Process of City Growth in America* NY: Cambridge University Press.
Rosen, P., ed., 1986, *Narrative, Apparatus, Ideology: A Film Theory Reader* NY: Columbia University Press.
Rossell, D. 1998, *Living Pictures: The Origins of the Movies* Albany: University of New York Press.
Ruiz, R. 2005, *Poetics of Cinema* Paris: Editions Dis Voir.
Russett, R., and Starr, C., eds., 1976, *Experimental Animation: An Illustrated Anthology* New York: Van Nostrand Reinhold Company.
Savlov, M. 2004, 'Film Listings: Code 46', *Austin Chronicle*, 19 September 2004.
Seigworth, G. J. 2005, 'From affection to soul' in Stivale, C. J., ed. *Gilles Deleuze: Key Concepts* Montreal and Kingston, Ithaca: McGill-Queen's University Press, pp. 159–69.
Shaviro, S. 1993, *The Cinematic Body* Minneapolis: University of Minnesota Press.
Shawhan, J., '"Qui Est Sylvie Braghier?": Identity and Narrative in Olivier Assayas' Demonlover', *The Film Journal* Available at www.thefilmjournal.com/issue6/demonlover.html.
Simmel, G. 1950, *The Sociology of Georg Simmel* Glencoe, IL: Free Press.
Slusser, G. 1999, 'The Forever Child: *Ender's Game* and the Mythic Universe of Science Fiction', in Westfahl, G., and Slusser, G., eds. *Nursery Realms: Children in the Worlds of Science Fiction, Fantasy, and Horror* Athens and London: University of Georgia Press, pp. 73–90.
Smith, A. 2004, 'Interview with Tim Robbins on Code 46' *Cinema Confidential*, 8 April, 2004.
Smither, R. B. N., ed., 2002, *This Film is Dangerous: a Celebration of Nitrate Film* Brussels: FIAF.
Sobchack, V. 1990, 'The Virginity of Astronauts: Sex and the Science Fiction Film' in Kuhn, A., ed., *Alien Zone: Cultural Theory and Contemporary Science Fiction Cinema*, London and NY: Verso, 103–15.
——, 1992, *The Address of the Eye: A Phenomenology of Film Experience* Princeton: Princeton University Press.
——, 1994, 'The Scene of the Screen: Envisioning Cinematic and Electronic "Presence"', in H. U. Gumbrecht and K. L. Pfeiffer, eds. *Materialities of Communication* Stanford University Press, pp. 83–106.
——, 2000, *Meta-morphing: visual transformation and the culture of quick-change* Minneapolis: University of Minnesota Press.
——, 2004, *Carnal Thoughts: Embodiment and Moving Image Culture* Berkeley: California University Press.
——, 2004, 'The Scene of The Screen: Envisioning Photographic, Cinematic and Electronic "Presence"', in *Carnal Thoughts: Embodiment and Moving Image Culture* Berkeley, Los Angeles and London: University of California Press.

Solomon, C. 1987, 'Animation: Notes on a Definition', in C. Solomon, ed. *The Art of The Animated Image* Los Angeles: The American Film Institute.
Stacey, J. 2003. 'She is Not Herself: The Deviant Relations of *Alien Resurrection*' *Screen*, 44.3, 251–76.
Stam, R. 2000, *Film Theory: An Introduction* NY: Blackwell.
Standage, T. 1999, *The Victorian Internet* London: Berkley.
*Star* Toronto, 1897, 'Fad Legislation Beaten by a Technicality.' 9 August, 1.
*Star* Toronto, 1907, 'To Inspect Theatoriums.' 25 April, 3.
Stern, M. 2004, 'Jurassic Park and the Moveable Feast of Science', *Science as Culture*, Autumn 2004, 133, 347–72.
Stiegler, B. 1994, *La technique et le temps*, Paris: Galilée/Cité des sciences et de l'industrie.
——, 2001, *La technique et le temps 3*, Le temps du cinéma et la question du mal-être, Paris: Galilée.
Stivale, C. J., ed., 2005, *Gilles Deleuze: Key Concepts* Montreal and Kingston: McGill-Queen's University Press.
Strachan, J. D. et al., 1997, 'TFTR DT Experiments', *Plasma Physics and Controlled Fusion*, 39, B103–14 Available at http://www.wsx.lanl.gov/ricky/disrupt.htm.
Strauven, W. 2006, *The Cinema of Attractions Reloaded* Amsterdam: Amsterdam University Press.
*Telegram* Toronto, 1908, 'Another Theatre Panic.' 18 January 1908, 10.
*Telegram* Toronto, 1897, 'Prize Fight Pictures, Controllers Oppose Them.' 5 August 1897, 6.
Tesson, C. 2001, 'La Révolution selon Rohmer', *Cahiers du Cinéma*, 559, 41.
Thacker, E. 2004, *Biomedia* Minneapolis: University of Minnesota Press.
Thaller, B. 2005, *Advanced Visual Quantum Mechanics* NY: Springer Science.
Thompson, K. 1998, *Storytelling in the New Hollywood. Understanding Classical Narrative Technique* Cambridge: Harvard University Press.
Thrift, N., undated, 'Closer to the Machine? Intelligent Environments, New Forms of Possession and the Rise of the Supertoy', Available at http://ggy.bris.ac.uk/staff/information/thrift_papers/closer_to_the_machine.doc.
Titford, J. S. 1973, 'Object-Subject Relationships in German Expressionist Cinema' *Cinema Journal*, 13.1, 17–24.
Toffler, A. 1970, *Future Shock* London: Bodley Head.
——, 1980, *The Third Wave* London: Collins.
Toronto, 1890, *Consolidated Bylaws*. No. 2453 License Fee Schedule for Amusements. Section 43, Subsection 19.
Toulmin, V., Popple, S., and Russell, P. 2004, *The Lost World of Mitchell & Kenyon: Edwardian Britain on Film* London: BFI.
Truffaut, F., with the collaboration of Helen Scott, 1985, *Hitchcock: The Definitive Study, Revised Edition* London: Paladin.
Turkle, S. 1998, 'Cyborg babies and Cy-Dough-Plasm: Ideas about Self and Life in the Culture of Simulation' in Davis-Floyd, Robbie, and Dunit, Joseph, eds. *Cyborg Babies: From Techno-Sex to Techno-Tots* London and NY: Routledge, pp. 317–29.
Turney, J. 1998, *Frankenstein's Footsteps: Science, Genetics and Popular Culture* Yale University Press.
Uricchio, W., and Pearson, R. E. 1993, *Reframing Culture: The Case of the Vitagraph Quality Films* Princeton, NJ: Princeton University Press.

Valverde, M. 1991, *The Age of Light, Soap, and Water: Moral Reform in English Canada, 1885–1925* Toronto: McClelland & Stewart.
——, 2003, 'Police Science, British Style: Pub Licensing and Knowledges of Urban Disorder', *Economy and Society*, 32.2., 234–52.
Van Dijck, J. 1998, *Imagenation: Popular Images of Genetics* London: Macmillan.
Virilio, P. 1989, *War and Cinema: The Logistics of Perception*, Patrick Camiller, trans. London and NY: Verso.
Waxman, S. 2006, 'Cyberface: New Technology That Captures the Soul', *New York Times*, October 15, 2006, AR1.
Weber, S. 1996, *Mass Mediauras: Form, Technics, Media*, Stanford: Stanford University Press.
Weigel, S. 2005, "Phantombilder," in O. Grau and A. Keil, eds. *Mediale Emotionen. Zur Lenkung von Gefühlen durch Bild und Sound* Frankfurt: Fischer.
Weingart P., Muhl C., and Pansegrau P. 2003, 'Of Power Maniacs and Unethical Geniuses: Science and Scientists in Fiction Film', *Public Understanding of Science*, July 2003, 12.3, 279–287.
Williams, A. P. 1996, 'The Silent Threat: A ReViewing of the Sexual Other: in *The Phantom of the Opera* and *Nosferatu*', *The Midwest Quarterly*, 38.1, Autumn 1996.
Williams, L. 1998, 'Melodrama Revised', in N. Browne, ed. *Re-figuring American Film Genres: History and Theory* Berkeley, Los Angeles and London: University of California Press, pp. 42–88.
——, 2000, 'Discipline and Fun: *Psycho* and postmodern cinema', in Gledhill, C., and Williams, L., eds. *Reinventing Film Studies* London: Arnold, pp. 267–81.
Winthrop-Young, G. 2002, 'Drill and Distraction in the Yellow Submarine: On the dominance of war in Friedrich Kittler's media theory', *Critical Inquiry*, 29.4, 825–55.
Wollen, P. 1980, 'Cinema and Technology: A Historical Overview', in de Lauretis, T., and Heath, S., eds. *The Cinematic Apparatus* London: Macmillan, pp. 14–22.
Wood, A. 2002, *Technoscience in Contemporary American Film: Beyond Science Fiction* Manchester: Manchester University Press.
——, 2007, *Digital Encounters* London: Routledge, 2007.
*World* Toronto, 1907, 'Managers Will Assist Preventing Nasty Plays.' 27 April, 6.
*World* Toronto, 1908, 'Panic at St. Catharines, Spark Ignited Combustible Film.' 16 January, 1.
*World* Toronto, 1911, 'Moving Picture Blaze.' 14 August, 1.
Young, P. 2006, *The Cinema Dreams its Rivals: Media Fantasy Films from Radio to the Internet* Minneapolis: University of Minnesota Press.
Youngblood, G. 1970, *Expanded Cinema* New York: E. P. Dutton.

# Index

Abbott, Stacey, 199n5
Abel, Richard, 82
Abraham, Farid F., 69n2
Adorno, Theodor, 175
'advermovies', 21, 43–47
advertising: and World Wide Web, 43–47
affect: and animation technique, 211
affect: in Deleuze, 145, 155n5
affect: and film theory, 15
affect: representation of, 16, 142, 144, 147–148, 151–153
affect: and spectatorship, 183, 214–225
affection-image (Deleuze), 145
agency: and spectatorial practice, 129–141
*A.I.* (film). See *Artificial Intelligence: A.I.*
Aitken, Ian, 161
Akbar, Abbas, 154n3, 155n9
Aldiss, Brian, 182n5
alternate reality games (ARGs), 43, 45
Althusser, Louis, 214, 239
*Angel* (TV series), 200n16
animation: and digital technology, 16, 190–191
animation: and film theory, 184, 197, 201–213
animation: techniques, 203, 205–212
anthropomorphism: in German language, 89
any-instant-whatever (Deleuze), 201–213
any-space-whatever (Deleuze), 222
apparatus theory, 9–13, 214–215, 232
archaeology (Foucault): and film history, 232–233, 238
architecture, 15, 126–7
architecture: technological interfaces as, 131
archives: and technological change, 231
Arnheim, Rudolf, 18n7

Arnheim, Rudolf: *Film as Art*, 8–9
*Arrival of a Train at La Ciotat* (film), 181
Artaud, Antonin, 100
*Artificial Intelligence: AI* (film), 52n7, 171, 177, 178, 182n5
Assayas, Olivier, 142, 144, 145, 148, 153, 156n10
*As You See* (film), 240n5
attention: and aesthetic strategies, 16, 144
attention: and subjectivity, 161–162
attention: and technological interfaces, 129–141
Atom Entertainment, 51n4
*Audio and Video Walks* (artwork), 220
Augé, Marc, 147, 149
Aumont, Jacques, 159, 164
automatic writing, 100, 102
automaton. See doubles

Barry, Nora, 51n1
Barthes, Roland, 69, 159
Batchen, Geoffrey, 233
Baudry, Jean-Louis, 10–12, 172, 173, 174–175, 215, 224n1, 232, 239
Bazin, André, 68, 98, 160, 161, 201, 213n1, 227, 236, 239
Belton, John, 17n1
Benjamin, Walter: *Arcades Project*, 39–40, 51n5
Benjamin, Walter, commodity culture, 40–41
Benjamin, Walter: distraction, 38–40, 160, 161, 162
Benjamin, Walter: shock, 93, 223
Benjamin, Walter: spectatorship, 126
Benjamin, Walter: technological change, 37, 40, 42, 50
Bergson, Henri: affect, 145, 154n4, 155n5, 211, 214, 219, 222
Bergson, Henri: and cinema, 88, 102, 221

Bergson, Henri: duration, 96–97
*Berlin Files, The* (artwork), 220
B. F. Keith's (theatre chain), 84
*Bicentennial Man* (film), 171, 173
*Billboard* (magazine), 81, 82
biochemistry: visual imaging techniques, 61
biotechnology: film as, 106
BitTorrent (software), 3
Bitzer, Billy, 159
*Blinkity Blink* (film), 206
blogs. *See* weblogs
*Blue Angel, The* (film), 199n1
BMW: online advertising campaigns, 44, 45–47
BMW Films, 42, 43–44, 45–47, 50–51
Board of Police Commissioners (Toronto), 86
bodies: and spatial aesthetics, 144
Bogard, William, 39
Bogue, Ronald, 98, 155n4
Bolter, Jay David, 17n1, 165, 240n2
Booth, Michael R., 47
Bordwell, David, 213n1, 215, 228
Bossin, Hye, 79
Bottomore, Stephen, 83
Bourdieu, Pierre, 138–139
Bovin, Jan-Olov, 62
Bowley, David, 69n5
Bowser, Eileen, 157
Boyertown (Pennsylvania): 1908 theatre fire, 75–76
Braidotti, Rosi, 224n3
Brakhage, Stan, 6
Brandt, Nat, 75, 83
Braun, Marta, 234
Broadfoot, Keith, 204
Brown, Tom, 17n3
*Bubble* (film), 4
Buck-Morss, Susan, 40, 47, 51n5
Bunin, Lou, 209–211
Bunton, Robin, 118
Burch, Noël, 159
Butler, Judith, 118
Butler, Rex, 204

*Cabinet of Dr. Caligari, The* (film), 94, 95, 101, 102
*Calendar* (film), 164–165

Cameron, James, 169, 176
Canada: film exhibition and distribution practices, 23–36
*Canadian Moving Picture Digest*: campaign against 16mm exhibition, 23, 28
Canguilhem, George, 71
Canning, Peter, 209–211
capitalism: and commodity culture, 40–41
capitalism: and film industry, 40, 175, 180
Cardiff, Janet, 220
Cardinal, Roger, 125
Cartwright, Lisa, 105, 106, 107, 216, 222, 224n2, 232
Casetti, Francesco, 9, 18n8
Cawley, John, 208
cellular phones. *See* mobile phones
celluloid: safety concerns, 75, 76–77, 79, 81, 85
censorship, 77, 79, 80
Cézanne, Paul, 162
CGI. *See* computer-generated imagery
Charcot, Jean-Marie, 235
Charity, T., 180
Chicago (Illinois): 1903 theatre fire, 75, 83
Chicago (Illinois): film censorship movement, 80
children: and cinema audiences, 80, 83, 174–176
children: and media effects, 177
children: representations of, 128, 168–182
Chomón, Segundo de, 228
Chun, Wendy, 88
cinema: and technology, 1, 5, 14ff
cinema: as technology, 1, 3, 6ff
cinema: death of, 3
cinema: technological identity of, 4
cinema of attractions: and new technologies, 157, 169, 229
cinema of attractions: and 'web cinema', 38–39, 50
cinema studies. *See* film theory
Cinematograph Act (Britain), 82
cinephilia, 5, 176–177, 180, 230
*Cinéthique* (magazine), 9

Claerbout, David, 66–67, 68
Clampett, Bob, 209–211
classicism: as dominant mode, 228
Clément, Catherine, 95
clocks: represented in films, 193–197, *194*
cloning: cinematic representations of, 110–111, 113–114, 115–117, 121
*Code 46* (film), 105, 109, 110–115, 118–119, 121, 122
cognitivism (film theory), 215
Cohl, Emile, 204, 228
Comolli, Jean-Louis, 12, 224n1, 239
commodities: and consumer culture, 40–42, 46, 47, 50, 230
computer games. *See* video games
computer-generated imagery (CGI), 169
computers: and spectatorial practice, 28, 41
Cook, David, 6, 7
Cooper, John, 28–29
Cooper Organization. *See* Motion Picture Exhibitors and Distributors of Canada
Corliss, Richard, 177
Craik, W. A., 79
Crary, Jonathan, 130, 141, 161–162, 235
crowd. *See* masses
*Crown Fountain* (sculpture), 67–68
Cubitt, Sean, 3, 13, 89, 219–220
Culhane, Shamus, 210
cybernetics, 221
cyberpunk, 111–112, 113

*Daily Standard* (St. Catharines), *76*
Damasio, Antonio, 214, 222
*Dark City* (film), 134
Darley, Andrew, 106
Deleuze, Gilles, 72
Deleuze, Gilles: affect, 145, 149, 154n2, 184–185
Deleuze, Gilles: difference, 156n10
Deleuze, Gilles: and digital technology, 103–104
Deleuze, Gilles: and film animation, 201–213
Deleuze, Gilles: influence in film studies, 88, 201

Deleuze, Gilles: temporality and duration, 68, 69
Deleuze, Gilles: theory of cinema, 88–90, 96–104, 155nn7–8, 162, 191–192, 196, 198, 214, 216, 219, 232, 238–239
Deleuze, Gilles: theory of subjectivity, 220
Deleuze, Gilles: virtuality, 221–222
*Demonlover* (film), 126, 142–148, 150–153
De Niro, Robert, 116
Department of Energy (U. S.), 55
Derrida, Jacques, 91, 164
desktop video, 47–49
Dickson, W. K., 236
Didi-Huberman, Georges, 235
digital cinema, 13
digital technology: and advertising, 47
digital technology: aesthetics of, 126, 142–156
digital technology: affect and embodiment, 216
digital technology: cinematic representation of, 145–147
digital technology: desktop and DIY video, 47–49
digital technology: and film theory, 89, 103–104, 189, 217–218, 226–240
digital technology: as progress, 227
digital technology: precursors of, 190, 228–229, 231–236
digital technology: and representational practice, 157, 166, 193
digital technology: and sound, 219–220
digital technology: and spectatorial practice, 41–42, 132–133, 140–141, 176, 216–220, 229
digital technology: as threat to film, 1, 5, 23–5, 176, 184, 189, 226–227
Dirac, Paul, 65
discourse networks (Kittler), 90–91, 238–239
distraction: in film theory, 160–162
distraction: and interface design, 130

distraction: and new technologies, 157
distraction: as spectatorial practice, 16, 38–39, 50, 157–167
distribution: Canada, 27
Dixon, Wheeler Winston, 13
Doane, Mary Ann, 69, 176, 234
Dolly (sheep), 106–107, 110
doppelgänger. *See* doubles
doubles: and cinema technology, 15, 72, 88–104, 173
doubles: in Freud, 89
Douchet, Jean, 227
*Dracula* (novel), 200n10
Dreyer, Carl-Theodor, 104n1
Driessen, Paul, 137
Dube, Bryan, 42
*Duck Amuck* (film), 208
Duhamel, Georges, 100
Durand, Régis, 69
duration (Bergson), 96–97, 102
DVD: and cinephilia, 230

Eco, Umberto, 231
*Economist, The* (magazine), 230–231
Eder, Jens, 215
Edgerton, David, 18n6
Edgerton, Sam, 54
Edison, Thomas, 234, 236
educational films: exhibition of, 26
Egoyan, Atom, 127, 158, 164, 166
Eisner, Lotte, 93, 100
electricity: and development of cinema, 230–231
electronic presence (Sobchack), 148, 150–151
electron microscopy, 62
Elias, Norbert, 84–85
Eliasson, Olafur, 139
Ellis, Jack, 6–7
Elsaesser, Thomas, 93, 199n1, 199n3, 223–224, 235
*End of the World in Four Seasons, The* (installation), 137, 139
environment: media, 126
episteme (Foucault), 90
Everett, Anna, 51n3
exhibition: and digital technology, 24
exhibition: history of, 23–27
exhibition: independent, 23–36

exhibition: itinerant, 25–27, 29–30
exhibition: licensing and regulation of: Canada, 29, 32, 34, 75–86
exhibition: 'non-theatrical', 26–27
exhibition: and 16mm format, 23–36
exhibition: theatrical: competition and business practices, 31
exhibition: theatrical: and Hollywood cinema, 26
exhibition: and 35mm format, 23–36
expressionism: in German cinema, 88, 90, 93, 99–101, 103, 192, 196, 198, 199
*Eyes of the Mummy, The* (film), 104

Famous Players: and Motion Picture Exhibitors and Distributors of Canada, 29, 34
*Fantasmagoria* (film), 204
Farocki, Harun, 240n5
Fassbinder, Rainer Werner, 199n1
Faure, Elie, 99
*Faust* (film), 188
Federal Combines Investigation Act (Canada), 29
Feld, Steven, 199n2
feminism: and film theory, 216
field (Bourdieu), 138–139
film history: and technological change, 226–240
film industry: Canada, 27–28
film industry: Germany, 188
film industry: and technological change, 227–228
film societies: Canada, 26
film gauges, 15
film stock, 71
film theory: and film history, 226
film theory: and new media, 89, 226–240
film theory: and scientific films, 53–70
film theory: trends in, 214–217, 224
Fincher, David, 45
fire: and cinema safety concerns, 75–86
Fithian, John, 4
*Five Angels for the Millennium, The* (installation), 131

*flâneur*: and film spectatorship, 161
Flaxman, Gregory, 155n4
Flusser, Vilem, 231
Ford (company): sponsorship of films, 52n10
format, 19–21
Foucault, Michel, 72
Foucault, Michel: and epistemes, 90, 91, 238
Foucault, Michel: and governmentality, 105, 107, 115, 118
frame (film): and movement, 202
frame (film): and temporality, 53–57
frame (textual): and digital media, 218
Franklin, Sarah, 107–108
Franklin, Ursula, 2
Frayling, Christopher, 119, 120
freedom: and spectatorial agency, 137
Freud, Sigmund, 89, 94
Freund, Karl, 104n1
Fried, Michael, 70n21
Friedberg, Anne, 17n1
Frisby, David, 84
Frogier, Larys, 159
Fuery, Patrick, 164
Fumaroli, Marc, 166
functional equivalence (Bordwell and Thompson), 228

Galison, Peter, 61, 65
Gane, Nicholas, 88
gaze, the: and scientific films, 53, 59
Gaudreault, André, 38
gender: and cinema audiences, 83
gender: and film theory, 216
gender: and modes of agency, 138
genealogy (Foucault): and film history, 232–233
generative agency (McNay), 138
genomic science: cinematic representations of, 16, 72–73, 105–123
genre: and representations of science, 105, 109, 111, 122
German (language): anthropomorphism in, 89
Germany: cinema: expressionism, 88, 90, 93, 99–101, 103, 192, 196, 198, 199

Germany: cinema: history of, 187, 189–190, 199
Germany: cinema: industry, 188
Germany: cinema: and national identity, 189–190
Germany: Romanticism, 89–90, 93–94
Germany: Weimar cinema, 16
Germany: youth culture, 189–190
Godard, Jean-Luc, 127, 158, 160, 164, 166
*Godsend* (film), 105, 109, 110–111, 114, 115–118, 120–121
*Going Forth By Day* (installation), 131
*Google Video*, 3
governmentality (Foucault), 72, 107, 113–115, 118, 121
Graham, G. G., 25
gramophone, 91
'Grand Café' legend, 176
Grant, Barry, 111
graphic mode (Manovich), 231
Gray, W. C., 26–27
Green, John C., 30
Grieveson, Lee, 80
Griffin, John, 79
Griffith, D. W., 200n13
Grosz, Elizabeth, 224n3
Grusin, Richard, 17n1, 165, 240n2
Guattari, Félix, 145
Gunning, Tom, 3, 38, 39, 157, 169, 229
Gutteridge, R. W., 79

Haase, Christine, 200n9
habitus (Bourdieu), 138–139
*Half-Life 2* (video game), 132
Halle, Randall, 200nn7–8
Hamacher, Kay, 69n12
Hamm, Nick, 110
Hansen, Mark, 104, 141, 154n4, 214, 218–219, 222
haptic perception, 127, 144, 146, 151, 217
Haran, Joan, 110
Harries, Dan, 38–39
Hayles, N. Katherine, 135
Haynes, Roslynn, 119, 120
Heath, Stephen, 3, 232, 239
Heidegger, Martin, 238–239

Heiser, Jörg, 220
Hendershot, Heather, 35
heterodyne detection, 58–59
Highfield, Roger, 106
Hills, Matt, 109–110, 115
*Hire, The* (advertising campaign), 45, 50
*History Lessons* (film), 163
Hitchcock, Alfred, 158, 175, 191
Hockney, David, 235
Hollywood: and capitalism, 175, 180
home video. *See* video
Horner, George, 6
horror films: and representation of science, 109, 111, 115, 118, 122
*Hostage* (advertising campaign), 46
Huillet, Danièle, 127, 158, 163, 166
*Hulk, The* (film), 114, 134
Human Genome Project, 108, 119
Hutchins, Edwin, 135
Huyssen, Andreas, 83

IBM: scientific films, 62
iconicity: and scientific films, 66
ideology: and film theory, 224
imaginary (Lacan), 92, 103
IMAX, 20
immigration: and cinema audiences, 77–78, 83
Independent Motion Picture Exhibitors Association, 33
Independent Theatres Association of Ontario, 31
indeterminacy, 161, 167n3
indexicality: and animation, 207
indexicality: deconstructed, 231
indexicality: and digital technology, 89, 176, 189, 191, 217, 227, 232
Industrial Light and Magic, 228
Ingersoll (Ontario): 1908 theatre fire, 75
*Inland Empire* (film), 4
instant, the: as film-theoretical concept, 53–57, 66–69
interfaces: and user agency, 16, 129–141
interferometry, 58–59
intermediacy (Deleuze), 201, 204–209
Internet. *See* World Wide Web

interval, the: and narrative logic, 142, 143, 148–149, 152, 153, 154
iPod, 230
*Iron Giant, The* (film), 181n1
Iroquois Theatre (Chicago): 1903 fire, 75, 83
Isin, E. F., 78

Jacobs, Lewis, 82
Jameson, Fredric, 151
Jancovich, Mark, 82
Jane Addams Hull House (Chicago), 80
*Jimmy Neutron: Boy Genius* (film), 173
Jones, Chuck, 184, 207–208, 212
Jonze, Spike, 51n6
*Jurassic Park* (film), 107–108

Kafka, Franz, 239
Kant, Immanuel, 56, 220
Kay, Harold: campaign against 16mm, 28, 31–32
Keenan, Thomas, 88
Keil, Andreas, 215
Kember, Sarah, 117, 119
Kelly, Kevin, 228, 232
Kirby, Lynne, 159, 161
Kittler, Friedrich, 72
Kittler, Friedrich: and digital technology, 103
Kittler, Friedrich: influence in film studies, 88
Kittler, Friedrich: theory of cinema, 88–96, 98, 99, 101–104, 232, 235, 238–239
Klein, Melanie, 216
Klein, Norman M., 212
Kodak: and 16mm format, 26
Kracauer, Siegfried: distraction, 160–161, 162
Kracauer, Siegfried: Weimar cinema, 88, 93–96, 99–101, 199n3
Krämer, Peter, 175
Kristeva, Julia, 224

Lacan, Jacques, 59, 91–92, 174, 220
*Lady and the Duke, The* (film), 165–166
Laine, Tarja, 218
Landecker, Hannah, 106

Lang, Fritz, 188
Lastra, James, 12–13
Latour, Bruno, 77, 105
LeBon, Gustave, 85
Leibniz, Gottfried, 97
Leigh, Danny, 44
Lemke, Thomas, 118
Lenburg, Jeff, 210
Lenoir, Denis, 152
Leslie, Esther, 37
Lessing, Gotthold, 56
Levin, Thomas, 160
Levin, Thomas Y., 235
Lewis, Ray: campaign against 16mm, 23, 28, 32–34
light: conventionalized in scientific films, 62–64
light: as thematic element in films, 196–198
literature: description in, 159
Livermore Laboratories, 55
Loiperdinger, Martin, 240n7
*Lola* (film), 199n1
*Lost in Space* (film), 171
Loyal, Steven, 85
Lubitsch, Ernst, 104n1
Lucas, George, 228
*Lucky Star* (advertising campaign), 43, 44
Lumière, Antoine, 3
Lumière brothers, 3, 228–229, 233–234, 235–236
Lunenfeld, Peter, 41–42
Lye, Len, 6
Lynch, David, 4
Lyotard, Jean-François, 239

Macpherson, C. B., 84
Manet, Édouard, 162
Mann, Michael, 43
Mannoni, Laurent, 234
Manovich, Lev, 1, 13, 38–39, 190, 192, 197, 218–219, 229, 231, 238
*Man with a Movie Camera* (film), 229
Marey, Étienne-Jules, 6
Marin, Louis, 159
Marks, Laura, 217–218
Marshall, P. David, 38
Marvin, Carolyn, 17n2

Marx, Karl: commodities, 40–41
masses: and cinema audiences, 81–82
masses: psychology of, 84–85
masses: and urban modernity, 83–84
Massumi, Brian, 154n5, 224
*Matrix, The* (film), 134
McLaren, Norman, 6, 205–207, 208–212
McLuhan, Marshall, 91, 94
McNay, Lois, 138–139
McSwain, James B., 81
Mebold, Annke, 20
mediality (Kittler), 91
Méliès, Georges, 3, 228–229
melodrama: used in advertising, 47
memes, 48
memory: as film-theoretical concept, 69
Mercedes-Benz: online advertising campaigns, 43, 44
Merleau-Ponty, Maurice, 137
Messter, Oskar, 228, 234
*Metropolis* (film), 188
Metz, Christian, 9, 174–175, 224n1, 232, 239
Michalka, Matthias, 237
Michelson, Annette, 239
military: uses of film technology, 54–56, 103, 235, 237
Miller, George Bures, 220
Miller, Toby, 20
*Minority Report* (film), 132, 133–134, 135, 136, 139
Minsky, Marvin, 182n4
mirror stage (Lacan), 92–93, 174, 214
mobile phones, 230
modernity: and urban masses, 83–84
Moller, Olaf, 189
Morris, Peter, 79
Morsch, Thomas, 216
Motion Picture Association of America (MPAA): and film piracy, 24, 36n1
Motion Picture Censorship and Theatre Inspection Branch (Ontario), 29, 36n2
Motion Picture Exhibitors and Distributors of Canada, 28–29, 33–34

Motion Picture Theatres Association of Ontario, 33–34
movement: cinematic representation of, 183–184, 192–193, 202–204, 207, 221
movement-image (Deleuze), 68, 97, 103, 155n7
MPAA. *See* Motion Picture Association of America
Mulvey, Laura, 69, 215, 224n1, 239
*Mummy, The* (film), 104n1
mummy-complex (Bazin), 98
Münsterberg, Hugo: *The Photoplay*, 7–8
Murnau, F. W., 187, 188–189, 193, 197, 198
music: and animation techniques, 208
Muybridge, Eadweard, 6

narrative: and spectatorial practice, 131
narrative: thematizing of technology, 88, 90, 94, 96
narrative: and technological development, 157
narrative: unconventional strategies, 126
Natali, Maurizia, 167n1
National Association of Theatre Owners, 4
National Association of Theatre Owners: and digital theatrical exhibition, 24
National Film Board (Canada), 30
National Film Society (Canada), 26
neurobiology: and film theory, 214, 222
New German Cinema. *See* Germany – cinema – history
new media, 19–20
new media: as enabling piracy, 24
nickelodeons: audiences, 75–86
nickelodeons: licensing and regulation, 75–86
nooshock (Deleuze), 98–99
norm, 71–73
*Norman McLaren: Creative Process* (film), 208
normativity, 73

*Nosferatu* (film), 183, 187, 188–189, 192–199
Novak, William J., 81

occasionality (Toby Miller), 20
Ontario (Canada): regulation of cinemas, 78–79, 81, 86
Ontario Board of Censors, 29
Ontario Treasury Department Inspection Branch, 29, 32
Oppenheimer, J. Robert, 54
O'Riordan, Kate, 110
O'Sickey, Ingeborg Majer, 189, 198–199
Owen, Clive, 45

Pabst, Georg Wilhelm, 199n1
*Pandora's Box* (film), 199n1
Panofsky, Erwin, 238
*Paradise Institute, The* (artwork), 220
Parisi, Paula, 228
Park, Robert, 85
Pashler, Harold E., 136
*Passion* (film), 163–164
Pathé: development of film technology, 26, 236
Paul, Robert, 236
Pearson, Roberta, 82, 200n13
peer-to-peer (P2P) networks, 42
Pendakur, Manjunath, 27–29, 33
Peranson, Mark, 142
Perez, Gilberto, 163, 165
Petersen, Alan, 118
Petro, Patrice, 199n3
Phantasmagoria (projection device), 193
phenomenology: and film theory, 217
philosophy: and cinema, 96–97
photography: and spectator practice, 159
physics: visual imaging techniques, 61
*Pinocchio*, 171
piracy: and threat posed by new media, 24
piracy: film industry concern with, 24
Pisters, Patricia, 156n10
Plateau, Joseph, 6
*Pleasantville* (film), 134
Plensa, Jaume, 67–68
Pleynet, Marcellin, 9
Poinsot, Jean-Marc, 159

Popple, Simon, 106
*Porter, The* (advertising campaign), 52n8
Porter, Edwin S., 159
presence: as film-theoretical concept, 68
Price, Harry, 30
projectionists: licensing of, 79
projector: development of, 237–238
Prosser, Jay, 69
prosumers, 37, 51n2
protocinematic devices, 190–191, 193, 219, 232–236
psychoanalysis: and film interpretation, 94
psychoanalysis: and film theory, 214–216, 223
*Psycho Kid* (video), 48–49, *49*
punctum (Barthes), 159–160

quantum mechanics, 65
Quilley, Stephen, 85

Rabinow, Paul, 117
Rank, Otto, 89, 94
Rapatronic camera, 54–55
Raynaud, Émile, 236
Raza, Ghyslain, 42. *See also* Star Wars kid
Reeve, Christopher, 107
reproductive technologies: cinematic representation of, 110–111, 114, 115–117
Reid, Stephen, 45
Reiger, Stefan, 221
Richter, Hans, 184, 212
*Road to Guantánamo, The* (film), 4
Robbins, Tim, 123n3
robots: representation of, 16, 128, 168–182
Rodowick, D. N., 98, 154n4
Rohmer, Eric, 158, 165–166
Romanticism: Germany, 89–90, 93–94
Romney, Jonathan, 164
Rose, Nikolas, 107, 118
Rosen, Christine M., 81
Rosen, Philip, 240n6
Rossell, Deac, 236
Ruiz, Raul, 158, 166–167

*Run Lola Run* (film), 183, 187, *188*, 189–192, 193, 195–196, 198
Russell, Patrick, 106
Russett, Robert, 212
Ruyer, Raymond, 104

Sadoul, Georges, 236
St. Catharines (Ontario): 1908 theatre fire, 75–76
scanning: and spectatorship, 125
*Scenario of the Film Passion* (film), 163–164
Schreck, Max, 193, 197
Schuberg, John, 30
Schwarzenegger, Arnold, 173
science: and uses of film, 53–70, 234
science fiction: children in, 170
science fiction: representation of science, 109, 111, 113, 121–122, 178–179, 180–181
scientific films: representational conventions, 14, 53–70
scientists: cinematic representations of, 109, 112–114, 116–117
scientists: media representations of, 119–121
Sedgwick, Eve Kosofsky, 216, 222–223, 224n2
Seigworth, Gregory J., 154n2, 155n5
*7 Years Later* (advertising campaign), 44
*Shadow of the Vampire* (film), 197
Shaviro, Steven, 216
Shawhan, Jason, 154
Simmel, Georg, 84
Soderbergh, Steven, 4
16mm: exhibition, 23–36
16mm: history of, 25
16mm: as threat to 35mm exhibition, 23–36
Slusser, George, 171
*Small Soldiers* (film), 179–180
Smither, R. B. N., 75
Sobchack, Vivian, 130, 148, 149, 150–151, 152, 178–179, 217, 237
Solomon, Charles, 205
Sonic Youth, 144, 146
sound: and digital media, 219–220
sound: and film history, 233

space: representation of: as affective, 126–127, 147, 149
space: representation of: and film technique, 189, 191
spectatorship: and affect, 214–225
spectatorship: as agency, 129, 137–139
spectatorship: attention and distraction, 126–127, 129–141, 144, 160–162
spectatorship: as embodied, 41, 50, 130, 135–136, 140, 144, 185, 214–225
spectatorship: in film theory, 92–93, 97, 125–128, 174–176
spectatorship: and interactivity, 41–42
spectatorship: representations of, 168–182
spectatorship: social aspects, 75–86
spectatorship: and technological change, 37–52, 129, 217
*Spider-Man* (film), 110
Spielberg, Steven, 52n7
Spinoza, Baruch, 97, 145, 214
spiritual automaton (Deleuze), 96, 97–100, 103
Stacey, Jackie, 114
Stam, Robert, 12
Standage, Tom, 234
*Star Kid* (film), 170, 174
*Star Wars* (film), 42, 175
Star Wars kid (SWK), 42, 46, 47–50
Starr, Cecile, 212
Stern, Megan, 108
Stewart, Garrett, 68
Stiegler, Bernard, 2
Stivale, Charles J., 155n4
Stoker, Bram, 200n10
Strachan, J. D., 69n2
Straub, Jean-Marie, 127, 158, 163, 165, 166
Strauven, Wanda, 17n3
*Student of Prague, The* (film), 94
*studium* (Barthes), 159
subjectivity: cinematic representation of, 113–115
subjectivity: constituted by cinema, 160–161
subjectivity: constituted by technology, 88, 111, 142–156
subjectivity: and doubles, 89
subjectivity: and 'electronic presence', 150–151
subjectivity: and film theory, 91, 214–216, 222–223
subjectivity: and spectatorship, 216, 220–223
subway films, 159
Superior Road Attractions, 30
*Swarm of Angels, A* (film), 51

technical standard, 19
technology: cinema *and*, 16
technology: cinema *as*, 16
technology: concept of, 14
technology: definition of, 2
technology: development and change: and capitalism, 40
technology: development and change: and concepts in film theory, 5, 53–70, 89, 201
technology: development and change: and concepts in film history, 6–7
technology: development and change: and film industry, 188
technology: development and change: and medium specificity, 226–240
technology: development and change: narratives of, 226–240
technology: development and change: new evoking old, 190, 226–240
technology: development and change: and nostalgia, 176, 217
technology: development and change: popular discourse of, 187, 190
technology: development and change: representations of, 168, 172
technology: development and change: and spectatorial practice, 11–12, 37–52, 129
technology: digital, 1
technology: human interface with, 130–131, 136, 140–141, 168–182
technology: and innovation, 5
technology: as mediating subjectivity, 88–104, 142–156

technology: pre-cinematic, 183
technology: and representational practice, 157–167, 191, 192, 199
technology: representation of: as aestheticized, 108, 144, 145–146, 169, 172, 188
technology: representation of: allegories of cinema, 169–174, 176–181, 189, 190, 196–199
technology: representation of: as threatening, 168
technology: as social agent, 77, 79–80
technoscience (Latour), 105, 108, 112–114, 121
television: and film history, 234
television: and film spectatorship, 37, 41
television: and indeterminacy, 167n3
television: and new technology, 229–230
television: representation of, 164
television: as threat to 35mm exhibition, 23
*Tel Quel* (journal), 9
Tepperman, Charles, 20
*Terminator 2: Judgment Day* (film), 127, 168–173, 176, 180
Tesson, Charles, 166
texts: modes of engagement with, 131
Thacker, Eugene, 109, 115, 116
Thaller, Bernd, 65, 66
theatrical exhibition. *See* exhibition
35mm: dominance of format threatened, 23, 25, 35
35mm: exhibition, 23–36
Thompson, Kristin, 215, 228
Thrift, Nigel, 179
time: in Bergson, 96–97
time: experience of, 148–149, 220–221
time: representation of: and cinema, 189, 191, 193–197, 206–212
time: representation of: conceptualized in film theory, 53–57, 66–69
time: representation of: in scientific films, 53–57, 64, 66–69
*Time* (magazine), 175
*Timecode* (film), 134, 136, 137, 139

time-image (Deleuze), 97, 103
*Titanic* (film), 134
Titford, J. S., 90
Toffler, Alvin, 51n2
Tomkins, Silvan, 216, 222–223, 224n2
Toronto (Ontario): early film exhibition, 80
Toronto (Ontario): regulation of cinemas, 77–78, 86
Toulmin, Vanessa, 106
toys: and mass media, 179–180
Truffaut, François, 175
Turkle, Sherry, 178
Turney, Jon, 108, 119
*24* (TV series), 129
*2001: A Space Odyssey* (film), 181n4
Tykwer, Tom, 187, 189, 191, 193, 195, 200n14

uncanny (Freud), 89
unrepresentability: and visual imaging techniques, 61
*Unwritten Law, The* (film), 80
urbanization: and development of cinema, 230–231
Uricchio, William, 82

Valverde, Mariane, 77, 78
Van Dijck, José, 119
VCR: and new technology, 229
VCR: and spectatorial practice, 41
*Vertigo* (film), 191
Vertov, Dziga, 229
VHS: and spectatorial practice, 41
video: formats, 20
video: home video: as threat to 35mm exhibition, 23
video: and nostalgia, 217
video games: aesthetics of, 148–149
video games: and film narratives, 191, 195–196
video games: as interfaces, 132–133, 139
video games: and new technologies, 229
Viola, Bill, 131, 139
viral video: and advertising campaigns, 43

viral video: and memes, 48
Virilio, Paul, 102, 232, 235
virtuality (Deleuze), 221–222
vision: conventions of in scientific films, 62–64, 65–66
Volvo: online advertising campaigns, 43
Von Sternberg, Josef, 199n1

war: and cinema technology, 56, 103, 235, 237
Waxman, Sharon, 156n11
Web. *See* World Wide Web
'Web films', 37–52
Weber, Samuel, 167n3
weblogs, 52n9
Weigel, Sigrid, 215
Weimar cinema. *See.* Germany – cinema
Weingart, Peter, 119
Welles, Orson, 181n3
Wentz, Jan, 44
Whitecross, Matt, 4
Williams, A. P., 199n4
Williams, Linda, 47, 169
Wilmut, Ian, 106
Winnicott, Donald, 216e

Winterbottom, Michael, 4, 18n5, 110, 113, 119
Winthrop-Young, Geoffrey, 88, 103
Wollen, Peter, 158
women: and cinema audiences, 83
women: cinematic representations of, 189, 197
women: and social roles, 187–188
women: and theories of spectatorship, 216
Woo, John, 46
Wood, Aylish, 108
World Wide Web (WWW): and cinema, 37–52
World Wide Web (WWW): and spectatorial practice, 37–52
World Wide Web (WWW): as user interface, 130, 135
Wright Wexman, Virginia, 6–7

Young, Paul, 105, 108
Youngblood, Gene, 237
*Your Double Lighthouse Projection* (installation), 139–140
*YouTube*, 3, 37, 39

Žižek, Slavoj, 224, 239